Given by Class of 1935
1934.

THE ITALIAN THEATRE

Joseph Spencer Kennard, Doctor of the Sorbonne, Paris.
After a painting by Henry Salem Hubbell, 1931.

THE
ITALIAN
THEATRE

*

FROM ITS BEGINNING TO
THE CLOSE OF THE SEVENTEENTH
CENTURY

BY

JOSEPH SPENCER KENNARD

NEW YORK

William Edwin Rudge

1932

PRINTED IN U.S.A.

AS A TRIBUTE
TO THE LOVING CO-OPERATION
OF MY WIFE
E. H. K.
THIS WORK IS GRATEFULLY DEDICATED

FOREWORD

A HISTORY *of the Italian Theatre should mean more than a study of important Italian plays. It should reflect the successive phases of the Italian social conscience, and through the succeeding centuries of the national evolution, depict the changing life of the Italian people. Such a theatre presumes to photograph life, not omitting its crudities and cruelties. It will also interpret the national character, and portray the historical background. It is also the theatre of psychology, presenting the struggle between the flesh and the spirit, the losing and winning of Mansoul. It is also the teatro di poesia, wherein reality is transformed by the poet into drama. More even than all this; its stage is the world, since the church, the civilization, the literature of Western Europe, of which the theatre is a part, are all of Italian origin.*

To compass adequately, within a few hundred printed pages, a subject so vast, so varied, is impossible. For the privilege of saying a little, the author has been obliged to omit much, to compress more, and sometimes, perhaps, to appear dogmatic and superficial.

To my wife, for her constant help and encouragement, to the Printing House of William Edwin Rudge for this distinguished example of the printer's art, and their unfailing courtesy; and to those others who have been helpful, I am grateful.

J. S. K.

New York
November, 1931

CONTENTS

CHAPTER X

THE SEVENTEENTH CENTURY:

Political situation of Italy at the beginning of the seventeenth century: The moral conditions: Corruption of the clergy: The intellectual revival in the seventeenth century: The patrons of the universities and academies: The founding of the libraries.

General characteristics of the tragedy in the seventeenth century Italian theatre: The sacred tragedies: Andreini's *Maddalena*: Tragedies of the Jesuit School: Scamacca's *Oreste*: Other followers of the classic tradition:

The *Crispo* of Savaro: His *Emiddo*, the *Celinda* of Miani: The use of Longobard history, Nolfi's *Romilda*: Mamiano's *Lucrezia*: The use of extra-Italian scenes: Cevoli's *Ormondo*: Delfino's *Cleopatra*: Bonarelli's *Solimano*: Graziana's *Cromuele*.

The meaning of the term *tragicomedy*, the shift from verse to prose: The translation of French tragedies: The pastoral drama and fable: The marine fable, the *Filli di Sciro* by Bonarelli: Andreini's *Florinda*.

Influence of the scenarios of the improvised comedy: Influence of Spanish dramatists: Buonarroti's *Fiera*: The use of *scherzi*, dialect, and satire: Immorality of the seventeenth century comic theatre: Defence of it by Cecchini.

BIBLIOGRAPHY

A complete bibliography of the matters here considered would require more than a large volume, even if such a compilation were possible. The titles here selected, together with the various supplementary bibliographies will probably suffice for most readers. The two works by A. d'Ancona, on the Italian theatre and the Italian literature are most important, and have been invaluable to the author.

ADEMOLLO, A. *Intorno al teatro drammatico italiano dal* 1550 *in poi.* "Nuova Antologia," 1881. *Il Carnevale di Roma nei secoli XVII e XVIII.* Rome, 1883. *Una Famiglia di comici italiani nel secolo decimotavo.* Florence, 1885. *I teatri di Roma nel secolo decimosettimo.* Pasqualucci, Roma, 1888.

AMBRA, Lucio d'. *Le théâtre contemporain en Italie.* "La rev. d'art dramatique," ANNÉE 17, p. 273–286. "La rev. d'art dramatique," Paris, 1902. N. S., v. 5, pp. 345–350.

ANCONA, A. d'. *Origini del teatro italiano.* Turin, 1891. 2 VOLS. *Manuale della letteratura italiana.* (With Orazio Bacci.) Florence, 1904–1908. 6 VOLS.

ANTOLINI, Patrizio. *Notizie e documenti Farrarese.* Ferrara, 1889. ATTI., V. 2, p. 33.

BARTOLI, Francesco. *Scenari inediti della commedia dell'arte.* Firenze, Sansoni, 1880. *Notizie istoriche de' comici italiani che fiorirono intorno all'anno MDL fino a'giorni presenti.* Padua, 1782. 2 VOLS.

BASCHET, Armand. *Les Comédiens italiens à la cour de France sous Charles IX, Henri III, Henri IV et Louis XIII.* Paris, 1882.

BERRET, Paul. *Des Conditions de representation de la comédie latine.* "Rev. d'art dramatique." Paris, 1899. N. S., v. 7, p. 174.

BLACK, John. Translation from the French of Goldoni's *Memoirs.* London, 1814. 2 VOLS. Same, abridged, with essay by W. D. Howells. Boston, 1877.

BROCCHI, Virgilio. *Carlo Goldoni a Venezia nel secolo XVIII.* Bologna, 1907.

BROGNOLIGO, G. *Nel Teatro di C. G.; Il Cavaliere e la Dama; Le Femmine puntigliose; La guerra.* Naples, 1907.

BROSSES, Le Président des. *Lettres familières écrites d'Italie en* 1739 *et* 1740. Fourth edition. Paris, 1885. 2 VOLS.

Buckley, Eric R. *The Staging of Plays 300 years ago.* "Gentlemen's Mag.," London, 1901. v. 291, pp. 288–297.

Campardon, E. *Les Comédiens du Roi de la Troupe Italienne pendant les deux derniers siècles.* Paris, 1880. 2 vols.

Caprin, Giulio. *La Commedia dell'arte al principio del secolo XVIII.* "Rivista teatrala italiana." Naples, 1905.

Carducci. *I Corifei della Canzonetta nel secolo XVI.* vol. xviii in Antologia di Critica Letterari Moderna.

Casanova de Seingalt, J. *Mémoires écrites par lui-même.* Nouvelle édition collationnée sur l'édition originale de Leipsick. Paris, no date. 8 vols.

Castelnuovo, A. *Una Dama Veneziano del secolo XVIII.* Nuovo Antologia, Jan., 1882.

Chambers, E. K. *The Mediæval Stage.* Oxford, 1903. 2 vols.

Clodel, Judith. *Le théâtre italien.* nouv. rev., n. s. Paris, 1900. Pp. 601–612.

Cuman, Arpalice. *La riforma del teatro comica italiano e Carlo Goldoni.* "L'Ateneo Veneto." anno 22, v. 2, p. 293; anno 23, v. 1, p. 80; v. 1, p. 197.

Dejob, Charles. *Les abbés,* etc. "Rev. prolit. et litt. Rev. Blue. Paris, 1898. ser. 4, v. 10.

Diderot, D. *De la poésie dramatique* (1758). Garnier, Paris, 1875.

Douhet. *Dictionnaire des Mystères.* Paris, 1854.

Durand. *Le culte catholique dans ses cérémonies,* etc. Méguignon, Paris, 1868.

Fainelli, Vittorio. *Chi era Pulcinella?* Gior. Stor. d. lett. Ital. Torino, 1909. v. 54, p. 59.

Funck, Brentano. *Les théâtres dans l'ancienne France.* "Minerva," Paris, 1902. v. 4, p. 526.

Gantheron, René. *Le théâtre italien en France.* série 2, tome 35, pp. 307–343.

Gherardi, E. *Le théâtre italien de Gherardi.* Paris, 1721.

GIACOMO, Salvatore, di. *Cronaca del teatro San Carlino,* 1738–1884. Trani; V. Vecchi, 1895. (Collezione Storica Napoletani, v. 1.)

GRIMM, Le Baron de. *Correspondance littéraire,* etc. (1753–1790). Paris. 16 VOLS.

HASTINGS, Charles. *The Theatre.*

HAWKINS, F. *Annals of French Stage.* Chapman and Hall, London, 1884. 2 VOLS.

HILLEBRAND, K. L. *Des Conditions de la bonne comédie.* Durand, Paris, 1863. *Études historiques et Études italiennes.* Frank, Paris, 1868.

JULLEVILLE, Louis Petit de. *Les Mystères.* Hachette, Paris, 1880. 2 VOLS. *La Comédie et les Moeurs en France au Moyen Age.* L. Cerf, Paris, 1885–1886. *Histoire de la littérature française,* VOL. I, M. A. *Histoire du théâtre en France.* Paris, 1880–1889.

LEROY, Onésime. *Études sur les Mystères.* Hachette, Paris, 1837. *Histoire comparée du théâtre.* Paris, 1844.

LUCAS, Hippolyte. *Histoire philosophique et litt. du théâtre.* 1862. 2 VOLS. in 1.

LUNGO, Isadoro Del. *Medio evo dautesco sul teatro.* "Nuovo Antologia." v. 98, p. 23.

MAGNIN, Charles. *Les origines du Théâtre moderne.* Hachette, Paris, 1838. "Journal des Savants," 1848, p. 199; 1849, p. 14; 1860, p. 537.

MANTZIUS, Karl. *A history of Theatrical Art.* VOLS. I AND 2. "Middle Ages and the Renaissance." VOL. 2.

MARCHESI, G. B. *I Romanze dell'abate Chiari.* Bergamo, 1900.

MASI, Ernesto. *La Vita e le opere di C. G.* Bologna, 1880. *La Vita, i tempi, gli amici di Francesco Albergati.* Bologna, 1878.

MENGHINI, Mario. *Bibliografia del dramma It.* "Rivista della Biblioteche." Firenze, 1896. VOL. 6, pp. 65–77.

MÉRIL, Edelestand du. *Histoire de la comédie.* Didier, Paris, 1864. *Origines latines du Théâtre moderne.* Franck, Paris, 1849. *Dictionnaire des Myst.*

MOLIÈRE. Cf. M. A. D. Regnier's collection, *Les Grands Écrivains de la France.* "Molière."

MOLMENTI, P. G. *La Storia di Venezia nella vita privata dalle origini alla caduta della republica.* Fifth edition, profusely illustrated. VOL. I, *La Grandezza;* VOL. II, *Lo Splendore;* VOL. III, *Il Decadimento.* Bergamo, 1910.

MURATORI. *Annali d'Italia.* Venice, 1848. VOL. VII.

MORICE, E. *Historie de la Mise en Scène,* etc. Paris, 1836.

NERI, Achille. *Carlo Goldoni.* Pavia, 1907. *Bibliografia goldoniana.* Giorn. degli eruditi e curiosi. Padua, 1883. VOL. III.

ORTOLANI, Giuseppe. *Della Vita e dell'arte di C. G.* Venice, 1907.

PARFAICT, Frères. *Histoire de l'ancien théâtre italien depuis son origine en France jusqu' à sa supression en l'année* 1697. *Suivie des extraits ou canevas des meilleurs pièces italiennes qui n'ont jamais été imprimées.* Paris, 1767.

PARMA (City of Parma). *Esposizione, Litt. del Teatro a Parma.* "L'illustrazione italiana," Milano, 1913. ANNO 40. pp. 308–309.

PETIT DE JULLEVILLE. See JULLEVILLE.

RABANY, Charles. *C. G. Le théâtre et la vie en Italie au XVIIIe siècle.* Paris, 1896.

RASI, Luigi. *I Comici italiani, Biografia, Bibliografia, Iconografia.* Florence. VOL. I, 1897; VOL. II, 1905.

RAYER. *Histoire universelle du Théâtre.* Franck, Paris, 1869.

RICCI, Corrado. *I teatri di Bologna nei secoli* 17. "Storia aneddotica." Bologna, 1888.

RICCOBONI, Luigi. *Histoire de théâtre italien depuis la decadence de la comédie latine.* Delormel, Paris, 1728. *Histoire de l'ancien théâtre italien.* Paris, 1730. 2 VOLS. *An historical and critical account of the theatres in Europe.* London, 1741.

RUGGERI, Luigi. *L'Archiconfraternita del Gonfalone.* Roma, 1866.

SACCHETTI, Renzo. *Le théâtre italien.* "Rev. d. rev." VOL. 30, p. 611.

SAINT-EVREMOND. *De la Comédie Italienne.* Paris, 1777.

SAINTSBURY, George. *Short History of English Literature.* London, 1908.

SANCTIS, Francesco di. *Storia della letteratura italiana.*

SAVIOTTI, Alfredo. *Feste e spectacoli nel seicento.* "Gior. Storia della letteratura italiana." VOL. 41, p. 42.

SCALA, Flaminio. *Il Teatro delle favole rappresentative,* etc. Venice, 1611. Collection of 50 scenarios.

SCHERILLO, Michele. *L'Opera Buffa Napoletana.* Milano, 1916.

SEICENTO (seventeenth century). *La Vita Ital^{ne} Nel Seicento.* Firenze, 1894; Milano, 1895.

SEMAR, John. *Pre-Shakespearean Stage.* Florence, 1913.

SEPET, Marius Cyrille Alphonse. *Le drame chrétien au Moyen Age.* Didier, Paris, 1878. *Origines catholiques du théâtre moderne.* P. Lethielleux, Paris, 1901.

SOLERTI, Angelo. *Le origini del melodramma.* Fratelli Boca, Torino, 1903. *Gli Albori del Melodramma.* Remo Sandron, Milano, 1904–1905. 3 VOLS. Is chiefly a collection of plays. *Musica, Ballo e Drammatica alla Corte Medicea, dal 1600 al 1637.* Bemporad, 1905.

SOUBIERS, Albert. *Le Théâtre italien,* etc. Paris, 1910.

STENDHAL. *La vie de Metastasio.*

TAMMASO, Niccolò. *Storia civile della Letteraria.* Turin, 1872.

TIPALDO, G. di. *Biografia degli Italiani illustri.* Venice, 1837.

VATASSO, Marco. *Per la storia del Dramma sacro in Italia.* Tip. Vaticana, Roma, 1903.

LIST OF ILLUSTRATIONS

VOLUME I

The plates either face the page designated or are grouped after it.

*Frontispiece: Joseph Spencer Kennard, Doctor of the Sorbonne, Paris.
After a painting by Henry Salem Hubbell, 1931.*

The Italian Theatre

THE
ITALIAN THEATRE

CHAPTER I

THE ORIGIN OF THE ITALIAN THEATRE, CLASSICAL AND CHRISTIAN

The pagan Roman theatre as one of the sources of the Italian theatre, a comparison of the Greek and Roman theatre with reference to the benefits and liabilities resulting from the imitation of Greek art: Native Latin drama: the *satura, satire,* and *atellana*: Latin poets important for their influence upon the Italian theatre: Plautus, Terence, and Seneca: Antagonism of the early Christian Church to the corrupt Augustan theatre: Rise of pantomimic art, *Chirosofi* and *Panfoni, cantico* and *fantoccio*: Satirization of the Church by the mimes: Their persistence past the tenth century: The writings of Hrosvita.

The Christian Church as the second and more important source of the Italian theatre: Elaboration of Church ritual: Gradual dramatization of the Roman liturgy: Evolution of the liturgical drama: Consolidation of episodes, apocryphal insertions of characters and narratives: Growing complexity of scenery with consequent shift from ecclesiastical locale: Change to the vernacular: Reasons for the Church's policy in enriching the ritual suggested: Typical sacred drama.

THE Italian Theatre is the child of the pagan Roman theatre and the Christian Roman Church; and the pagan Roman theatre itself is the child of the Greek theatre and of an Italian civilization earlier than that of Rome, which flourished in the Campania until it was finally absorbed by the Roman power.

Great as was the Roman debt to the theatre of Greece, Rome lost more than she gained by her imitation. So great was the difference in the substance of the two races, so vast their divergence in form of government, that the transplanted Attic comedy and tragedy never became truly acclimated on Latin soil; and the Roman imi-

3

tations of Greek plays were either un-Attic in their spiritual content or, if truly Greek, were an exotic product, foreign to Roman genius. Differences of heredity and environment forbade the successful transplanting of the Greek theatre to the Latin soil.

The Greek theatre was spontaneous and normal, the highest product of Greek art, and that most honoured by the people. The tragic poet presented upon the stage the story of the national heroes and the glorious traditions of immortal Hellas; and between the poet who breathed the atmosphere of art and the spectators who possessed an unequalled sensitiveness to that art, there was perfect harmony. A new spectacle at Athens brought throngs from every part of Greece; both the writers and the actors of great tragedies were highly honoured, and might even hold high office. In the name of the nation, the most illustrious magistrates conferred the palm upon the authors of those monuments of the human mind; for in Greece, the theatre, both tragic and comic, was encouraged by the state, and was held in honour by the entire nation; hence the Latins were eager to transplant the Greek drama to Rome.

But how different were the conditions in Rome during the first centuries of the Christian era. The Roman Emperor reigned by fear, or was under the control of those even more wicked and dissolute than himself. Voluptuousness was ostentatious; and the common people were scourged by usury and rapine. Civilization was preparing itself for dissolution; and the literary movement responded to this moral condition. The Athenians considered the theatre as a tribune in which the poet filled the office of an orator; but in Rome the play only amused the people and caused them to forget their lost liberties. Hence political comedy was impossible in Rome; and exiled Naevius, dying miserably at Utica, was a warning against discussing political questions on the stage.

Equally true is it that every condition was lacking in Rome for the production of good tragedy. Even if tragic genius had existed,

Maccus as Punchinello

it would not have been appreciated by the common people, or have been tolerated by the tyranny of the state; nor would actors of character have been found to present it, for the whole profession was held in abject contempt, and classed with rogues and panders, declared infamous by the law and unworthy of military rights or civil honours.

There had, however, been a Latin drama which preceded that imitated from the Greek. In its earliest scenic form this was called *Satura,* an intermingling of dialogue with music, song, and dance. However decent this form of dramatic representation may have been at first, its recited dialogue called *diverbii,* accompanied by songs and dances, finally became so licentious that it was suppressed by law. It was succeeded by the *Satire,* a moral and didactic composition, frequently in dialogue. This was the most purely Latin expression of the Roman theatre.

Another early form of drama, was the Atellanian fable (*favola atellana*), so called from the Etruscan city Atella. These *Atellanæ* first ridiculed the rural customs and speech of the neighboring Campania, and then made sport of the trivial happenings of the provincial cities and of amusing types of small-town people. These caricatures finally developed into absurd stage figures with a fixed stage personality; and, when the *Atellanæ* had become the most popular representations of the Roman stage, these became masks for comedy or farce, under the names of Macco, Pappo, Buccone, Manduco, Casnare. Because of the licentious speech permitted this form of dramatic composition, these masks became extremely popular and survived for centuries.

These then, are the sources of the Roman theatre: the native *Atellanæ* derived from the neighboring Etruscan Campania, the native Latin *ludi,* and the Greek theatre. The intermingling of these was not favorable to the development of a high form of Roman drama. The native Latin *ludi* were so stifled in their infancy by the highly developed transplanted Greek drama, that we shall never be able to judge to what excellence they might have finally arrived. For although the rude, indigenous scenic representations continued to be presented in Rome, they were always overshadowed by the borrowed Greek theatre. Since the perfected Greek drama was the product of a soul and a civilization essentially different from the Latin, these Latin imitators of the Greek masters of tragedy failed to equal the greatness of the Greek originals. At their best, the dramatic works of the Latins were only imitative; and since those written in the finest period of Latinity have perished, it is impossible for us to know the real value of the best product of the Latin imitators of the Greek theatre.

The three Latin playwrights who most influenced the Italian theatre are Plautus, Terence, and Seneca. Plautus arrived in Rome from Sarsina, a city of Umbria, at the time when the armies of Hannibal were overrunning Italy, and his plays soon won the favor of the people. So great was his popularity that many comedies written by unknown writers were produced under his name. Of the twenty-three Plautian plays accepted by Varrone as genuine, twenty have survived; and we are able, therefore, to form a better judgment of his work (and, for a similar reason, that of Terence) than of that of the other Roman comic poets. Undoubtedly, Plautus possessed the qualities of a great comic poet; and had it not been for the obstacles in Roman government and life, he might have given to the world comedies equal to some of the Greek classic models. But Roman tyranny forbade his attacking specific vices or criticizing the government, and permitted him to rail at vice only in a general way. So he avoided dangerous allusions and protested that his comedy was intended merely to amuse. As a result, Plautus exerted little influence on public life or private morals, since a moral end was prohibited in comedy, and the comic poet remained merely a buffoon. Notwithstanding such limitations, Plautus produced several remarkable plays. In both the *Trinummus* and the *Persa* there are masterly representations of a chaste and high-minded daughter contrasted with an ignoble father; both are true to life. The unclean jests and phrases and ugly pictures scattered through these plays reflect Roman life. Had they been omitted, Plautus would have had no audience; and posterity would have lacked these faithful pictures of Roman life in the most corrupt days of the Republic. Plautus was not only the first, the greatest and most fertile Latin writer of true comedy, but he was also the one who exercised the most influence on the Italian Theatre.

Of his many rivals and imitators, Cicilio Stazio was most famous. But Terence was the most able, and the most admired, translated, and imitated. These two comic writers differed utterly. Terence possessed the Hellenic soul; and he so thoroughly understood the quality of the Greek drama, and so caused the Attic comedy to flourish in Rome that his plays present the most perfect comic art in Latin literature. And yet this very excellence killed national Latin comedy. In every age, the people go to the theatre for pleasure; and when his most delicate and tender play, the *Ecira,* was given, Terence had the humiliation of beholding the spectators interrupt the representation by rushing from the theatre in order to view the rope-dancers and acrobats, and applaud the gladiators in the circus.

Latin tragedy is represented by the ten plays attributed to Seneca. But these were literary exercises rather than plays designed to be performed upon the stage, since there was no liberty in Rome, and tyranny was too fearful of the truth of tragedy to tolerate its performance. When we consider his exasperating style, his lack of scenic effect and of ideas, his strange images, his exaggerated epithets, his rhetorical travesties of the characters, we marvel at Seneca's immense fame in imperial times. Christian writers, unable to resist the influence of the relics of Roman literature and seeing the tragedies of Seneca highly honoured, cited his sententious sayings and moral maxims and constructed many imitations of his plays.

As the Empire grew more corrupt, as æsthetic sentiment declined and sensuality increased, the plays of Plautus, Stazio, Terence, Seneca, and the other playwrights of the Republic were more rarely performed. The people became infatuated with scenic spectacles which delighted the eye and, through their gross realism, roused the passions. During the last years of the Empire, the sensuality of the *mimes* and the gladiatorial combats had so corrupted the whole Roman world that sorrow and death must be real and not simulated. The artistic imitation of theatrical representation had lost its appeal.

In the first age of Christianity, pagan Rome sometimes protested against this corruption of art and morals; but it was the early Christian Fathers and the Church Councils that most vigorously fulminated against the corrupting spectacles. St. Chrysostom writes of "the dissoluteness, the diabolical pomp, the waste of time, the appeal to the emotions, the meditation of adultery, the school of fornication, the exercise of intemperance, the exhortation to immodesty, the occasion for laughter, and the example of uncleanness," which characterized the theatre of his time.

Contrary to the assertion of many writers, both comedy and tragedy were sometimes represented in Rome in the first centuries after Augustus, though the theatre had been shorn of its glory. Neither Fate, nor gods, nor the ancient myths retained their hold on a people who had become sceptic and without patriotism. Inevitably the drama, which is always the reflection of its age, had lost its substance. It had become a literary exercise. There could be no worship of art as a sacred thing, no inspiration of genius, when philosophers laughed at the ancient faith and ridiculed religious traditions.

This change was gradual. The pantomimic art of expressing an action or a thought by gestures was first introduced into the spoken drama as an ornament or symbol. Encouraged by the emperors, pantomime soon became a separate art; and its performers were the idols of prince and populace. These actors were called *Chirosofi* and *Panfoni*, that is, men who with knowing hands can express anything. The pantomime, performed at first by a single actor, then later by several, represented the thought by gestures. Another actor, probably hidden, chanted with instrumental accompaniment the *Cantico,* which set forth the subject. Public taste demanded that scenes of the utmost obscenity be openly enacted on the stage; and thus the theatre became a school for the corruption of morals. Realism could go no further than it did when, in some pantomimic representation, Domitian ordered that in place of a lay figure (*fantoccio*) a live man should be crucified and then devoured by a bear.

Even after the Christian Church had become the state religion, the Fathers of the Church and the Church Councils fulminated their anathemas, and evoked the civil laws against the mingling of men and women and even young girls in the theatre, where they were swayed by the representation of the most passionate emotions. Yet, deaf to the invectives of their teachers and to the decrees of the law, Christians left the churches empty, and rushed to attend the immoral games and pantomimes. This was an open sore in the early Christian Church; and the prohibitions of Church Councils and the anathemas of popes against theatrical spectacles continued up to the time of the rebirth of the Drama in the Church itself.

There was, however, another and less-avowed reason why the Church attacked the *ludi;* for the theatre had, in its turn, attacked the Church. The *mime* added to his repertoire the figure of the Christian. He wore the costume of bishop or of priest, and ridiculed the ministers and proselytes of the new religion.[1] The war between the Church and her most audacious adversary continued until the Church itself so popularized the religious drama that the pagan *ludi* were effectually suppressed.

No positive answer can be given to the question as to when the pagan, immoral *ludi* and games inherited from Rome ceased to be presented in some form in Christian Italy.[2] But, after the eleventh and twelfth centuries, when the liturgical drama, which was born within the Church and governed by the clergy, had assumed a sufficiently dramatic character, the people seem to have renounced the profane spectacles in favor of those given in the churches. Even as late as the tenth century, however, the church authorities continued to fulminate against both people and clergy for participating in these reminders of the obscenity of paganism. Not only the feasts of the saints but also the heathen festivals of Bacchus, patron of the vintage, and of Janus and the festive days of the Kalends of January, were celebrated equally with Easter and Christmas and the Ascension. The feasts of the martyrs and the dedications of the churches competed with clamorous merrymakings in the streets, with games and horse races, with *mimes* with lewd words and gestures, and with irreverent and obscene songs sung by choirs of women. So little did the people reverence the House of God that they considered it as a common meeting-place; and the dances and coarse amusements and songs were often carried from the streets and squares of the city into the very church itself, in which the people sometimes slept. Even as late as 1210, Pope Innocent III was obliged to condemn theatrical performances in the churches and the clergy who took part in them, as did both Church Councils and Synods, and even the civil powers.[3]

Before quitting this subject of the influence of the pagan theatre upon the Christian, mention should be made of the writing of Hrosvita, a nun of the monastery of Gandersheim. Although she was a German, and the form of her writings is that of the *sacra rappresentazione,* she belongs to this tenth century and wrote in

Latin six dramas: *Gallicano, Dulcizio, Callimaco, Abramo (Abraham), Panuzio, Sapienza*—all of them directly inspired by Terence. "I did not refuse," she writes, "to imitate in my writings Terence, who to-day is so much read by many. It has been my aim to substitute for so many incestuous turpitudes of feminine lusts, the chaste actions of the holy virgins, which I have celebrated according as the smallness of my talent permitted me." We know also that Terence and Plautus were widely read in the very numerous copies of their works made by the monks.

Child of the classic Roman theatre, without doubt, yet the Italian theatre owes even more to the Christian Church. Always the Italians have been peculiarly responsive to the dramatic art. And when, after centuries of endeavor, neither religious nor civil prohibition sufficed to turn Christian converts from the pagan *ludi,* then the Church, by the elaboration of the ritual, by the solemn majesty of a visible contemplation, and by symbolical expression of the mysteries of the faith, so appealed to the dramatic inclinations of worshippers that they abjured the profane and shameless heathen spectacle.

How interesting the situation: two religions, two civilizations, pagan *ludi* and Christian ceremonial, coexisting, contrasting, contending; each appealing to the emotional and dramatic instincts of a race.

Such is the first period in the development of the Italian Theatre. The pagan scenic spectacle continues, and contests for favor with Christian liturgy and ceremonial which continually grow richer and more dramatic. Then comes the second period when, the Church having triumphed, the true Christian drama appears, which owes nothing to pagan art, and of which the final development is the *sacra rappresentazione.* And then we have the third period, with its revival of the ancient Latin culture, of which the imitation of the ancient classic theatre is but one of many aspects.

If we disregard unimportant surviving remnants of the antique theatre, Italian dramatic art in the Middle Ages was the fruit of religious inspiration and ecclesiastical ceremonial.

An adequate development of the gradual elaboration and dramatic accretions of the Church ritual, from its Apostolic simplicity to the period of its greatest richness, would require a volume. St. Justinian in his first *Apologia* indicates to us the austerity and sobriety of the celebration of the Eucharist in the second century. Already, as early as the fourth century, this service had become so enriched and complicated and required so many actors as to have become in fact a dramatic representation;[4] and the *Ordines Romani* of the eighth and ninth centuries relate how much more elaborate and dramatic was the Mass as celebrated in Rome by the Pope himself, the whole complicated liturgical ritual being now rigorously fixed and requiring to be exactly carried out. By the eighth and ninth centuries, the Roman liturgy, through the dialogue form of the responsory psalm and antiphon, through the interrogations and affirmations between the principal celebrant and the inferior ministers, and through the continued actions and movements of the priests, had already attained to the position of a dramatic performance. And this was still further developed in the ritual which was written in the monastery of San Gallo and which from there spread throughout Christian Europe toward the end of the ninth century. But it is in the introit of the Easter Mass and office of Soissons that we have these two dramatic elements of dialogue and action so fused and harmonized and the symbols presented in such concrete and material form that we have a real theatrical setting with the appropriate stage-properties.[5]

The first of the liturgical dramas which had begun to be represented in the churches in the tenth century, had as their subject the Biblical account of the birth and death of Christ. Next were introduced other events from the life of Jesus and episodes from the Acts of the Apostles, and then events from the Old Testament, the exact words of the Bible being always used. Next we have the linking of various Biblical episodes together with amplifying and connecting pieces. At first, these additions to the Biblical text were mere isolated short scenes which corresponded with and explained some chapter in the Gospel, each inserted in its appropriate place in the liturgical office according to the religious festival that it was intended to celebrate. These additions necessarily brought about the next change: the use of other than the exact Biblical language. Gradually the cycle of the dramatic compositions became more varied in its happenings and more human in its personages. The people were soon satiated with seeing the repetition of the same events, and desired that not only the personages of the Biblical story but also men like themselves should appear in the drama. And so we have the subjects chosen from the mediæval traditions of the lives of the saints and other stories.

When these dramas have become more ample, composed of several scenes, and richer in events and personages, the actors explain the events, and instruct or entertain the audience in long speeches. Imaginary personages are introduced into the Bible story; as, for example, the merchant who sold to the Magdalene the perfume she poured on the feet of the Holy One. Satan and the lesser devils become common characters on the stage, each speaking his appropriate part and delighting the audience with burlesque and even with obscenity. As the stock of legends was great and constantly growing, and as everything was availed of which would add novelty or variety, there were hundreds of these dramas. Some of these were a mere crude cutting up of the legend into scraps which were distributed as dialogue without any attempt at originality. By joining, however, several of these compositions, one vast drama was at times created, which might require several days for its performance.[6]

As the action grew more varied, so of necessity the scenic setting and mechanism became more complicated. In fact, it had by this time become convenient, for both church and spectacle, that the latter be moved from the church into a better adapted place. Mechanical paraphernalia and scenic illusion were introduced to represent the places where the action occurred; and stage costumes appropriate to the characters represented were used. The actors, also, endeavored to understand and express the psychology of the characters, and to give attention to gestures and inflection. In the first period, the representation had been purely an ecclesiastical ceremony, closely connected with the church *offices,* given in the church and participated in only by the clergy, and not recited but sung, so as to show its close connection with the church rite. But, when the drama had been moved out into the great square of the city or into the open fields, and the actors were the common people, and the sacred text was merely an excuse on which to hang an almost free scenic composition, the drama lost its hymnal character; and musical instruments and a different kind of music were introduced. As Magnin says, "The spectacle is truly religious and edifying, but it is no longer an ecclesiastical office; the drama is still sacerdotal, but it is no longer liturgical; and the abundance of the interwoven material shows well to what extent the clergy have had to concede to the lay spirit." In all this, however, the greatest change was the passage from the Latin idiom to the vernacular. This change of idiom was achieved very gradually at first, a few words of the vulgar tongue insinuating themselves into the text. Of all Christian countries this change came latest in Italy. But, by the time we have arrived at the full development of the *sacra rappresentazione,* Italian is used exclusively.[7]

Any attempt to fix an exact date when the liturgical drama passes into the *sacra rappresentazione* must be academic and futile, for the reason that we have not sufficient knowledge of the character of those early thirteenth-century religious spectacles. Uberto Benvog-lienti relates that "about 1200 there was represented [in Sienna] on Good Friday by decree of the Commune, the Passion of our Lord; and those who represented such figures were paid by the public." But we know nothing of the content or language of this represen-tation. Apostolo Zeno relates that on the *Prate della Valle* in Padua, in 1243, there was given a "spiritual representation"; but whether this was pantomime or spoken drama, and if spoken, whether given by the priests in Latin or by the people in Italian, whether a strictly liturgical or a religious feast, we do not know; and one guess is as good as another.

It is an interesting speculation whether, even if the Christian Church in its first contest with paganism had not enriched its ritual so as to form a counter-attraction for its converts in order to draw them away from the immoral *ludi,* it did not hold within itself the germ of such a complexity of symbolical ceremonies as must have inevitably evolved into an elaborate liturgy in which to celebrate the mysteries of its faith and the magnificence of its com-memorative feasts in memory of its saints and martyrs. The repro-duction by action of the events in the life of Christ, accompanied by the scenic surroundings, was sure by its symbolism to appeal to the dramatic instinct and, at the same time, to present a spectacle appealing to the eye.

Hymns and reading from the Old and New Testaments, and homilies and prayers, were the simplest form of Sunday worship among early Christians. But there were also the *agapi* (love-feasts) and the commemoration of the Last Supper. Yet in the second century Justinian writes:

On Sunday, when time permits, the memorials of the Apostles or the writings of the prophets are read; [then follow the sermon and prayers]; and then bread, wine, and water are brought; the presi-dent prays and renders thanks; the people respond *Amen*. To each is distributed his portion of the blessed elements, and to the absent they are sent by means of the deacons.

Here we already have a certain dramatic action in which priest, deacon, lecturer, and the people take part.

For the *Procession of the Sepulchre,* a sepulchre was actually raised in some part of the church; and the solemn procession moved with the waving of banners, the gleaming of candles, and the ringing of bells; and when it had arrived at the sepulchre, the two deacons acting as angels ask, "Whom seek ye here in the sepulchre, O Christians?" And the two priests acting as Marys respond, "Jesus, the Nazarene, crucified, O celestial ones." Then the angels reply, "He is not here; He is risen." And the Marys exclaim "Alleluia! To-day the Lord is risen. Let thanks be given to God. Say *eja* [come]."

The sacred drama at last is born.

NOTES

CHAPTER I

1. With the intention of holding up to ridicule the Christian rites, there was given in the presence of the Emperor Diocletian a mimic representation entitled *De mysteriis Christianæ observantiæ*. The actor Genesio lay stretched on the ground, pretending to be very ill; and there came to him two other actors dressed as priests, and an exorcist, who, after Genesio had expressed the wish to embrace the religion of Christ, solemnly baptized him; but then, to the profound amazement of the jeering audience, the actor suddenly and sincerely converted, told of the light that had dawned in his soul.

2. *Interdum ludi fiunt in ecclesiis theatrales; et non solum ad ludibri-orum spectacula introducuntur in eis monstra larvarum, verum etiam in aliquibus festivitatibus, Diaconi, Presbyteri et Subdiaconi insaniae suae ludibria exercere praesumunt. Mandamus quatenus, ne per huiusmodi turpitudinem Ecclesiae inquineter honestas prae-libatam ludibriorum consuetudinem vel potius corruptelam curetis e vestri ecclesiis extirpare.* Gregor: *Decret.*, III, 1, 12.

3. The Council of Treves, in 1227, forbade the priests *ludos theatrales fieri in ecclesia et alios ludos inhonestos.* In 1293, the diocesan Synod of Utrecht decreed: *ludos theatrales, spectacula et larvarum osten-siones in ecclesiis et caemeteriis fieri prohibemus.* And an edict of Alfonso X of Castile (c. 1260) shows that the civil powers sup-ported the ecclesiastical prohibitions. Therein it is prohibited for buffoon performances to be given in churches, or for priests to take part in them in their priestly vestments.

4. D'Ancona contends, however, that the real date of the beginning of the liturgical drama was the year 692, when, in an edict of the Council of Constantinople, the Fathers, "for fear lest the dogma of

the humanity of Christ should vanish among the subtleties of the
oriental symbolism, ordered that the Redeemer should be represented *humana forma* [in human form] in all the episodes of the
Passion, which the liturgy had hitherto avoided doing."

5. Though the plot and setting of the liturgical drama was at first very
simple, the instructions inserted in the liturgical books give directions as to how to secure the theatrical illusions necessary to the
spectacle; and the performers were dressed in costumes proper to
their historic character. And in order that the common people might
participate in the sacred rite, the liturgical drama preceded the regular religious ceremony or Mass which was afterwards celebrated.

The populace, however, desired to share in the acting by adding
to the sacred characters those of the common people; and in order
that they might clearly understand the words of such actors, they
wanted them to speak in their own language rather than in Latin.
The fact that the drama thus became secular was another reason
why it was moved out from the church. This secularizing becomes
still more marked when, instead of being an actual adaptation of
the Gospel text to scenic forms, it becomes a more or less diluted
paraphrase of the text, as, for instance, when the words of the Magdalene and of Mary become the long lamentations of impassioned
women.

6. Great indeed is the contrast between the liturgical drama of Soissons, a very brief dialogue between the two Marys beside the tomb
of Christ, and the drama *The Resurrection,* probably belonging to
the twelfth century and consisting of two parts: the first at the
sepulchre of Christ, the second representing His appearing to the
disciples in Jerusalem. In another liturgical drama, *The Appearance at Emmaus,* there are the three appearances: first at Emmaus,
then at Jerusalem in the absence of Thomas, and then when
Thomas is present. In other liturgical dramas, shorter compositions
were subsequently united in a more complex one, as in *L'Adora-*

tione dei Magi, in which is included both the adoration of the shepherds and afterwards of the Magi, each taken from an earlier composition. *The Raising of Lazarus* is also probably a composite of three earlier dramas, each dealing with a single scene.

7. In the earliest period, the Italian sacred drama was less fully developed than in other parts of Europe. But that such dramas were written in Italy is proved. According to Goussemaker the liturgical dramas *L'Annunziazione* (The Annunciation), *Il Giorno della Resurrezione* (The Day of Resurrection), *Il Sepulcro* (The Sepulchre), and the *Compianto delle tre Marie* (The Lament of the Three Marys) are of Italian origin and were presented by the clergy in the Cividale church. They were drawn from three codices of the cathedral of Cividale of Friuli, belonging to the fourteenth century; and two of them, the *Annunziazione* and the *Giorno della Resurrezione,* date back to a very remote period. The classic work of Alexander D'Ancona contains a list of such of these early liturgical dramas as remain to us.

There still remain some vestiges of the early liturgical drama in the ritual of certain of the religious festivals, as in the procession of the faithful on Palm Sunday, bearing palm branches to commemorate the triumphal entry of Christ into Jerusalem. In the office of the *Tenebre* (darkness) of Holy Week, the putting out of the lights signifies the darkness that was upon the earth at the moment of the Crucifixion. And the *office* of the *Passio* is purely dramatic. Cf. *Journal des savants,* 1892, p. 682.

Regarding the origin of the French theatre, the complex question is well summed up in the following extract from the *Historie de la litterature Francaise,* of Petit de Julleville (II, 400):

"In the midst of the liturgical office, too short for the people's taste, the priests inserted, at the solemn fêtes, above all at Christmas and Easter, a dialogued performance of the gospel scenes commemorated on those days, such as the Nativity of Jesus or the Resurrection. The drama was short, reduced to its essentials, a simple paraphrase of the sacred text. It was written in Latin and, originally, in prose. The actors were priests and clerks. The performance was wholly grave, solemn, hieratic. It is this ancient form of drama which we call the *liturgical drama*. Little by little, poetry, first in Latin, afterwards in the vulgar tongue, and, with the poetry, individual inspiration, crept into the liturgical drama and altered its primitive character. The religious dramas were still acted in the churches, where the Latin was mixed with French; but when the popular idiom had entirely supplanted the Latin, the drama issued from the church and passed from the hands of the priests into the hands of the laity. This evolution seems to have been accomplished in the twelfth century."

And, be it also noted, the French mystery-plays undoubtedly influenced the Italian drama.

CHAPTER II

THE CHRISTIAN CHURCH AND THE MEDIÆVAL THEATRE

The relation of the drama to contemporary Italian life: Early history of the Roman Catholic Church: Ascendancy of Church over State: Conflict between Empire and Papacy: Penance of Henry IV: Distinction between the early Christian Church of the Apostles and Romanized Church: The latter's influence upon all intellectual and artistic activities: The Church's organization of the theatre.

Additional sources of the Christian Drama: the laud: Cult of the *disciplinati* and Flagellants and their lauds: Classification of the laud: Its evolution into dramatic form—the *Devotioni*: Cyclical Drama: Connection of the laud with religious text and liturgy: Spread of the *Devotioni*.

The *Sacra Rappresentazione*. Variant synonyms: Florentine *Sacre Rappresentazioni*, their versification: Date of the earlier types: Popular festivals considered as one source: Mechanism of the *Sacre Rappresentazioni*: Locale: Actors: Details of the staging: Examples of scenic contrivances: Content of the *Sacre Rappresentazioni*: Illustrations of dialogue: The stock characters.

Transition from solemn themes to the comic: Satirical types: Final performance of *Sacre Rappresentazioni* in Florence: Performances in Ferrara, Modena, and Perugia: Distinction between Florentine types and other Italian presentations: *Intermezzi*: Inroads of chivalric and profane themes.

"ALL the world's a stage," where each man plays his part: and conversely, it is true that the actor's supreme endeavor is so to interpret real life that his audience shall feel that they are actually present and participating in some event which is happening before their very eyes. No matter how great may be its other merits, the play which the actor chooses as his medium cannot be a good play if it is false in its representation of the real life that it assumes to represent.

The purpose of this history is to give to the modern reader a progressive revelation through these centuries of Italian life—life as it is pictured in these old plays, and set within the frame of life as it was actually lived in Italy at the time the play was written. Each should interpret the other; and both are necessary in order to give

21

that re-creation of the past in its entirety which must be the aim of every honest historian. It will be necessary, therefore, sometimes to interrupt the consideration of the play (which is after all only the mimesis of life) in order to consider the real life in which these plays were created and which they assume to interpret. If we are successful in this, we shall have the play, the author of the play, and at least so much of actual contemporary history, that from these three elements, we shall obtain a vivid revelation of the Italian life of the period under consideration.

The Church, the Empire, and the Commune not only controlled Italian political life during the Middle Ages, but were also the essential elements of the civil and private life of the Italian people during that period. It was an iron age, full of vileness and violence and rivalries for dominion. But it was also in some respects a splendid age, full of contrasts, full of life, an age in which are to be found the beginnings of what was later to become the great Italian Renaissance.

The Roman Catholic Church is the most remarkable human institution that the world has ever known; and the Roman Catholic Church is the first essential element in the Italian life of the period we are considering. How the primacy of the Church passed from Jerusalem, where the Redeemer had lived and taught and died and the great Apostles had received the Holy Ghost, and how, passing by Antioch and Alexandria, it came to Rome, is too vast a subject for this chapter. The fact remains that, in the Synod of Constantinople in 347, the bishop of Rome was declared *first* in dignity and the bishop of Constantinople *second*. The marvelous fact, however, is this: that it required all the power of pagan Rome to establish the papacy, and without the papacy there would probably have been no Catholic Church. "Universality" and "perpetuity" were the two words that the name of Rome suggested to the minds of the pagan world. Rome, *caput terrarum* and *caput rerum,* in Christian thought also became *caput Ecclesiæ.*

The name "pontiff," once common to all the bishops, was reserved to the bishops of Rome, as was that of pope; and this spiritual monarchy was strengthened by the power of such popes as Leo I, who obliged Attila to turn back from the gates of Rome and mitigated the horrors of the invasion of Genseric. The very barbarians who destroyed the Occidental Empire accepted Christianity, and bowed before the authority of the Pope of Rome.

From the outset, however, this claim of supremacy was disputed. The first Christian emperor, Constantine, himself claimed the title of *pontifex maximus*. He exiled bishops and convoked synods; and many of the succeeding emperors went much farther. Costanzo in the Synod of Milan of 355 flings in the faces of the astounded bishops the *placito: Canone e la mia volontà*. He in fact assumes to be both pope and emperor, and drives into exile Pope Liberio when the latter dares to oppose him.

Nevertheless, the Church grew in strength as the State grew more feeble and gradually died. For the peoples of the earth, who for so many centuries had been accustomed to look to the throne of Caesar as the source of power, found it not difficult likewise to associate spiritual supremacy with the Imperial City, towards which all religions had flowed, and which had awed even barbarian invaders by something mysterious and spiritual in its majesty. And when the Church had grown strong in its Roman organization, had succeeded to the ancient empire, and had erected the new empire, it was natural that she should want no masters over her.

But the passing of the Western Empire and the pretensions of its rulers to the headship of the Church as well as of the State, did not end the difficulties of the Roman Church. The despotism of the Emperors of Byzantium, the pretensions of the Greek patriarchs, and the nearer—and for that reason more dangerous—oppression of the Longobards succeeded. What a sense of relief must have risen in the heart of Leo III, on that Christmas day of the year 800, when, in the basilica of St. Peter's, he placed the imperial crown on the head of Charlemagne and felt that, after three centuries, the Western Empire had risen again to protect the Church, and that the hated Longobard domination had ceased forever!

And yet the pope was the vassal of Charlemagne, and the restoration of the empire was in itself a new source of danger to the papacy; and in succeeding years the bitter contest between empire and papacy was to fill the world with scandal and with clamour. Nevertheless, in spite of the pretensions of some of the successors of Charlemagne, and the weakness of some of the popes, the authority of the pontiffs continued to grow. And this authority was greatly increased, when, in 1059, Pope Nicholas II had a decree voted by the Lateran Council, by which the election of the pope was reserved to the College of Cardinals; while the people, the remainder of the clergy, and the emperor had only the right of approval. Then, in 1073, came that momentous event in the history of the papacy, the election of Gregory VII.

And now, let your imagination pass over less than four years since the election of this pope. It is January of the year 1077; you are in the courtyard of the castle of Canossa; the winter wind is bitter cold, and snow is on the ground. A man is standing there clothed in sackcloth of penance, excommunicate and cursed; for three days and nights he has been waiting there with bare head and feet, until another man shall admit him to his presence and bestow upon him absolution and pardon. That humble penitent is the great German Emperor, Henry IV, and the other man is a mere priest, "the servant of the servants of God," Pope Gregory VII. Can such a thing be? Such a thing certainly was; the historical fact cannot be disputed. Gregory VII dreamed of a universal theocratic monarchy; and he almost made his dream come true.

Vividly does Carducci picture him: "A Tuscan and of the people," he appears in history "like one of the Cyclopean walls of the

Etruscan cities near which he was born: in the shock of the en-
counter with him, the German halberds shivered to splinters; and
the wrath of the Salic emperor foamed in impotence at his feet."
He and his immediate successors made the power of the papacy
the supreme power of the Middle Ages. The will of the pope is the
will of God himself. Innocent III calls himself vicar of Christ, no
longer vicar of Peter. The pope is the judge of the earth. The emperor has now become the creature of the pope, who has the right
to depose him. Otto IV, crowned by Innocent III, was called "king
of the Romans by the grace of God and of the Pope." But the popes
not only exercised a lofty sovereignty over temporal princes; they
themselves finally assumed the crown of secular princes, with the
title of pope and king. Liudprand, Pepin, Desiderio, and Charlemagne, all contributed to the growing State of the Church. In the
first years of the ninth century, it comprised the Roman duchy and
almost the whole exarchate of Ravenna, the Pentapolis, and an
important part of the duchy of Tuscany.

And this Roman Church, my reader, is the first vital element in
the life of the Italian people at that period in their history which is
covered by the plays we are now considering. In a very real sense
we may say that the Italian Theatre during the Middle Ages *is*
the Roman Church, so intimate is the connection. The liturgical
drama, the *laudi* and *devozione,* and the *sacra rappresentazione,*
originated in the Church. At first they were a part of the Church
services in which the actors were the priests; when at last they came
out from the Church doors into the *piazza* and were performed by
laymen, they were still Christian religious performances.

These, then, are the essential facts that give significance to a
study of the Italian theatre at this period of its development. In the
first place, the only form of Christianity that had importance to the
vast mass of Italians was something vastly different from the early
Christian Church of the Apostles. It had become a Romanized ec-

clesiastical institution and an important temporal power. And, in becoming Romanized, it had also become largely paganized, and had transferred to its own use the gods and goddesses of the Latins that still remained alive, by making them into saints. It had sanctified the Pantheon and Colosseum, and had clothed the saints with the spoils of heathen poets.

And in the second place, this Romanized church not only claimed supreme political power, but had penetrated into every phase of human thought and into every form of art: attributing to the Virgin Mary something of the cult of Vesta; crystallizing the Aristotelian system into scholasticism; robing science in the cowl of theology; vaunting for herself the preservation of ancient civility, the perpetuation of the Latin language not only in her church services and in books of learning, but also in such magnificent Christian odes as the *Dies Irae* of Tommaso da Celano, the *Stabat Mater* of Jacopone da Todi, and the *Pange Lingua* of Tommaso d'Aquino; and availing herself, as we have seen in these chapters, of the new vernacular language in the cries of terror, compassion, and adoration, and the exalted fantasies and visions of Christian souls, and in substituting for the Roman pagan theatre a Roman Catholic Christian theatre, founded upon the liturgy of the Church, the contents of the Holy Scripture, and the legends of saints and martyrs. You cannot understand the Catholic Church of these centuries, nor can you appreciate this early Italian theatre, unless you appreciate how closely Church and Theatre were then interrelated.

To trace the origin of an important literary movement is interesting. The sudden disappearance of such a literary expression, at the very culmination of its development, is astonishing. We note the Paduan *ludi;* and we have in the Friulian cyclical representations of 1298 and of 1303 the highest development of the liturgical drama; and apparently at this very time it ends. Those representations remain detached facts, without apparent connection with the later vernacular sacred drama. Some other source, therefore, some new element, must account for the beginnings of that vernacular sacred drama, which occupies so important a place in the history of the Italian Theatre, the *sacra rappresentazione*. This new element, introduced about the middle of the thirteenth century, comes from the lauds. And where did the lauds originate, and what was their cause, and what is their character?

In Perugia, proud city of magnificent distances, in Perugia, in 1258, an old hermit named Ranieri Fasani, abandoning his cave, suddenly appeared in the streets and implored the sinful people to appease the divine wrath and glorify Christ by the shedding of tears and the torture of their bodies. Other hermits followed the example of Fra Ranieri. A marvelous revival of faith, a whirlwind of religious mania, surged through the city, and the fire spread like a conflagration.

With stupefaction Italy saw entire populations in great processions, calling themselves *Disciplinati di Gesu Cristo,* passing along the slopes of Umbria and spreading over the land. In the bitter winter cold, with bare breasts and shoulders and feet, with groans and cries, imploring the mercy of God, they confessed their sins and lashed themselves till the blood flowed. The Alps and Appenines heard their cries of terror and those lyrics of ardent love, called *laudi* because of their praises of God, the Virgin, and the saints. This flood of Flagellants passed the confines of Italy and poured into Provence, Burgundy, Germany, and Poland, announcing the reign of the Holy Ghost and the arrival of the Crucified One to punish the wickedness of men, as had been prophesied by Gioachino and Segarelli.[1]

Pope and civil authorities disapproved; but even when the frenzy of that extraordinary year, 1260, had passed away, and the lauds no longer were sung by excited processions under the serene skies, in

almost every city and village these *Disciplinati* formed themselves
into fraternities and retired to chapels or churches where they could
execute their discipline, recite their prayers, and sing their lauds.
For it was impossible that such deep emotion as that felt by the
Flagellants should be expressed only in beatings and groans. The
primitive canticles in which those humble laudators of God sought
to express the passions and affections of the soul, were rude and
unformed verses; but they were of a lyric character, a popular form
of sacred chant.[2]

The singing of the laud was thus peculiar to the *Flagellanti, Disciplinati, Scopatori,* or *Battuti;* and, unlike the hymn, it is the improvisation of ignorant men, and is sung in Italian and not Latin,
the language of the hymn. For the laud is of the people, ardent,
fervid, and disconnected; while the hymn is of the church, ecclesiastical and grave, and preserves the rules of its pagan source.

Of the three forms that the *laudi* assumed, lyrical, narrative,
and dialogue, the latter gradually prevailed. The parts were assigned among the different brethren according to that character of
the sacred drama which each one had been chosen to represent.
When it became the turn of his character to speak, the brother to
whom such part had been assigned, recited or chanted his strophe
while sitting or kneeling in his own place.

But since these Gospel scenes were in fact little dramas, the passage from declamation to scenic representation readily took place.
Here we have the germ of the Italian sacred theatre. And, the laud
having become a dramatic performance, costumes were required
appropriate to the sacred character represented; and the proper
scenic mechanism and properties were provided.[3]

The two *devozioni* of Holy Thursday and Good Friday show
how far, even before 1350, the lauds had advanced from the rough
and semi-lyric lauds of the *Disciplinati*. These two *devozioni*, while
borrowing something from other sources, strictly follow the Gospel

story. It is certain that each was given in the church as a part of the preaching service; and since God the Father and Satan and angels and devils and the dead participated, it must have been an imposing spectacle.[4]

As in these cases, so in many others: different compositions were united; and sometimes these in turn were combined and assumed the proportions of a great cyclical representation, of which the most noted example produced in Italy is the *Passion of Revello,* presented in that city in 1490. This great Piedmontese cyclical drama is, in construction, versification, and proportions, influenced by the French mysteries, and is unique in Italian literature. It is composed in pure Italian and not in the dialect of the people. Thus with the growth of culture, especially in the cities, with the changed conditions of times and writers, the primitive crudeness and humility of the early lyric lauds had changed to the more perfected form of the *lauda dramatica.* We are thus prepared for the *sacra rappresentazione,* though it is not easy to explain the change of strophe and rhythm, since the *sacra rappresentazione* from its beginnings is composed in verse of eleven syllables and in *ottava rima.*

The foundation of the dramatic laud is the liturgy and not the liturgical drama, although the latter would seem to stand as an intermediary between them. It was linked directly with the evangelical texts; and, at least in Umbria, it was the custom to pass directly from the ritual readings to the dramatic laud. It is true that the dramatic lauds were also influenced by certain ascetic writings of the later Middle Ages, such as the *Pianto della Vergine Maria* (Lament of the Virgin Mary); but this influence was subordinate to that of the sacred texts and the liturgy.

The many examples of Umbrian spiritual poetry that still survive, show how large was the family of religious troubadours and minstrels even in that single province; and, notwithstanding the large number that must have perished, about one hundred dramatic lauds have been preserved. That they were the work of many authors is indicated by their different qualities; but, with the exception of Jacopone da Todi, few of the authors of the lauds will ever be known by name. Their work was devout and not literary.[5]

We have now come to the conclusion of another period in the evolution of the Italian theatre.[6] It is a long road from the primitive Umbrian lauds to their latest highly developed form in the most elaborate of the *devozioni;* and wide was their spread from Perugia, the city of their origin, until they had penetrated into all the provinces of Italy. It is a period remarkable for its contribution to the drama. It is impossible to think of these Umbrian lauds without picturing those Flagellants, poor *Disciplinati di Gesu Cristo,* marching in processions of thousands through snow and ice and bitter winds, lashing themselves and imploring mercy for their sins; that whirlwind of religious awakening that seizes an entire population. It is the most dramatic, and one of the most important events of the Middle Ages.

Having considered the two earlier forms of the sacred drama— first, the liturgical, which, after having its genesis and ultimate development into a cyclical representation in Padua spread into the conterminous provinces; and then that second phase, which first appeared in Umbria as *laudi,* attained its most perfect form in the *devozione,* and passed from Umbria with the institution of the *disciplinati* into every part of the Italian peninsula—we are now prepared to discuss its last and most perfect form, which appeared in Florence, and which was named *sacra rappresentazione.*

Though representations under this title were produced in other parts of Italy, the true *sacre rappresentazioni* were not only Florentine in their origin, but they differed in character from those representations in other Italian cities, which were for the most part mute and symbolical pantomime.

Another name much used for the sacred drama is *mistero;* and the *rappresentazioni* are sometimes called *miracoli,* as are *Stella* and *Santa Maria Madallena;* and among other titles of later origin, the name *commedia spirituale* was given to the *Malatesta* of 1569 and to the *Anima* of 1575. But the generic name *sacra rappresentazione* has come to be accepted for the type of sacred drama that originated and chiefly flourished in Florence. In their first and finest period, from the middle of the fifteenth to the latter part of the following century, they were truly Florentine, being but slightly influenced by the latinizing mania of the age. Indeed they form an important part of the Florentine vernacular literature, with its richness of appropriate words, of picturesque phrases, and of elegance. These *sacre rappresentazioni* are truly important as monuments of the language, because in them the simplicity of the popular speech is frequently both tender and pathetic, and sometimes attains to real majesty of diction.

Being plebeian in origin and dramatic in content, the *rappresentazioni* were written in verse, as was all other Italian popular poetic literature. Unlike the Umbrian lauds, which first were written in eight-footed strophes, the *rappresentazioni* of Tuscany used the *ottava rima,* a metre which, though also used in the most sublime epic, was born and perfected among the common people.

And being in verse, the *rappresentazioni* were at first always sung, but not always in the same manner.[7] The lauds of the popular liturgy each had its own popular air; and the liturgical pieces, as the *Te Deum,* retained their own churchly music. It is probable, however, that, at a later date, parts of the *rappresentazioni* were declaimed and other parts sung.

Though it finally wandered far from its original content, and was often corrupted by foreign additions, yet the *rappresentazione* was essentially a devout and moral spectacle, fundamentally religious. Its arguments were originally taken from the Gospel and from pious legend, and were intended to be an exposition of the fundamental principles of faith and morality.

It is not easy to determine the date of these earliest compositions written in the vulgar tongue. The *Campagnia del Gonfalone* had represented the *Passion of Christ* and other mysteries in the Colosseum in Rome as early as the thirteenth century; and we have seen that in other parts of Italy the *devozioni* had developed into representations of a truly cyclical character, both being religious. On the other hand, the Florentines, being intensely democratic, for centuries delighted in popular festivals of scenic form; and, even when these were "Christianized," they revealed many traces of their pagan origin.

In Florence, the day dedicated to St. John the Baptist, patron saint and protector of the city, was celebrated with great pomp. In the early fourteenth century, Giovanni Villani describes a festival given by the Florentines on the Arno, and expressly states that it was an ancient custom of the land. This was not a mute, or pantomimic, spectacle. Under its Christian dress, we have here a continuation of the old Roman popular *ludi,* and no true *sacra rappresentazione*. And they were spectacles, not true drama; the few spoken words merely explained or connected the mute scenes or pantomime.

The *sacra rappresentazione* owes its birth to the union of these two sources. Founded on the Umbrian *devozione,* its earlier forms were permeated with the same religious spirit. Nevertheless, and notwithstanding the fact that ecclesiastical rites were sometimes performed on the stage, and at times given in churches, unlike the *devozione,* the *sacra rappresentazione* is a genuine theatrical composition, separated from the Christian cult and independent of religious functions. And as a rule, the actors were youths of the town-folk, and neither ecclesiastics nor religious brothers of the *disciplinati*. When, to this religious foundation upon the *devozi-*

Remigio Canta Galina F.

CAPITANA DELL'ARMATA DI COLCO FATTA DALLI
SIG.r DEPVTATI

Battaglia Nauale rapp.ta in Arno per le Nozze del Ser.
Principe di Toscana l'Anno 1608. Giulio Parigi I.

Remigio Canta Galina F.

REALE DELL'ARMATA DEGL'ARGONAVTI DOVE ERA GIASONE RAPPRESENTATO
DAL SER.mo SPOSO

Battaglia nauale rapp.ta in Arno per le Nozze del
Ser.mo Prencipe di Toscana fauola ideata Giulio Parigi.

Arno Spectacles

Teatro, d'Arno, doue si corse il Palio, delle Fregate, et abbruscio la Naue d'Amore con tutti i Tormenti, intorno alquale giraua il carro del Gioco suo Amb.re con il Riso Diletto ontento, e altri affetti simili.

Arno Spectacle

Carro dell'Africa

Carro dell'Asia

Carro di Marte e di Venere

Arno Spectacles

Tav. 5.

TEATRO FATTO IN FIRENZE NELLA FESTA A CAVALLO PER LA VENVTA DEL SER.º PRINCIPE D'VRBINO
Qui scorre 92 Caualieri diuersi abattimenti e dopo in balletto si vide anora una famiglia a piedi di 300 persone, oltre i Carri e l'altra gente per diuersi seruitij

Iulius Parigi Inu.   Callot delineauit et f.

Florentine Spectacle

V · NO · DE · GL · ABBATTIMENTI · DELLA · GVERRA · D' AMORE.
FESTA · DEL · SERENISSIMO · GRAN · DVCA · DI · TOSCANA.

Io Callot F.

Florentine Spectacle

one, was added the inspiration of the Florentine popular festivals in honour of St. John the Baptist, the result was the true *sacra rappresentazione.*

Our earliest example of the Florentine sacred drama is found in the manuscript *Storia* (1454) by Matteo di Marco Palmierie, describing the *rappresentazione* of the Feast of St. John.[8] Here we have, in a sequence of spectacles, a summary of Paradise Lost, the giving of the Law to Moses, the annunciation, birth, death, resurrection and ascension of Christ, and the final Judgment. The mimic form still prevails; but unlike other Italian representations, mute shows with only a few words added to indicate the event, we have here a dramatic form, with brief dialogues drawn from the sacred text. It is a *sacra rappresentazione.*

Abraham, bishop of Souzdal, who came to the Council of Florence, describes the representations of the Annunciation and Ascension given in Florence in 1439 in the church of the Annunziata. The spoken part is restricted to the episode of the prophets and to the annunciation of the Angel; and the mechanism and the lighting evidently played the important part. Whether the words were spoken in Latin or Italian is not indicated.[9]

Before proceeding to an examination of a few *sacre rappresentazioni,* typical or selected because of certain characteristics, let us consider briefly the "atmosphere," place of performance, scenic settings, stage properties, and types of actors, which were common to most of these performances.

In France, the performance of the mysteries was a great festival, which frequently required several days for its completion. During the recital, the gates of the city were shut, and armed men patrolled the deserted streets, the entire population being at the Mystery. In the Florentine *rappresentazione,* though the drama was shorter, the actors fewer, and the audiences smaller than in the French performance, the poet nevertheless conceived the spectacle according to the gigantesque forms of that period. Embellishing it with the pomp of place and the magic of romance, and freed from the Aristotelian rules of unity of action, time, and place, he freely seized on all the expedients that history and legend and even his own imagination suggested, to weave the drama as he willed; and frequently he produced a spectacle of great splendor.

The place of the performance varied. Churches, oratories, the vast refectories of convents, were arranged for the theatre; frequently the performance took place in the open air upon a stage erected in the midst of a flowery field or under the green foliage of shady trees. The churches of Santo Spirito, the Carmine, San Felice, or the open spaces in front of these were used; and the *Compagnia del Vangelista,* the most famous of all the Florentine companies performing *sacre rappresentazioni,* possessed a field of its own. The usual hour for the performance was Vespers.

We have a characteristic description of a typical audience at one of these Florentine sacred festivals. As the people assembled they laughed and shouted, the children screaming and throwing eggs and apples, and everyone trying to get the best seats. But during the recital we have the impression of a devout and quiet audience. Although women were probably permitted at such a religious spectacle, and men of mature years also attended, the audience was largely composed of youths, since the chief object of the spectacle was to inspire them to good conduct. Probably many, perhaps all, of the spectacles were free. Surely Lorenzo de Medici would not have asked pay from citizens who came to see the spectacles which he had composed and in which his children acted.

The dramas were acted by companies of young boys. In Modena, there was the company of *San Pietro Martre;* in Rome, the company of the *Gonfalone;* in Florence, the most celebrated was the company *del Vangelista.* These boys were dressed in costumes appropriate to the characters they represented, and were trained by the *Festaiolo,* who was at the same time director, head actor, and prompter.

There has been much discussion and some uncertainty as to the scenic setting and the mechanism and "properties" used in the *sacra rappresentazione.* Some French scholars hold that the scene of the French mystery play was a great edifice, with Hell at the bottom; and, above that, as many stories or floors as there were important places where the action took place; that above the topmost floor was placed Heaven; and that each of these floors was divided into as many compartments as there were places in those regions mentioned in the play.

But the more generally accepted view of the "scene" of the mystery play is that of Paulin Paris, professor of the College de France.[10] An open-air theatre about one hundred feet long extended in front of the lowest seats of the spectators. Below the front part of the stage, and concealed by it, was the infernal region, which opened to afford passage to the devils, and into which they cast the souls and bodies of sinners, and from which issued flames and smoke. On the front part of this platform, the actors stood and spoke their parts, issuing from compartments or booths representing palaces, temples, cities, or wherever the action took place, and returning to the appropriate apartment when they had finished speaking.

When the places between one scene and the next were supposed to be separated by a great distance, or by a space of many years, the actor passed out of sight behind his compartment and issued from the same or another compartment a little later, in order to give to the members of the audience the illusion of the passing of time or of distance.

In a few yards of boards were represented desert plains or boundless seas, or countries separated by hundreds of miles; and these vast distances were traversed in the few seconds required for the actor to pass from one to the other compartment of the stage. The eye of the spectator thus took in at one glance all the scenes of the representation: Heaven, where the Angels and God in Trinity sat on a magnificent throne; below this, the earthly scenes; and, at the bottom, Hell.

The settings for the Umbrian *devozioni* were not dissimilar, since the drama itself was not unlike, and it is probable that most of the earlier *sacre rappresentazioni* used a similar scenic setting. In the later transformations of the *rappresentazione,* when the attempt was made to reduce it to the regular form of the ancient drama, the scene was based on perspective. The edifices were constructed so as to resemble reality. If it were a city, the characteristic monuments were seen in the distance, and all were united into a whole by the *scenario* or back-cloth (*prospettiva*). The only difference arose from the fact that relatively the Italian spectacle was usually more simple than the French. The written scenic indications, found in every Italian *rappresentazione,* show that there were always several scenes.

These *rappresentazioni* were almost all founded on saintly legends, mainly recitations of miraculous events, which must be exactly performed before the eyes of the spectators. Nothing was left to the imagination; nothing took place behind the scenes; hence, mechanical aids were necessary to accomplish these results.

In *Abel and Cain,* Hell's mouth opens; "And then, you shall see the soul carried by the Devil into Hell." In the *Santa Cecilia,* "the heaven opens and the Angels come for her soul and carry it into Heaven." In the *Annunziata,* Filippo Brunelleschi so contrived the stage machinery that "one saw high up a heaven full of living figures moving, and an infinity of lights appearing and disappearing. Twelve children dressed as Angels . . . appeared as though they danced"; over their heads were "three circles or garlands of lights, formed of certain small lamps that . . . from the ground

SCENA GROTTA DI VULCANO 1702

Inferno

appeared to be stars; and the frameworks, being covered with cotton wool, appeared as clouds."

"Also from above there descended a luminous *mandorla*," in which there was "in the guise of an angel, a boy of about fifteen." And when the *mandorla* came to rest, the angel came out upon "the stage, saluted the Virgin and delivered his announcement"; then he returned on high. "The angels circling in the heaven above, singing, . . . it really appeared to be Paradise, especially because there was a God the Father surrounded by angels, which, . . . with infinity of lights and sweetest music, verily represented Paradise."

Animals frequently appeared on the stage. In the *Santa Margherita,* there is a dragon; and in *Santa Cristina,* there are two great serpents. With ropes and pulleys the souls of the righteous are drawn up into heaven, and the angels are let down; and through trap-doors the devils and the wicked go down into Hell. When the saint is about to be killed or tortured, a puppet is substituted; and when a "spot-light" is required to shine on an actor, a highly polished basin reflects the sunlight.

After considering these exterior surroundings and settings and mechanisms, let us examine the content of the *rappresentazione* itself. It is a dramatic composition which proposes to show the punishment of vice and the reward of virtue. The lives of holy men and women, as found in the Scriptures, in the lives of the saints, and in holy legends, are the material. Scene follows scene, from birth, through a life of suffering and final martyrdom for the Faith, to the entry of the holy person into eternal bliss. It is a composition in dialogue, which has a beginning, a progress, and an end, and which has as many scenes, performed in as many places, as the subject requires. To accomplish this, many actors, human, celestial, and infernal, appear. Scattered through the scenes of the *sacre rappresentazioni* are to be found a procession of human personages of every rank and quality, and possessing every virtue and every vice: kings, queens, courtiers and beggars, thieves and wastrels, priests, monks, nuns, judges and physicians, shepherds, peasants, and robbers. Truly here all the world is indeed a stage; and found upon this stage, each man and woman plays a part. Here also appear God the Father and Jesus and the Virgin, angels and heavenly messengers, Satan and devils from Hell.

Monks, priests, physicians, and judges are the special butt of the writers of these dramas that often mirror the times and give us precious information as to the social, moral, and religious conditions of the Italy of those times. Here also we have the manner of thought of the common people in the fifteenth and sixteenth centuries.

In the *Conversione della Scozia,* we have this conversation between two doctors:

> Let us upstairs be going
> And praising ourselves, we will keep on saying,
> Except ourselves, no other save God could
> have healed him.
>
> . . .
>
> Fortune is ever friend of the audacious,
> And the world to-day belongs to the presumptuous.
> And our art, deprived of these two Virtues,
> Is much like Zero multiplied by Zero.

In the *Rappresentazione di Susanna* is pictured the corruption of justice by the same judges who are afterward inflamed by Susanna and condemn her to be stoned. Bankers and merchants are usually depicted as usurers. In *Sant' Onofrio,* two merchants say: "Some stupid fellows look on usury as sinful, yet those poor silly creatures must surely see that he who has not money is not valued." Soldiers are always represented as bullies and cowards, the very scum of the galleys. Precious rogues, knaves, and rascals are the beggars. (*Poverelli di Cristo,* Christ's Poor, they are called.) Rogues and rascals also are the wild and disobedient youths, who are introduced to point a moral for the education of the young—chief object of many *rappresentazioni.*

In *San Giovanni Gualberto,* the chaplain announces that two priests have come, each seeking appointment to the same parish. The simoniacal bishop thus replies to him:

> Call each of those priests alone into a cellar,
> And learn which one has got the mighty dollar.
> The one thou seest that has more will for spending,
> Bring him in here: to him I'm first attending.

In the *Miracolo di un Monico* (Miracle of a Monk), in *Sant' Orsola,* and in *Sant' Onofrio,* to mention three out of many, we have the monastic life presented, and almost always in dispraise. It will not do to say these accusations come from irreligious and unfriendly writers. For these are sacred representations, religious drama, written and acted with the direct purpose of teaching a religious or moral lesson.

Many peasant interludes are found in the representations, as in that of Joseph (Giuseppe).

> Beco, good day; and where might you be going?
> Look if you have got a *grosso* you can lend me. . . .
> That I could buy a little grain . . .
> I've left at home my wife who's crying,
> With children six, and they're of hunger dying.

To-day we have a last reminder of the shepherds of the *Rappresentazione della Nativita* (Nativity) in those Abruzzesi fife-players who on Christmas eve play their rustic pipes under all the Madonnas of Rome.

The women's parts in these representations are always acted by boys, since it would have been a scandal for girls to mingle with the boys in the dramatic companies. Mostly they are comic characters, gossips and huckstresses, usually quarreling. The women characters nearest to real life are the heroines borrowed from profane legends, as Stella, Uliva, and Rosana. But the women "Saints" are all of the same type, and not at all feminine. Without earthly desires or temptations, they long for heaven and the sacred nuptials with Jesus. Outrages against their modesty or cruel lacerations do not anger them.[11]

Since Heaven and Hell held such prominence in many *rappresentazioni,* and since elaborate stage machinery was used for representing these places, it follows that divine and diabolical personages must be among the actors. God the Father is "a great King who sits upon a most excellent seat, with a benign, compassionate, and paternal countenance." Usually His will is made known by heavenly messengers, or by a mysterious voice; but Jesus frequently descends on the earth to help his followers.

In those representations called *Miracoli della Madonna,* the Virgin bears a leading part. Satan and his ministers play a prominent rôle in very many of these dramas. In most cases, the Devil is costumed as such; but sometimes he takes human form. In *Pellegrino,* he presents himself as the Apostle James; in *Sant' Onofrio,* as a hermit.

And, finally, it was customary for the *rappresentazione* to have both a prologue and a leave-taking. The "annunciation," or prologue, chanted by an angel, merely hints at the drama about to be performed, and begs for the indulgence of the audience. It is usually very short. The *licenza,* or leave-taking, sung at the end, was usually entrusted to the same angel who had delivered the "annunciation." Sometimes, in place of the *licenza,* the piece terminates with the *Te Deum* or some ecclesiastical or popular song.[12]

QARTA SCENA DI MARE

Scena di Mare

Now that we have visited the stage, and examined the little compartments in the rear representing a country or city or desert or royal court or battlefield or forest or ship tossing on an angry sea, as the case may be, in which some part of the action of the drama takes place, and from which the appropriate actor emerges at the proper time; after looking down into the Inferno from which the devil will emerge with his imps, to tempt the saint or to seize the sinner; after gazing into the sky-scenes, where Paradise is found, and where God the Father sits on a gorgeous throne surrounded by Angels, all gleaming and flashing with lights; after examining the complicated stage-machinery and properties; after conversing with some of these Florentine youths who will soon be acting the varied human, divine, and infernal characters of the sacred drama, and considering the metre and canto of the composition, and admiring the vigorous Tuscan vernacular in which it is written; seating ourselves among this expectant and laughing audience made up of every class of the great Florentine democracy, men, and women, and especially youths, who cease their chatter and listen reverently, as also we do, when the "Angel" advances and makes his bow, and in short strophes briefly outlines the drama, and begs for quiet and reverential attention from the audience: after this preparation, let us now examine the drama itself.

The most ancient of these *rappresentazioni* were written by Feo Belcari (1410–1484) about 1450. Grave, dignified, and solemn are his *Abraham and Isaac* and *The Angel Raphael and Tobit*. Serious also is the *St. John and Paul* of Lorenzo de Medici the Magnificent. Very solemn and pitiful is the *Last Supper and Passion* (*Cena e Passione*) by messer Pierozzo Castellani. But in the majority of *sacre rappresentazioni,* where the personages of the play are drawn from daily life—robbers, rogues and peasants, kings and clerics, saints and assassins, doctors and dupes, judges and martyrs—the comic contends with the grave, and the laughter of the audience is provoked by many means. Bad boys quarrel and fight in the *Prodigal Son,* as do two beggars in the *St. Thomas,* both by Castellani. Indeed altercations and blows and killings are as favorite a source of amusement in the *rappresentazioni* as in many modern moving-picture plays; and were probably enjoyed by an audience of much the same character. At other times, the laughter of the audience was provoked by the use of grotesque names and by comic words which had no relation with the subject.[13]

Satire as well as comicality is found in many of these dramas, as in *Sant' Orsola* where astrology is derided, and in *Sant' Onofrio,* also by Castellani, where the idle life and gluttony of the friars is held up to ridicule. The *Rappresentazione di Biagio Contadino,* although it preserves the outer form of the sacred drama, is almost classic Grecian in the bitterness with which the speeches of the demons lay bare the intrigue of the Italian courts and the depravity of contemporary customs. Here also is comedy almost suggesting the modern novel. That it ends in tragedy is to be expected, since all such compositions were bound to have a religious aim.[14]

San Giovanni Gualberto, which was exceedingly popular in Florence, is another example of what might be called the satiric drama. It is a grandiose spectacle of chivalric suggestion, with splendid banquets, tourneys, royal courts, a coronation, woods and caverns.[15] In another composition, *Rappresentazione quando Abram caccio Agar sua ancilla con Ismael suo figliuolo,* the poet has a distinct moral purpose. In the contrast between Isaac and Ishmael are shown the reward of a virtuous youth and the punishment of one who is idle and inclined to evil living.[16]

The entry of Charles VIII into Florence in 1494 is the last record we have of a *rappresentazione* in that city in the fifteenth century. In his honour, the *Vergine Annunziata* (Annunciation of the Virgin) was represented with ingenious and marvellous artifice in the church of San Felice in Piazza; which was so pleasing and "delightsome to him that, having seen it once publicly, he wished to see it other times incognito and privately."

Probably these representations were too theatrical for Savonarola, as there is no mention of them in Florence during his time. Writing about 1547, Giorgio Vasari says that the *rappresentazioni* had in his time almost ceased to be given. To the great delight of all the people, the *Annunziazione* was repeated in Florence on the arrival, in 1566, of Giovanna d'Austria, wife of Francesco de Medici. "There was given," says Vasari, "the so famous and in old times so celebrated *Festa* of San Felice, so called from the church, where it used formerly to be given."

True *sacre rappresentazioni* were not confined entirely to Florence. In Pistoia, in 1516, a fraternity was founded, like those in Florence, composed wholly of youths, which was called *Compagnia della Purità,* which gave true spoken *rappresentazioni* in the Florentine manner. A document of 1462 shows that sacred plays (*ludi*) were barred by both the civil and ecclesiastical authorities. But we have the record of two such given in 1518. Corio relates that in Milan in 1475 "on the piazza of the seraphic and divine Francesco, there was given by some Florentines, the *Spectacle of the Resurrection of the Son of God,* at which were present more than eighty thousand persons; a thing verily great in the opinion of all." It is probable, however, that this was a mute spectacle.

In Ferrara, in 1481 and again in 1490, performances were given before Duke Hercules. Mention is also made of performances in Modena and Perugia, and elsewhere in the Peninsula. In fact, to give a sacred spectacle was a common way of honouring princes when entering an Italian city, as when the *Signoria* of Lucca joyously entertained Sigismondo, King of the Romans, in 1432, with a "most beautiful *rappresentazione* at San Senzio, to give pleasure to the Emperor, who with much delight came to see it with many of his Barons."

Nevertheless, there is a vital difference between the whole class of Florentine representations and those given in other parts of Italy. These are not true dramas: even though we sometimes find in them dialogue and songs, both Latin and vernacular, and choruses and monologues illustrative of the action, yet are they addressed to the eye rather than to the ear; miming holds preëminence over recitation.[17]

In Florence, on the contrary, while we also have purely spectacular performances—and even in the most rigid *rappresentazione,* there is a strong appeal to the eye—yet they are true dramas, versified action *in modo di recitazione.* And thus to Florence belongs the honour of having created a new form of dramatic composition. But even in Florence this form ceased to be given. Departing from its primitive popular simplicity, it added Latin imitation; and theological subtlety replaced the early simplicity of the legend. Allegories and symbols were substituted for the dramatized stories; music and theatrical abuses changed the nature of the devout spectacle.

The almost universal sources of these representations are the Bible and the lives of saints and martyrs, and similar material drawn from Christian legend; and custom required a literal reproduction of every detail of historic or legendary reality, so that nothing was left to the imagination of the spectator. In that favorite form of this drama, the martyrdoms, all the gruesome particulars are reproduced before the eyes of the audience. We have the decapitations, and the amputations of breasts and other members. Real flames are frequently used. In the actual decapitation, a puppet (*fantoccio*) was substituted; but sometimes, through excessive zeal, great suffering was inflicted on the one tortured.

There was, however, opportunity for invention in the *intermezzi* or interludes introduced between the scenes of the actual drama. At first these were of modest proportions, merely explaining the

ne

legend. But as time went on, these *intermezzi,* amplified without relation to the real drama, invaded the place given to dramatic recitation, and, with the aid of the music and the stage mechanism (*ingegni*), attracted the whole attention of the spectator, much as the pantomime had invaded and finally subordinated the pagan drama.

Cecchi says that the *intermezzi* were "a modern thing"; and Lasca says that the taste was corrupt and that the interludes "overshadowed the play, and made it appear poor and unworthy." The *rappresentazione* of *Saint Uliva* is an example of this transformation. When festivals or other merrymakings are mentioned in the legend, splendid banquets are often introduced into the *rappresentazione* with real food and wine. In their later and degenerate forms, almost no representation was without music and dances; and even hunts and battles added to the magnificence of the sacred spectacle.

Life and movement and joy sprang from the "sacred drama"; and little remained that was sacred, save the title. Instead of the Bible and the lives of the saints, the chivalric and feudal world, profane legends and popular tales, become the material for these representations. The *rappresentazione* of *Stella,* like those of *Santa Uliva* and *Rosana* and *Santa Guglielma,* presents tradition. Jousts are fought with great glitter of arms and blare of trumpets in *Stella* and *Uliva.* In the interludes of *Uliva,* Jove is invoked, and various classic fables are represented, and nymphs appear dressed in white and shepherds hymning the Golden Age.[18]

A far, far cry from the hieratic solemnity of the early representations of the Passion of our Lord! The true *sacra rappresentazione* had ceased to function. The age demanded a new form of drama. A most interesting period in the history of the Italian Theatre, after a life of more than one hundred years, now passed from the stage. What succeeded we shall consider.

NOTES

CHAPTER II

1. "In the year 1260," says a writer of that time, "while all Italy was defiled by many wickednesses, a sudden and fresh commotion occupied first the Perugians, then the Romans, and afterwards almost all the Italian populations, who were in such wise overcome by the fear of God that, noble and ignoble, old and young, and even children of five years old marched processionally through the squares of the city, naked, with only their shameful parts covered, having thrown aside all restraint; and, each holding in hand a leathern scourge, with groans and cries they lashed themselves severely on the shoulders until the blood came.

"Having given free vent to their tears, as though with the very eyes of their bodies they beheld the Passion of the Saviour, they implored, weeping, the mercy of God and the assistance of His Mother, entreating that, as to innumerable other sinners, so also to them, penitents, their sins might be forgiven.

"And not only by day but also by night, with lighted candles, during a most bitter cold, by hundreds, by thousands, by tens of thousands they went around to the churches of the cities, and humbly prostrated themselves before the altars, preceded by priests with crosses and banners. And the same did they in the villas and *castelli,* so that fields and mountains seemed alike to resound with the voices of those who called upon God.

"Then were the musical instruments and the love songs silenced; only the lugubrious chant of the penitents was heard everywhere, as well in the cities as in the country; at the wailing modulation of which the hardest hearts were softened, and the eyes of the most obstinate could not restrain their tears.

"Nor did the women hold aloof from such great devotion, but in their own rooms not only the women of the common people but also the noble matrons and delicate virgins with all modesty did

46

likewise. Then almost all discords were turned to concord: the usurers and rapacious hastened to make restitution for the wrong done; men stained with divers crimes humbly confessed their sins and corrected their pride. The prisons were opened, the prisoners liberated, and the exiles had liberty to return to their homes.

"In short, men and women manifested as much sanctity and mercy as though they feared that the divine power wished to consume them with celestial fire, or to shake with vehement earthquakes, and with other plagues, with which divine justice is used to avenge itself on the wicked.

"At such sudden repentance, which spread beyond the confines of Italy through divers provinces, not only ignorant men but also the wise marveled, wondering whence came so great a vehemency of fervor: the more so as this unheard of form of penance had not been instituted by the Supreme Pontiff, who was then residing in Anagni (Avignon) nor persuaded by the labour or eloquence of some preacher or other authoritative person, but had had its beginnings among persons of simple life, whose footsteps others, learned and unlearned alike, immediately followed." D'Ancona, *Origine del Teatro Italiano*, I, pp. 105–107.

2. It would be difficult to find examples of lauds in the vulgar tongue before this age; but their existence is possible. It is noteworthy, however, that St. Francis at the time of his conversion, used the French language to praise God: *Laudes Domino cantabat lingua francigena. ... Infra se insum bulliens, frequenter exterius gallicum erumpebat in jubilum*. And in a hymn to his name: *Seminudo corpore Laudes decantat gallice*. But when he began to wander about the Marches, singing, as the "Fioretti" say, *e laudando magnificamente Iddio* (and magnificently lauding God), it is probable that he magnified the Creator and the works of His hands in the language of the common people, as he did in the canticle known as the *Canticle of the Sun*.

The populace, in 1399, had not yet wholly left off the use of the

Latin canticles, as Sant' Antonio attests: *Cantando laudi et inni in latino et in vulgare* (singing lauds and hymns in Latin and in the vulgar tongue), especially that sequence to which it is said that Gregory gave birth: *Stabat Mater Dolorosa, etc.*—Lami, *op. cit.*, pp. 622, 640.

3. A ritual of the fourteenth century belonging to the *Disciplinati* of San Domenico in Perugia, indicates that it was the custom first to perform the discipline, and after that to sing the lauds on Sundays, and on Holy Thursday during the ceremony of the "washing of the feet." The brothers wore appropriate garments for the ceremony; and it is reasonable to suppose that, together with the dress, there was also the appropriate setting for the representation.

The inventory of the fraternity shows that among other things they possessed "two black robes of zendado for angels," and "a shirt for the Lord of Good Friday" and "a black gown for the Madonna," and "three caps, one grey, one white, the third yellow, each with hair," and "two beards of hair, the one white, the other black," and "a white woolen mantle for the Devotion for St. John," and "thirteen mantles for Apostles," and "a mantle for an old Jew," and "two pairs of wings for angels," and "a tunic for Christ," and "a cross and a column for the Devotion."

4. These *devozioni* contained in the Palatine Codex No. CLXX, bear, written at the end, the date MCCCLXXV; but critics agree that they were probably composed in the first half of the 14th century.

5. In all three of the most ancient codices of lauds that have survived to us, the popular language of Umbria is used; and without doubt these served for the offices of the Confraternities. Each book contains both lyric and dramatic lauds; the former were sung univocally, and in the latter, the dialogue was distributed among the various brothers, each of whom recited in his turn the words of the character he represented.

6. Until a recent discovery of Professor Monaci's, our knowledge of the laud was chiefly confined to the lyric form. But it is now possible to trace the dramatic lauds of Italy from their present day form in the countryside spectacles of Tuscany, all the way back to the very birth of the spiritual drama in the vulgar tongue of those thirteenth-century peasants, and to note the form of evolution.

7. Hence it is that the lauds of the *Santa Margherita* are set down as to be sung like the *vaghe montanine* by Sacchetti.

There are also found songs for two and three voices, as in *San Tommaso,* in *Saul,* and elsewhere; and songs in unison, especially those of invocation or prayer, for more persons. And at times the voices must have been accompanied by instruments, as is expressly said in regard to a *canzonetta sopra suoni gentili* (to sweet sounds) in *Costantino,* and to two stanzas sung by dancers in the *Conversione della Maddalena* (Conversion of the Magdalen). A violin, a viola, a lute, served the reciter to make the perfect intonation, and to maintain it true and continued throughout his part.

8. "For *San Giovanni* the form of the *festa* . . . was re-ordered in this manner: that on the 21st day, the show was held. On the 22nd day, there moved first the cross of Santa Maria del Fiore, with all their boy clerics, and behind them six singers; secondly, the companies of Jacopo the cloth-cutter and Nofri the shoemaker, with about thirty children dressed in white, and angels; thirdly, the edifice of San Michel Angelo [St. Michael Angel] above which was God the Father in a *nuvola* [cloud];[1] and in the piazza, before the *Signori*[2] they gave a Representation of the angelic battle, when Lucifer with his accursed angels was driven out of heaven; fourth, the company of ser Antonio and Piero di Mariano, with about thirty children dressed in white, and little angels. Fifth, the edifice of Adam, which in the piazza gave a representation of when God, after He

1. See Vasari's *Lives of Cecca and Brunelleschi.*
2. Probably the *signoria,* i.e., rulers of the city.

had created Adam and afterwards Eve, gave them the commandment, and their disobedience up to the chasing of them from Paradise, with the temptation of the serpent, and other things pertaining; sixth, a Moses on horseback, with much cavalry of the principals of the Children of Israel and others; seventh, the edifice of Moses, which made in the piazza the Representation of when God gave them the law; eighth, more prophets and sibyls with *Hermes* and *Trimegisto* and other foretellers of the incarnation of Christ; ninth, the edifice of the Annunciation, which gave its Representation; tenth, Octavian the emperor with much cavalry and with the sibyl, to give the Representation of when the sibyl predicted to them that Christ should be born, and showed them the Virgin in the air with Christ in her arms.

"And it happened that, the edifice being before the *Signori,* and Octavian having dismounted and ascended on to the lower part of the edifice, or into the church, to begin his Representation, there arrived a German, who had on him only a thin shirt, and at the foot of the edifice demanded, 'Where is the king of Rome?' Some replied: 'Behold him here'; and showed him Octavian. He mounted on to the edifice; many believed that he was one of those who had to take part in the *festa* and hence did not prevent him. He first took the idol which was in the said temple, dashing it into the piazza; and turning to Octavian, who was dressed in violet velvet brocaded with richest gold, he took him, flung him among the people in the piazza; and then clung to a column to climb up to certain children who were above the said temple in the form of angels; and here came forward some of these standing around with the sticks they had in their hands, and beating him severely with difficulty brought him to the ground; whence, rising, and attempting again to climb up, beaten with blows from above and below he was overcome.

"Eleventh, *Templum pacis* (Temple of Peace) with the edifice of the Nativity to give its Representation; twelfth, a magnificent and triumphal Temple as edifice, in which octagonal temple ornamented with the seven Virtues around, and on the east with the Virgin with the new-born Christ, and Herod, the Representation was given around the said temple; thirteenth, three Magi with cavalry composed of more than 200 horses ornamented very magnificently, came with offerings for the new-born Christ; the passion and the Sepulchre were left out because it did not seem that they were in keeping with a *festa;* fourteenth, a troop of Pilate's horse-soldiers set on guard at the sepulchre; fifteenth, the edifice of the Sepulchre, when Christ rose again; sixteenth, the edifice of Limbo, whence he brought forth the Holy Fathers; seventeenth, the edifice of Paradise, where he set the said Holy Fathers; eighteenth, the Apostles and the Marys who were present at the Assumption. Nineteenth, the Edifice of the Ascension of Christ, that is when he ascended into heaven; twentieth, cavalcade of three kings, queens, damsels, and nymphs, with cars and other appurtenances to the life; twenty-first, the edifice of the Quick and the Dead; twenty-second, the edifice of the Judgment, with plentiful tombs, Paradise and the Inferno, and its Representation, as by faith we believe it shall be at the end of the world. All the aforesaid edifices gave their Representation in the piazza before the *Signori,* and lasted until 16 o'clock [i.e. 4 p.m.]."[3]

Translated from D'Ancona *Origine,* etc., Vol. 1, pp. 228–229.

9. "A learned Italian man," so writes the Russian bishop, "has executed in Italy a magnificent work. In a convent of Florence there is a great church dedicated to the name of the Virgin, at the entrance door of which rises a tribune of ten steps [feet] and a half, whereunto leads a little stair cleverly constructed. The tribune and the stairs are both covered with curtains. The tribune represents the celestial sphere, whence God the Father sends the angel Gabriel to the holy Virgin: in it there is a throne, whereon is seated a man of majestic aspect, dressed in sacerdotal robes, with a diadem on his

3. Cambiagi, *Memorie istoriche reguardanti le feste solite farsi in Firenze per la nativita di San Giovanni Battista,* etc. Stamp. Granducale, 1766, p. 65.

head and the gospel in his left hand, as is customary to represent God the Father. Around him and at his feet stand in beautiful order many children. Seven circles surround the throne and the children, and of these circles the smallest has a diameter of about two *braccia*; then there is another larger by two spans, and so on; and in these are placed thousands of little oil lamps lighted.

"The moment of the great and miraculous spectacle having come, many people gather in the church, with eyes fixed upon the platform in the midst. After a little the curtains with the draperies are lowered, and, on the magnificent seat near the little bed is seen he who represents the Virgin. On the same platform are seen the four Prophets, each one of whom has a writing in his hands which contains the ancient prophecies as to the birth and incarnation of Christ. They move about on the platform, each looking at his script, and extending the right hand towards the tribune, which is yet veiled, and say, 'thence comes the salvation of men'; or, discoursing with one another, 'the Lord comes from the South.' Then they dispute together for about half an hour. Above, on the tribune, is seen God the Father surrounded by more than five hundred burning lights, which gyrate continually and go up and down. Children dressed in white, representing angels, surround him, some with cymbals, others with flute or cithern, making a spectacle gladsome and of indescribable beauty.

"After some time the angel despatched by God descends upon two ropes to announce the conception, and being arrived before the Virgin Mary, who is reposing, presents himself to her courteously, holding in his hand a little branch. Then follows the Annunciation, which is an abbreviation of the *Ave Maria,* and the Virgin rising quickly responds with sweet and modest voice: 'O youth, how dost thou dare to approach my threshold and penetrate into my house? What insensate discourses are these, that God will be with me and become incarnate "in my womb?" I do not trust thy word, since I am not experienced in marriage and know no man. Get thee hence, O youth, that Joseph may not see thee, while thou tarriest talking in my house, and cut off thy head with an axe. I pray thee, depart, or he will drive me too from the house.' Then, seeing her fear, the Angel answers her: 'Fear not, O Mary, I am the angel Gabriel whom God sends to announce to thee the conception of his Son. Believe in what I tell thee: thou shalt conceive without seed; the Holy Ghost shall come upon thee, and the power of the Almighty shall overshadow thee.' The Angel commits to her the beautiful little branch, and reascends; Mary remains standing, following him attentively with her eyes.

"In the meantime there goes forth from God a fire, and with a noise like thunder directs itself to the three ropes towards the middle of the platform, there, where the prophets were, rises in flames and gives off sparks in such wise that all the church is full of it; . . . fire advances ever greater and more resounding from the high tribune, lighting the lamps in the church, but without burning the garments of the spectators or doing them any harm. When the angel arrives there, whence he descended, the flame ceases, and the curtains close once more.

"This marvelous and most cunningly devised spectacle saw I in the city of Florence, and I have described it as best I have been able; but it is impossible to do so well, so marvellous and inexpressible was it. Amen." (Abbreviated from D'Ancona, *op. cit.*, p. 249, *et seq.*)

This description shows clearly that the most striking part of the spectacle was the mechanism. The spoken part was secondary.

10. Before entering into a garden, a temple, a house, the characters walk, speak, act; nor do they remain inside their dwellings save when they are obliged, as the holy Virgin in her oratory at the moment of the angelic salutation, Jesus Christ in the temple when he disputes with the Doctors, St. Peter, in the antechamber of Caiaphas, when he denies his Master—*De la mise en scene des Mysteres, Leçon du 7 mai 1855 au College de France*. See also Septet, *Esquisse d'une Representation dramatique a la fin du XV*

siecle, Paris, Palme, 1868; and now also P. DeJulleville, 1, 305 *et seq*. But Mr. V. Fournal in his *Curiosites theatrales,* Paris, Garnier, 1878, follows the ancient hypothesis of the *etages*. Also in the *Nativity* published by Jubinal, 11, 70, it seems that the ordinary manner was to recite inside their own houses: *Cy voisent hors de leurs eschaffaults et regardent le ciel* (Here they come out of their scaffoldings and look at the sky).

11. In the *Conversione della Maddelena* (Conversion of Mary Magdalen) are vivacious dialogues between two gossips who dispute in church over the best seats.

12. In some *rappresentazioni,* in place of the Annunciation, a short dialogue scene is given before the main play, as in the *Miracolo della Maddalena*. In the *Invenzione della Croce* there are found at the beginning some interesting *frottole* (ballads, songs), as also in the *Abramo e Agar* (Abraham and Hagar).

13. Thus, in the *Rappresentazione di Santo e Daria* is a character called the "huntsman," with these lines:

> Up quickly Gherardino and Zanabone,
> Giovan del Bruca, Marcetto and Fracasso,
> call Buriasso and Lorenzone,
> and Tinca, and Zeta, Morgante and Marmasso,
> and Coccodrillo and Bobi del Falcone,
> and Bertuccin who goes with his neck lowered.

And, in the *Rappresentazione di Teofilo* (of Theophilus), the Hebrew enchanter thus evokes the phalanxes of the devils:

> O Beelzebub, great prince of Inferno
> with Cerner, Malataca and Calcabrino,
> and Lastaroc and all thy government;
> come all of you to my dominion.

But the most curious names were those reserved for the robbers or assassins, of whom are "Quattrocento," "il Moscra," "il Tinca," "il Scaramuccia," "il Tagilagambe," "il Carapello," "il Branco," "il Cuccudrilla," "il Bertuccione," "il Carpigna," "il Scalabrino," "il Ciuffagno."

14. Biagio is a wicked, insolent, and avaricious peasant, in whose orchard is a tree reputed to produce delicious figs. The peasant had constructed a hut near the fig tree, and spent every night there on guard against thieves. A gentleman resolves to punish the insolent fellow and gathers together a party of merry companions, who mask themselves in the form of demons, while their leader gets himself up in the semblance of Beelzebub. Having arrived in front of Biagio's, they halt, and Beelzebub asks of each an account of what wickedness he had done in the world. Each says his part; the head demon applauds them; and, as a reward, orders each of them to climb the fig tree and eat a quantity of fruit in proportion to their evil deeds. Barbariccia gets six figs, Astaroth twelve, Farfarello twenty, Calcabrino thirty, Tirinazzo fifty; Squarciaferro, the wickedest, who is to have a hundred, leaps upon the tree, and finds not a single fig. But Beelzebub, to recompense him, orders him to enter the hut and devour the *contadino*. The terrified Biagio who, at every fig gathered by the demons, was ready to burst with rage, on hearing the cruel sentence, and seeing Squarciaferro coming, flees from the hut to the house, and terrified by fright, dies in his wife's arms. The drama closes with a little moral sermon to the peasants.

15. In *San Giovanni Gualberto,* the Angel announces the *festa* (fête) and explains the argument. The scene represents the house of a cavalier called messer Gualberto. A servant brings letters which announce that the cavalier's son has been slain. Gualberto laments his misfortune. Giovanni, his other son, swears and takes oath to Jesus Christ that, even if he should have to search the whole in-

habited earth, he will find that treacherous assassin and, in his blood, avenge his brother's death. He arms himself, mounts his palfrey, and, accompanied by his servants, gallops towards Florence, promising to return home avenged, for Easter day.

The scene changes to Florence on Good Friday. The murderer of the youth says that he wishes to go to church; and therefore no arms are necessary, since, on this holy day, the relatives of the dead man will not injure him. He meets with Giovanni, who permits him a last brief prayer to God before his death. The murderer kneels, confesses that he killed the youth and is not worthy of forgiveness, but implores Giovanni's pardon on this most holy day when God was crucified to redeem mankind.

Giovanni is touched; he embraces him; and together they enter the neighbouring church. Kneeling before the Crucified they thank him, the one for having been delivered from death, the other for having had the strength to forgive. The Crucified in token of approval bows his head; and Giovanni, having kissed his enemy, sets him free.

Then he calls his servants Gismondo and Arrichetto, and sends them to the tavern to have supper prepared. After the servants have gone, Giovanni returns to the church, prostrates himself before the altar, and prays God to show him the way of salvation; and concludes:

> And for thy love, O jocund Lord of mine,
> I'll father, mother, all the world resign.

Giovanni walks towards the monastery of San Miniato near the city, knocks at the door, and, telling his story to the Abbot, asks to be received as a monk.

The servants, not seeing their young lord, pay the host, and, on reaching home, relate to messer Gualberto the episode between Giovanni and the murderer. The cavalier fears that misfortune has overtaken him; and with piteous cries, his wife urges her husband to hasten with the servants to the place where they had left his son.

Arrived before the door of the monastery of San Miniato, messer Gualberto asks the porter if by chance a young man has arrived there. Giovanni, modestly refusing to go to his father, begs the Abbot to persuade him to consent to his son's obeying the divine call; and, in case Gualberto refuses, to bring him into the monastery which he himself will not leave.

At this reply brought by the Abbot, messer Gualberto storms and threatens, and declares that, at all costs, he intends to see his son again. When he has entered the monastery, imagine his indignation, and amazement at seeing the handsome youth clothed in a great rough cowl!

> Sure these great wretched friars have made all speed
> To clothe your body in their garb, my son,
> Still pains and passions fresh for me to breed.
> And you, Sir, give consent to what is done?
> Since he is in one of their frocks arrayed
> They think the world and Heaven's on their side;
> None's here could e'en say pap if he assayed,
> For all of you in here like pigs are styed.
> In evil hour get you back to the spade,
> You ugly crew, all hypocrites inside.
> And thou, wouldst blind like all these others be?
> Go quickly, get thy things and come with me.

The wretched father, after having vented his feelings and invoked death, falls down in a swoon.

The Abbot exhorts the monks to pray to God for the unhappy old man. He comes to himself again. But during the syncope, God has touched his heart; and he is content that his son should embrace the religious life. He asks pardon of the monks for his abuse of them, tenderly embraces his son, and departs.

In his final earthly hour, the venerable Abbot, when about to die, exhorts the monks to persevere in the way of the Lord; he asks their pardon for errors committed, and dies. The friars assemble to elect the new superior; and here the poet with rapid touches draws a repellent picture of the monkish manoeuvres. Giovanni has a majority of the votes to succeed the dead Abbot; but a certain don Roberto conspires with two of his confrères to buy the dignity from the Bishop of Florence.

The second part of the drama begins in Florence and is of the highest importance, since it differentiates this composition from other *rappresentazioni*.

Before considering the case of the Abbot, his chaplain tells the bishop that in the courtyard there are two priests who are contending for a vacant church. Monseigneur replies:

> Into a corner call each priest alone,
> And learn who's got most money to his name,
> And he whose purse weighs most shall be the one.

The honest chaplain has convinced himself that the people's protégé

> Is a good priest, but he's but poorly off,
> Nor would know how to make a blind man sing;

that is, would not be able to spend a soldo; the other has a little bag with him, and in it are two hundred fine ringing ducats. The bishop then replies:

> This one is very right; bring him in here.

Then begins the debate in the presence of the bishop. The peasants insist that, the church belonging to the people, only the people have the right of electing the parish priest; but Monseigneur appoints as parish priest the one who has secretly given him the money bag. And one peasant says to the others:

> Just see that vile accursed bishop, see!
> May he who trusts in him be cut to bits!
> The Turk who to his Mahomet bends the knee
> Has better conscience and a faith that better fits.

Now comes the story of Don Roberto to the friars who are with
him: "Here is a hoard of money," Don Roberto says, "With these
hundred ducats I will buy the office of Abbot. If I succeed, thou,
don Giovanni, shalt be prior; thou, don Arsenio, almoner; and
thou, don Pietro, treasurer. If we are in accord, the monastery shall
be wholly ours." And here they are before the Bishop, who tells the
chaplain to admit them:

> Let him pass in who to enrich me comes,
> Let all the others stay outside and bark.

The friars make their request, and jingle the sack of ducats. Monseigneur wishes to know if they are weighty, and accepts the bag of
gold; the appointment is made. The ambitious monk is recognized
by the monks as Abbot. He calls the tenants and threatens them if
they do not pay, while the tenants pour forth their rage against the
friar who has bought his place.

Giovanni, who can no longer endure the evil doings in the monastery, consults a saintly hermit who advises him:

> Get you into the market-place straightway,
> Where there's much people met to buy and sell,
> And there with such great fervour as you may,
> All that the Bishop's done, to them you'll tell;
>
> How San Miniato's sold for cash away,
> And all their simony thou'lt show forth well.
> Speak thou the words which God shall give to thee,
> And afterwards, my son, return to me.

The scene changes to the *Mercato Vecchio*. The people are clam-
ouring, hustling, pushing in that filthy Babel set in the very centre
of Florence. Giovanni mounts on a little wall and preaches against
the Bishop and the wicked Abbot. A citizen rebukes him saying:

> Put you no faith in this dishonest liar
> Who so as not to work became a friar.

The bishop hastens to the Market, abuses and beats the preacher, and threatens to burn him alive. Giovanni returns and tells the hermit, who counsels him to withdraw from a city which is so evil as to submit to such a wicked bishop.

The story next shows San Giovanni Gualberto retiring into the Apennines, whence after founding the famous monastery of Vallombrosa, he descends into the plain near to Florence and becomes abbot of San Salvi. The furious bishop hires a Spanish cutthroat to attack the convent of San Salvi and kill the monks. To the villain and his robber band, it is as though they were going to a wedding. They thank fortune which sends them a little work.

16. A father has two sons, one a sorry fellow, the other good. The former gratifies his every wish, is deaf to admonition, refuses all restraint. The second, dutiful, modest, industrious, intercedes for his misguided brother. The father, having learned that a representation was to be given dealing with the adventures of Isaac and Ishmael, invites his two sons to go to the fete.

They take their way towards Fiesole. Benedetto asks the *festaiuolo* (master of the ceremonies) the subject of the representation. The *festaiuolo* narrating the story, supplies that part which in the other *rappresentazioni* is usually taken by an angel. The dialogue becomes yet more animated, owing to the arrival of a hunchback who is to represent one of the personages; and the drama begins. When the story is ended, the father asks the wicked son how he has liked it. The boy is convicted of his sins, resolves to change his life, and, from the Ishmael that he had been, to become a new Isaac. The happy father clasps him to his breast and thanks the *festaiuolo;* and the *rappresentazione* closes with a brief salutation to the spectators.

17. Favoured in its rise by the most powerful family of the city, set up with liberal expenditure by pious fraternities, rendered splendid by the clever inventions of the best artificers, the *sacre rappresentazioni*

were in turn transplanted and imitated in other parts of Italy. In 1414, in Parma, a *rappresentazione* of the *Re Magi* was given by the doctors and scholars of the University; and there are vague notices of *ludi* in Rome in 1414, and of certain Neapolitan spectacles in 1423. At the Court of Amedeo VIII of Savoy, and probably in Turin, there was given with great magnificence in the April of 1427 the *ludo* of St. George.

18. Santa Guglielma, when iniquitously accused by her own brother-in-law, is condemned to death by the King, but is saved by a cavalier. She wanders through a desert, crosses the sea, arrives at a monastery, obtains from God the virtue of healing the sick, heals her own accuser of a terrible leprosy, and is finally reunited with her husband. Uliva, to escape the evil love of her father, cuts off her hands, and is abandoned in a wood. After having encountered the strangest adventures, and having miraculously reacquired her hands, and having become the wife of the King of Castile, she is exposed to the persecution of her royal mother-in-law, until her innocence triumphs and her sorrows come to an end. Stella, without any fault of her own, excites the envy of her stepmother, through whose hatred she is exposed to dolorous adventures not unlike those of Uliva. Rosana, who loves prince Ulimento, is torn from him by the order of the King and Queen, and sold to the Soldan, and is then liberated by the valour of her young lover.

The *rappresentazione* of *Stella* is one of the most vast and varied compositions of this character, and deserves special mention because it presents an intermixture of all the dramatic elements.

Frederic, Emperor of France, convokes his barons and announces that urgent state affairs require him to go to England. He commends Stella, his only child by his beloved first wife, to the loving care of the Empress. As the Empress is walking with her step-daughter in the palace garden, two passing merchants praise the beauty of the maiden.

The envious stepmother summons her faithful servants, Arnaldo and Ugo; and, after swearing them to secrecy, she reveals that it will soon be impossible to conceal the consequences of Stella's evil life. The culprit must die to save the royal honour. They must lead the maiden into a wood, kill her, and, as a proof, bring to the Empress the severed hands. Besides the money reward, they shall be raised to the grade of captains.

The assassins invite Stella to go with them to meet the returning Emperor, who is drawing near to the city. The happy girl hastens with them. After they have gone a long way in the wood, the assassins inform her that the Empress has condemned her to die. Stella with pitiful lamentations commends herself to the Virgin Mother of God, and pleads with her executioners not to kill her. Ugo and Arnaldo are filled with compassion; but, mindful of the danger of not fulfilling their oath to the Empress, they cut off her hands, which they carry to the Empress. In a quarrel over dividing the gains, Arnaldo slays Ugo.

The scene then changes from France to Burgundy. The son of the Duke of Burgundy goes hunting with his barons and, coming to the wood, hears poor Stella's cries. She refuses to tell him the cause of such cruel mutilation, but returns with him to court. Her wounds are dressed; and the young prince, attracted by her beauty, modesty, and noble manners, loves and marries her.

Again the scene changes back to the Emperor's Court. The Emperor, having returned from England, hears his daughter's supposed fate, and grieves inconsolably. His wife, to divert him from such sorrow, proclaims a tournament to which all the princes and barons of the empire are invited. The young Duke of Burgundy repairs thither to display his prowess; and, in combat with the Duke of England, obtains a triumph, and sits on the right hand of the august sovereign.

The scene is again in Burgundy. Stella has given birth to two sons. The old Duke despatches a messenger with the joyful news to his son. The Empress learns from the messenger that Stella is yet living, and trembles for her own life. The messenger, having received the Duke of Burgundy's letter in reply to that of his father, returns to the Empress; and from her hands drains a cup of drugged wine, and is overcome by deep sleep.

The wicked woman replaces his letter by another, counterfeiting the signature of the young prince, and praying his father to kill both the dishonest mother and the children since they were the fruit of adultery. The Duke, having read his son's letter, trembles with horror, and consults with his barons, who unanimously advise that the children and the adulteress be put to death. Poor Stella, dragged into a horrible wood and left there with her tender babies to be devoured by beasts, implores the protection of the Virgin. In the meantime, a hermit approaches and comforts her, and, to save her from the wild beasts, leads her to a neighbouring grotto and there leaves her. The sorrowing woman again prays to her celestial protectress. And behold, the Madonna descends to comfort her, and miraculously restores her hands, and then disappears.

The Prince of Burgundy returns to his father's court, hears the dreadful tale, and, horrified at the black treachery, hastens to the wood, where he encounters the hermit, who leads him to the cavern in which Stella had found shelter. The husband and wife weep for joy; the husband marvels at the new wonder of the hands, and understands the miracle of the Madonna. The royal couple arrive at the court amid the amazement of all. The mourning is changed into rejoicing; and, in the midst of a splendid banquet, Stella relates the pitiful history of her adventures. All marvel; and soon the husband and wife repair to France and appear before the Emperor. Imagine the joy of the bereaved father on finding his daughter restored to him. He orders the death of his impious consort, and, taking the crown from his own head, places it upon the tresses of his beloved and too unfortunate Stella.

CHAPTER III
(AN INTERCHAPTER)

THE ITALIAN COMMUNES

The Italian Commune as the basis of modern society: Its early history: In Milan; most affected by feudalism: In the lesser Maritime Republics: In Genoa; least affected by feudalism: In Venice; most important for the study of the theatre: In Rome; a type differing from the others because of the rivalry of Empire and Papacy: In Florence; latest and most glorious of all the communes:

IT is not possible truly to understand these plays, or to judge of the accuracy of their representation of contemporary life, unless we can enter into the minds of their authors and also participate, at least to some degree, in the social life of the audiences that listened to them. This social atmosphere, the daily life and thought and spirit of author and of audience, which must be a part of any true history of the Italian Theatre, is to be found in the Italian Communes. More than that, the Italian Communes were the greatest contribution which Italy made to Europe during the Middle Ages.

"The Italian Commune," says Villari, "is an institution which created modern society. The Middle Ages were unacquainted with the State; Europe was divided into feudal castles, into associations, almost into little groups and fragments. Above these fragments into which society was broken up, there were two great, two universal institutions: the Empire and the Church; but these two institutions, just because they were universal, could not favour the institution of the modern national State. The Middle Ages knew nothing of civil equality; the aristocracy was a separate caste from the rest of the population; it represented, in Italy, the foreign blood. The workers were not free. The Italian Commune proclaimed the independence of work, the equality of men. These are the foundations upon which modern society is based."[1]

64

The history of the Italian Communes is the history of the larger part of Italy for several centuries. Upon this history many books have been, and many more will be written. The present writer hopes to compose one. The subject is an inexhaustible mine of treasure. But nothing more than the briefest survey can be attempted in this chapter.

At the outset, it must be remembered that not all Italy was under Communal government. To southern Italy came the Normans, shortly after the year one thousand, as the allies of the Pugliesi; and in less than one hundred years they had dissipated the fragments of the old Longobard, Greek, and Communal institutions, and, after many vicissitudes, ruled over most of that large part of Italy which finally became the Kingdom of the Two Sicilies. All this region, then, is outside of the Communal regime, as it was also outside of the reconstituted Western Empire.

If we accept the claim that the Italian Commune is the first foundation of modern civilization, it is not difficult to understand that the Italian historian would fain believe that it is an old Roman institution which survived the feudal order; whereas the Germans see it as the offspring of Germanic individualism, an institution derived from the Conquest. The Italian Commune was, in fact, derived from many elements, including the old Roman tradition, the Church, and German feudalism; and the proportion of these elements will vary according to whether the Commune under consideration be Milan or Venice or Rome or Florence. Each one of these forms will be briefly considered as representing a different type, all uniting to make up the Italian Communal system; though each form had a different influence upon the Italian theatre.

From the fourth century, Milan was considered the second city of the Roman Empire; and its archbishop-hero, St. Ambrose, exercised an influence not so greatly inferior to that of the Pope in Rome, in a diocesan principality which extended from Genoa to

Coira, from Mantua to Turin, and which observed a distinct religious ceremony. The history of the city is summed up in the history of a succession of great men. After the barbarian conquest which left the marble city a heap of ruins and witnessed the massacre of more than thirty thousand of its inhabitants, and after the succeeding centuries of anarchy, came the first Otto and feudal tyranny; but it was an intelligent despotism and the beginning of a political renaissance. In the ninth century, Archbishop Ansperto wisely governed the city, rebuilt the ancient walls which had been destroyed by the Goths, and made its defences so solid that the people from the distracted countryside flocked within its gates, with the result that, in the eleventh century, it was the most populous city in Italy, numbering more than three hundred thousand inhabitants.

But greater than Ansperto di Biasonno of the ninth century, greater than Landolfo di Carcano of the tenth, was that man of iron will and great soul, Archbishop Ariberto d'Intimiano, who ruled the Milanese in the eleventh century and who holds a great place in the history of his city. That same Ariberto who had twice crowned Conrad King of Italy, does not hesitate—when that king attempts to take away the liberty of Milan and to enter the city with his army—to lead a citizen army against that king, to drive him from the walls, and to uncrown him. Supported by the affection of the Milanese people, he ignores his excommunication and deposition from the archepiscopal seat by the infamous Pope Benedict IX.

Here begins communal government. The king is uncrowned. From the public acts are removed every imperial date. Ariberto begins to draw, from the popular forces, elements of administration and government; and the prestige of feudalism has been shaken in the public mind by the successful defence against the Empire. The moment seemed ripe for the assertion of full communal liberty.

But Ariberto's spirit was not great enough to complete the work of political emancipation; and he fell back into the traditional alliance with the greater feudatories.

Then comes Lanzone, the noble rebel against his own order, the great vassal who makes common cause with the people; Lanzone who is neither Guelf nor Ghibelline; who substitutes for his own personal power the universal body of citizens, those common people who, together with the nobles, had fought against the Empire and defeated the Emperor, and now felt themselves no longer a servile flock but free citizens. Lanzone, who had been elected *Capitano del popolo,* in 1043, went to Germany and made a treaty of alliance with the Emperor. Long were the succeeding negotiations both with the Emperor and with the different classes of the citizens; but finally, on May 5, 1055, at the solemn Diet held in the meadows of Roncaglia, the necessary ordinances were sanctioned and became a part of the public law of the Realm. After centuries of strife, the universal body of citizens had attained their civil emancipation; and there arose in Milan the sovereign and autonomous commune.

A "sovereign and autonomous commune," we have said; but it will be remembered that we also have said that the "ordinances" became a part of the public ordinances of the *Realm*; for though the rights of all the citizens have been equalized into a "Commune," we are still upon feudal soil; still supreme is the authority of the *Sacro Impero Romano e Germanico.* Large as may be the liberty of government of the citizens within their own walls, no one questions the authority in the Imperial Diets of him who is Roman Emperor and King of Italy, and judge and arbitrator between city and city. And for centuries to come, in all the communes, there will be need for constant watch and struggle to retrieve and maintain the already established *buone consuetudini*—good custom.

Amalfi, Pisa, Genoa, and Venice, at the time we are now consid-

ering in our history of the Italian Theatre, possessed many traits in
common in which they differed from the communes of Milan and
Florence and Rome. The Commune of Amalfi requires only brief
mention. Like a brilliant comet it lighted the Italian sky for a
moment; and, like a comet, it was soon extinguished, as was the
splendour of Naples, Sorrento, and Gaeta, before the rising greatness of Pisa, Genoa, and Venice. From Arabia and Egyptian
Alexandria, from Africa and Antioch and Sicily, from every port
in the world, rich treasures were poured into Amalfi. Wherever
the tides of commerce flowed, its ships and its sailors were found.
And then, in the beginning of the twelfth century, came the Norman hosts; and the liberty and prosperity of Amalfi were extinguished in blood, leaving behind not a trace of influence upon the
Italian Theatre.

The Republic of Pisa, however, was, for a time, a fierce rival of
Venice for the commerce of the Orient. Cherishing as her heritage
the ancient Etruscan civilization and the Roman greatness, Pisa
did not fear to wage war with Genoa and Venice, and to challenge
and defeat the might of the Saracen armadas. Pagans, Parthians
and Chaldeans, Libyans and Turks, merchants and mariners from
every port of the then known world, thronged her streets, until her
maritime power was shattered in the battle of Melotia. Her literature and her art remained and grew more luminous; and her influence on the Italian Theatre was considerable.

Genoa, however, was the republic most feared by Venice: Genoa,
who more than once humbled the pride of the city of the lagoons,
destroyed her fleets, and seized her commerce. Long and bitter
were the wars, brief the truces. Sometimes Genoa and Pisa united,
as in the war against the Moors for Sardinia; and then Genoa and
Pisa fought each other for sixty years. But Genoa was never entirely overwhelmed. Though the Genoese quarter of Acre was
burned to the ground and their navy destroyed in a most bloody

battle by the Venetian Lorenzo Tiepolo in 1256; and though again in 1261, in the waters of Trapani, the Venetians seemed to have forever shattered their power, yet, in the proud victory of Curzola, the armada of Genoa completely shattered the Venetian fleet, and brought back five thousand prisoners to Genoa. For our purpose, the important thing to remember is that, of all the communes, Genoa was least influenced by Feudalism; and that from 958, she enjoyed her liberty. Her maritime rivalry with Venice and Pisa, and this fact of her communal liberty, are constantly reflected in the plays of Genoese inspiration.

To Italians, the significance of the great war lies in the fact that the *Veneto* of the Romans is now Italian. This dream and, for centuries, most ardent desire of every true Italian, has now become an historic fact. "Unredeemed Italy" is at last Italian, and never again will be subject to foreign dominion. How every fair-minded and intelligent man in all the world must rejoice that this act of justice has at last been accomplished, and that—from the eternal snows of the Corinthian and Tyrolese Alps to the warm waters and brilliant sun which bathe the shores of the Adriatic Gulf—those historic lands and cities have at last returned into the bosom of Mother Italy! And how large a place they have occupied in the literature, and especially in the theatre, of Italy; this Italian *Veneto,* of which beautiful Venice herself, so long groaning under the yoke of the foreign oppressor, is the exquisite crown.

Not here is it possible to consider the founding of Eraclea, Jessolo, Murano, Malamocco, and Torcello, in the Venetian lagoons, by the Italian inhabitants of the *Veneto,* fleeing from the Hunnish hordes that poured down over the Alps in the fifth century. Is it not written in the chronicle of Altino? And how they drained fens and marshes, planted vineyards, reclaimed fields, straightened winding canals, and sank cisterns? Has not Cassiodorus told us? We know that the first government was that of the maritime trib-

unes (*Tribuni Marittimi*) elected by the people; and we know that
Paoluccio Anafesto, the first Doge, was elected in 697, and we
know that when Pepin, Charlemagne's son, attacked the Venetian
duchy with his army and ships, the people, under the advice of
Doge Agnello Partepipazio, sought refuge in the island of Rialto.
And tradition says that Pepin suffered so great a defeat that the
waters were dyed red with the blood of the slaughtered Franks.
Certain it is that at Rialto began the magnificent city of Venice.
The many small islands were united by bridges, a magistracy was
created, and the new city was embellished.

How fortunate might we suppose this city. Unlike the other
Italian communes, here was no faction of Guelf and Ghibelline
waging fratricidal warfare; no mingling of two races of victor and
vanquished to raise high towers in narrow streets from which to
fight between themselves; no Germanic Emperor to demand an
oath or to bring his armies within her confines. She alone will
never be vassal of Church or Emperor. Surely we may expect
Venice to develop her truly imperial prosperity in tranquillity.
Alas, the domestic life of Venice was a succession of internal discords from century to century. Often the battle raged furiously
between her leading men. Stern Pietro Candiano and his son are
slain in the palace, and their slaughtered bodies left unburied out
of scorn. A Caloprino slays a Morosino; and later the Morosini
hack to pieces three Caloprini. Thus through all the Middle Ages,
probably more than any other Italian commune, does Venice present a picture of the fury of the factions.

Notwithstanding these internal discords and the rivalry of the
other maritime communes, the city increased in population and
prosperity. In 1006, Doge Orseolo II completed a part of the basilica of San Marco and the ducal palace, conquered the Dalmatian
maritime cities, established quiet in the fevered city; and the Adriatic, freed from Narentano pirates and the Saracens, became a

Venetian lake. Her ships were to be found in all the ports of Africa and Asia. Durazzo was captured; the Byzantine Empire was saved from the Normans; unexplored seas were traversed; and a separate quarter of Constantinople became in fact a Venetian city. Her power dominated the Orient. Within the city were the hum of industrial activity, manufactures of every species of textiles, foundries and workshops; and, later on, the greatest arsenal in Europe created her ships. Her government, midway between the tyranny of a single autocrat and the democracy of all the citizens, was ruled by the *Ottimati,* or noble families, a form of government that, in spite of its defects, gave independence to Venice for centuries.

For many reasons, the history of the Venetian Commune possesses an interest far surpassing that of any, or all, of the other maritime communes. Indeed, this interest is greater than that of any other commune in Italy except possibly that of Florence. The Commune of Venice is unique in the history of the world. To the student of the Italian Theatre, Venice, its customs, and its history, are of surpassing importance. No other city in the world so truly reflects its history, its customs, the very psychology of its people, in its theatre. Here was born and lived the greatest of all the writers of Italian plays, and one of the most prolific. And these plays are Venetian. More than that, they are Venice itself, its customs and its people of every rank.

But besides Venetian Goldoni, by many considered the most popular playwright the world has ever known, there were many other Venetian writers of plays, and many other plays in which the life of Venice is reflected, some of which will be considered in this history. Venice is unique: unique in her origin, and her saints and festivals; unique in her form of communal government and in the character of her people. This very brief reference to Venetian history should be helpful to an understanding of the Venetian theatre, which has an interest all its own.

The Roman commune does not represent any type; it stands by itself. *Roma caput mundi regit orbis frena rotundi* was absorbed in the idea of universal domination. Her sovereignty had dominated the world; her civilization and law had been imposed upon Europe and Asia and Africa; and her people were still intoxicated with the terrible sound of her name and dreamed stupendous dreams. Even in this twentieth century, for one of her citizens to say, "I am a Roman," signifies to him something grandiose and imperial.

But Rome was also the seat of the Papacy. This was not accidental; without Rome there would not have been a Roman Catholic Papacy. The attributes of imperial pagan Rome were appropriated by the Church. Rome was also the fountain head of the Roman-Germanic Empire. It was the "Holy Roman Empire"; and from the time when its first Emperor, Charlemagne, was crowned in Rome, his successors were accustomed to consider their solemn coronation in Rome as a part of the Imperial formula. And the Roman people, believing that they themselves were the supreme authority, welcomed both Papacy and Empire within their city, not as masters but as evidences of their own sovereignty.

But, as if there were not enough confusion in the fact that Roman people, Roman papacy, and the crowned head of Holy Roman Empire, each claimed supreme authority in the city, there came down from their castles and fortresses in the hills about Rome, the most haughty, most cruel, most insolent nobility that the world has ever seen, and took up their residence within those tragic walls. These nobles bring their armed retainers in from the country and also organize the people into armies. The temples of antiquity, the arches, the baths, the Coliseum, are turned into fortresses. The beautiful marbles and statues are torn down and built into bulwarks. There are inextinguishable ferment, violence, victories, defeats. There are the wars of the factions: nobles fight against nobles; again they unite to oppose the emperor within their walls;

and there is always the pope to fight or to oppress. Tumult and horror are for centuries the ordinary form of life; permanent anarchy and confusion are the expression of the history of the Roman commune.

As early as the beginning of the eighth century, mention is made of the Roman duchy; and the people strive to have a duke of their own election. From this time until the fifteenth century, when Martin V, definitive founder of the temporal power of the popes, finally destroyed the remains of communal liberty, some sort of communal life, under various names, existed in Rome; but it was always under the shadow, and with the limitation, of the presence of the Pope and the influence of the Empire. Sometimes it was almost absorbed by one or the other of these two powers. Sometimes it seemed as if the people, conscious of their rights and of their strength, would be free from both these oppressions, as when, in 1143, they reconstituted the Senate, and declared the Republic to be restored and the temporal power of the popes to have ceased. Two years later, Arnaldo of Brescia came to Rome, and, with the cry, "No pope and no emperor. Let us ascend the Capital and restore the republic," recalled Rome to its ancient glory. Arnaldo was burned for this sin; and his ashes were thrown into the Tiber. But, though that dream of the Republic seemed to have vanished, it was never destroyed; and though popes may have seemed to have attained quiet and to have secured domination over the riotous city, the volcano was only slumbering.

How the power of the Bishop of Rome changed and gradually expanded into the enormous and universal power of the Papacy, has already been related.[2] The rise and progress of the papal temporal dominion in its contact and conflict with the people of Rome, who still cherished the old Roman idea that in them resided the right of universal dominion, is the most important fact in the history of the Roman commune. Rome was the prison, as truly as it was the throne, of the popes. It was the place of their martyrdom. How many popes were dragged from their churches and palaces, and outraged, beaten, and threatened with death, and sometimes killed! Against others, the gates of the city were shut; while others made shameful surrender to the mobs or to the nobles. Urban II, who could raise all Europe in crusade against the infidel, lived upon alms. Gregory VII brought a German emperor to his feet, yet was assaulted in the midst of the Christmas services, beaten, and dragged by his hair from church. In the never-ending war between national and imperial force, each side elects its pope and strives to remove the pope of the adverse party. This is the picture of the commune of Rome during the Middle Ages. And greatly did it influence the Roman theatre of these centuries.

Though Florence was the latest in origin, it was the most glorious of all the Italian communes. Situated in a valley, surrounded by a circle of castellated hills, fortresses from which the feudal nobles could threaten and dominate the city, it had not the room to expand which had Arezzo or Sienna, each standing on a hill, or Pisa and Lucca, each situated upon a plain. The antagonism between the city people gazing up at the hated feudal castles and foreign nobles looking down upon the despised city was more intense than in any other of the Italian communes.

The beginnings of Florence were humble. We know that it was sacked by Totila in 550; that it had sunk into such obscurity during the Longobard dominion that it is mentioned as a mere suburb of Fiesole. We know that Charlemagne, and after him many other Emperors, passed through it on their journey to Rome to be crowned; and that there was continual contact between Rome and Florence where some of the popes found refuge when fleeing from their own rebellious capital. But the first documentary evidence of a sense of citizenship is in 1063, when the Florentines rebelled against their bishop, whom they claimed to have been simoniacally elected through money paid to duke Godfrey, husband of Countess Beatrice, the mother of Matilda. In the account of the trial, municipal magistrates are mentioned, although it was still connected with feudal institutions.

Upon the death of the Countess Matilda in 1115, Florence found herself independent, owing to the contest between the Empire, which wished to resume its control over the Margravate, and the Church, to which Matilda had left all her possessions. Without contest or upheaval, those who had commanded the army and administered justice in the name of Matilda became the Consuls of the Commune and continued to exercise their offices in the name of the people. The real government, however, remained with the heads of the Guilds, or *Arti,* who with their adherents formed the Senate or Council. And back of these were the *Popolo,* the people, who in matters of great importance were gathered together in a Parliament. It is this democracy of government by the body of citizens, associated together in their consortium, or confederation of arts and crafts, and daily discussing public affairs, which partly explains the intellectual activity of the times.

The first period of Florentine history is that of continued war against the fortified castles upon the surrounding hills. Then came civil war against the conquered counts of these demolished castles, who were compelled to live within the walls of the city and under the laws of the Commune. It is a history of political and social communal transformations, internal wars and revolutions. These nobles, of Germanic origin and foreign feudalistic customs and traditions, fortified themselves in their palaces within the city, and attempted to live the same life they had lived in their castles upon the surrounding hills and to wage the same war. When the nobles were excluded from the government, they united with the heads of the chief Guilds against the lower classes, the *popolo minuto,* who at first only fought for a share in the government, but finally became the supreme power. Then came the Medici, and the Republic fell. The *Arti,* or Guilds, lost all political importance in this concentrated government; there were no longer privileged classes or hostile groups. The society of the Middle Ages had ceased to exist; moral decadence had begun; we have arrived at the Renaissance.

The history of the Florentine Commune is of absorbing interest. Here we see how the liberty of popular government unfolds from the first feeble feudal organization in which the nobles rule, through a government in which nobles and people unite, to the final type in which the people alone are supreme; every form of communal life is to be found in this evolution. Here we have the contest between Papacy and Empire, the two powers which dominate the Middle Ages; here we have the strife between two peoples compelled to live within the same city walls, German feudal nobles and Italian commons, with irreconcilable difference of ideals; here, in the tumultuous tragedies of its inner life, Florence presents the first germs of the modern State.

And the marvel of it all is that this unending strife, characteristic of all the Italian communes, and these political movements which stirred men's souls and roused their passions, also roused their minds and stirred their artistic faculties, making them alive, filled with that ardour of youth and resolution of manhood which not only enriched the cities with workshops and carried their commerce to the ends of the earth but also found its glory and crown in the beginnings—and more than mere beginnings—of the cosmopolitanism of art and dramatic representation which we are considering in these pages.

NOTES

CHAPTER III

1. Pasquale Villari, *Gli Albori della vita italiana.* See also: Francesco Lanzani, *Storia dei Comuni Italiani origini ac* 1313.

2. Cf. Chapter II, the opening section.

CHAPTER IV

THE FIFTEENTH CENTURY AND THE HUMANISTIC THEATRE

The fifteenth century a division between the Italian mediæval and humanistic theatres: Character of humanism in Italy in the fifteenth century: Petrarch's lost comedy: Vergerio's *Paulus*: University plays: Levico's *Catinia*: Alberti's *Philodoxus*: Pisani's *Philogenia*: Aretino's *Poliscena*: Piccolomini's *Chrysis*: Buzario's *Cauteriaria*: Medio's *Epiriota*: Poliziano's *Orfeo*: Boiardo's *Timone*.

AS in all evolutions that have not been interrupted by some abrupt cataclysm, so, in the gradual unfolding which marks the evolution of the Italian Theatre, there is no exact year to which we can point and say, "Here ended the Italian mediæval theatre, and here began the Italian humanistic theatre"; yet, for convenience of chronological division, the year 1400 may be accepted as the dividing line between the new and the old. This fifteenth century is the overlapping fringe between the old theatre and the new; and the year 1400 presents the humanistic theatre as its characteristic, because, from this date, Humanism is the prevailing note in all Italian literature, though there were still a few play-writers who composed in the "mediæval" manner, just as it is true that, as early as 1337, from the time of his sojourn in Rome, Petrarch, abandoning his scholasticism, became not only a Humanist but the father of Humanism.

Before considering the Humanistic Comedies, reflect for a moment upon the spiritual, intellectual, and social conditions of Italy during the period immediately preceding the Italian Renaissance.

During the fifteenth century there was an almost complete separation between the cultivated classes and the people. Humanists, intent upon the exploration of the classics, ignored the vulgar tongue. They thought and wrote in Latin. A polite public was formed, who, in the courts of princes and palaces of noblemen, amused themselves with ephemeral literature in the Latin tongue. Even when they wrote their mother tongue, men of humanistic culture loaded it with Latin.

The renaissance of Italian literature took place almost simultaneously in three centers: at Florence under the protection of the Medici, at Ferrara in the castle of the Estensi, and at Naples in the Aragonese Court. Rome, from the pontificate of Innocent VIII to that of Leo X, was almost dumb and deaf to literature; Venice waited till the period of the printing-press; Milan produced nothing. It was but gradually that the wave of national culture reached the minor states. The three cities to which Italy owed the resurrection of her genius were ruled by princes; and, from its commencement, the new literature felt the influence of courts.

The Humanists themselves constituted a new and powerful body, a nation within the nation, separated from its higher social and political interests, selfish, restless, greedy for celebrity, nomadic, disengaged from local ties, conscious of their strength, with the vast prestige of learning in that age swaying the intellectual destinies of the race. Insolent and ambitious in all that concerned their literary pretensions, these men were servile in their private life. They gained their daily bread by flatteries and menaces, hanging about the courts of petty despots, whose liberality they paid with adulation, or quickened with the threat of infamy in libels.

And it is precisely these characteristics of this Italy of the fifteenth century which is revealed in its *quattrocento* humanistic theatre. It is, indeed, the mirror which truly presents to our eyes the very life of the age. For, whether by intention or otherwise, every play reveals the author's own mental and spiritual evolution as it is developed under the influence of his age and environment. He may choose for the development of his plot some other age, some far distant country; yet that other age and country, and the personages with whom the author peoples the scene, inevitably interpret both the soul of the writer and the spiritual and intellectual evolution of his own age and country.

The Italian fifteenth century is an age which gave Giotto to art and St. Francis to humanity; an age in which Dante, instead of being the master and dominator, was in fact but its greatest product. It is the age of the Crusades; of Arnaldo of Brescia and his revolution against the papacy; of the League of Lombard States, of the Great Schism, of the Inquisition, of the founding of the universities, of St. Thomas Aquinas, of Savonarola, and of the Medici; the age of the *Trovatori* and of Provincial poetry, of Longobard legends and of Carlovingian epopee in Northern Italy; of Charles of Anjou; of the Sicilian Vespers; of the "Magna Curia" (Sicilian poetic school) and the Aulic lyric; of Norman civilization and of the great Frederick, and the other prince-poets in the South. It is the age of the revival of Aristotelian philosophy, of Latin religious and moral poetry, of the precursors of Humanism and Latin culture. And yet, at the same time, it was the age of *Dolce stil nuovo* (the sweet new style) and of literature in the vernacular. It was the age of the *lauda* and of the *devozione,* of the exodus of Greek scholars from Constantinople to Italy, and of the invention of printing.

To differentiate accurately between these social, spiritual, intellectual, and sometimes opposing energies, in this intermingling of old and new, of original and imitation; to assign to each of them their proper place in the history of thought; even to represent the Italian psyche of this period, interpreted by its dramatic production, is most difficult.

Janus-faced indeed was this Italian evolution: backward looking toward the setting sun, and striving to revive the old Roman civilization and old Latin literature; yet, with the other face, gazing into the luminous horizons of the dawning day and, in the new

Italian vernacular, endeavoring to express the Renaissance ideas and ideals, which were invading the universities and establishing civic liberty in the communes.

Janus-faced the spiritual and moral and political world. Everywhere old and new are in conflict; everywhere spirit and flesh contend. Brutal acts of violence, obscene literature, and immoral social life are contrasted with the preaching that Christ is King of Florence, and with St. Francis singing his *Cantica del Sole,* and with the rapturous emotion of mystics and ascetics. Everywhere is rebellion, upheaval, exaggeration, as the heritage of the past contends with the new conquest of the intellect. This is the characteristic of the Middle Ages.

Amid the purifying blaze of new ideals, the decrepit edifice of feudalism was crumbling away; and chivalry, born from feudalism, beautiful in romance, in real life was more often oppression. Its virtues were too often mere empty words, phantoms without substance, oppressing rather than protecting woman.

The growth of the commune (the commonwealth) is the greatest political and social affirmation of the Italian Middle Ages. To the individual, so long outraged and trodden down, it gave a new consciousness of the dignity of personality. With new institutions came new ideals; and relationships between men became more human. Men's souls saw new visions; to men's hearts came new ideals. The war between flesh and spirit is waged under new forms; and, though harmony between such opposed tendencies will never be attained, and the truth ofttimes is lost sight of in this struggle, yet spirit and intellect still will be reflected in literature and art, and inevitably appear in this new development of the Italian Theatre.

Two great men represent the opposing tendencies of this period. Dante in his *Divina Commèdia* looks backward into the Middle Ages, which he completed and closed with his disdain, his wrath, and the sublime imaginings of his lofty soul. Francesco Petrarca, the first modern man, the harbinger of the Renaissance, beholds the dawn. With him, we enter upon a new period of thought, and of the art of the theatre. Petrarch's single humanistic play forms a very small part of his literary accomplishment. It is, however, remarkable that the initiator of the humanistic play so conspicuously exemplifies in thought and character this period of unrest and contradiction. Restlessness and contradiction did indeed mark Petrarca for their own. To-day he writes like an ascetic; to-morrow he composes as a pagan: constantly inconsistent, torn by opposing desires; a modern man sick with hysteria and nerves. Sometimes for an hour he is lost in the mists of Ages; then, he beats his breast and asks mercy of God; but soon he emerges to write sonnets to the golden tresses of his lady-love. To-day he is humble, to-morrow arrogant; constant only in his love for Italy, for Rome, and for classic antiquity.

In another book, we have written about the nature of Petrarca's love for women. For Petrarca not to love and to die would be the same. Quinet has truly written: "The originality of Petrarca consists in his having been the first to feel that every movement of our existence may contain a poem; that there is not an hour of life which may not enclose an immortality." How unfortunate is it then that such a fervent supporter of Humanism should have composed only one humanistic comedy, and that that one has been lost.

In his letter to Giovanni Colonna di San Vito, brother of Stefano *il vecchio,* in reference to his *commèdia Philologia,* Petrarch wrote, "Quid multa? Meministi, credo in *Philologia* nostra, quam ob id solum ut curas tibi iocis excuterem scripsi, quid Tranquillinus noster ait." And some years later, in 1348 or 1349, when his Florentine friend Lap da Castiglionchio asked to see this comedy, he replied that this comedy of his youth was not worthy to be known of learned men; and, besides, he had not the manuscript with him; he had left it, perhaps at Avignon.

With the exception of this lost Petrarchian *Philologia,* the only other humanistic play that belongs to the fourteenth century is the *Paulus* of Pier Paolo Vergerio, senior of Capodistria, composed in Latin at Bologna probably in 1389 or 1390. This play, placed in Bologna, begins with a characteristic and original scene, which clearly presents the moral figure of the protagonist. Paolo is a youth of weak and changeable character; and his servant Herotes, a complacent executor of his master's desires, induces Nicolosa to sell her daughter Ursula to Paolo. Before leading her to his master, Herotes seduces the young girl, but persuades Paolo that he has procured him an intact virgin.

Paulus has certain exterior resemblances to the classical comedies of Terence; but its spirit, sentiments, and manners belong to the fourteenth century.[1] Like most of the Latin comedies of this century, *Paulus* reflects that contemporary Italian university life, to which, because of its importance in relation to the theatre, we shall give an interchapter. The personages of many of these plays are students; and they are frequently composed by students with lively imaginations. Two of these will illustrate the gaiety and licentiousness of these students and also their relations with Bologna townspeople. We will select a play which has neither title nor name of the author; he was probably a student. Like most of the Latin dramas of the *quattrocento,* this play reflects the vivacity and libertinism of Italian university students. Sharp, vivacious, rich in interest on account of the satire against the clergy and the realistic description of the university life, this play is disgustingly obscene. It describes a conspiracy of young and wild "contubernales" against Frate Janus to punish him for an unclean vice. There are pages which cannot even be summarized. In another play, the *Commèdia Elettorale,* some of the students of the University of Padua conspire against their co-disciple, Corrado Schutz. We live again in one of those glorious Renaissance universities. These persons really experienced the passions, and performed the actions, described in the *Commèdia*.

Also unknown are the authors of three other *quattrocento* Latin plays: the *Conquestio uxoris Canichioli Papiensis,* the *Comœdia Bile,* and the *Comœdia sine nomine.* The first is an obscene dialogue between Canicchiolo and his wife while they are both lying in the conjugal bed. It is inspired by the tenth story of the fifth day of the *Decameron.* The *Comœdia Bile* also is a vivacious trialogue between Bila, a spiteful, avaricious woman, and Aristanco, her husband, a jovial hospitable man, and Episcopo, a finished knave. In the *Comœdia sine nomine,* classical and mediæval elements so mingle that it is unlike any other *quattrocento* Latin play. It was probably composed by a Dominican friar between 1450 and 1460, and is dedicated to Cardinal Prospero Colonna, who died at Rome, March 24, 1463. The same mediaeval legend which inspired the unknown authors of *Rappresentazione di Stella* and the *Rappresentazione di Santa Uliva* likewise inspired the unknown author of the *Comœdia sine nomine.* In the two former, however, the Christian sentiment mingles with the spirit of adventure which belonged to the Middle Ages; while in the latter, the responses of the oracles and Apollo and Minerva and the priestess of Delphi are substituted for the angels and the Virgin; and the jousts of the Middle Ages are supposed to take place in classic Athens. The most interesting characteristic of the play is this curious anachronism, this strange mixture of ancient and modern manners and sentiments; it is a paganized *sacra rappresentazione.*

Siccone Polenton di Levico in the Walsugana in 1419 wrote a dialogue entitled *Catinia.* In his letter of dedication to Giacomo Badoer, the author called this work a "Fabula." Five men gaily eat and drink in an inn. "Nothing can be more worthy of man, nothing more pleasing to God than to find men peacefully drinking, eating, and rejoicing in good company." Thus the *Catinia* is apparently a hymn to gluttony. But it is more, since the substantial part of the comedy consists in a jesting and friendly dispute between Catinio and Bibio, interrupted continually by the observations of the others.

Contrasted with this merry dialogue of an already mature chancellor of the Commune of Padua, is the severely thoughtful work of a young student of the Bolognese university. The *Philodoxus* or *Philodoxeos* of Leon Battista Alberti was probably composed before the second half of 1426. The young Athenian Filodosso loves Doxia, also loved by the insolent Roman citizen Fortunio. The latter, aided by his friend Froneo, breaks into Doxia's house, but by mistake carries off her sister Femia. Finally Chronos, *"excubiarum magister,"* arranges everything. Fortunio keeps the ravished girl, and Filodosso marries the beloved Doxia. Doxia is glory; Femia, her sister, is fame; Filodosso loves glory; Fortunio pursues Fortune; Froneo is wisdom; and Chronos is Time, who solves difficulties. They are merely personifications of abstract concepts. Though greatly admired by his contemporaries, Alberti's comedy is cold and tiresome. The allegorical suffocates reality.

De coquinaria confabulatione or *Repetitio egregii Zanini coqui* and *Philogenia* were written by Ugolino Pisani. *Philogenia* preserves the type of the mediæval epic comedies and also of the sacred dramas; and the various events succeed each other without interruption and without logical division of the story into hours and days. It deserves consideration as being one of the very few humanistic comedies in which there is a real portrayal of character. Prodigio is a priest of easy morals and corrupt soul. Epifebo is a wild youth who hesitates at nothing in order to accomplish his purpose. Filogenia is weak but not vicious. She accepts the various vicissitudes of her successive amours as the necessary consequence of her first fault; nevertheless she suffers, and accepts the pain of marriage to a dolt as the only means of possessing her beloved

Epifebo. The conclusion of the comedy is effective. Epifebo gives to Filogenia a dowry and marries her to the stupid peasant Gobio, who sets out for his country home leading his supposed virgin bride, while another peasant, Salino, walks ahead, blowing on his pipes a *tur lu ru tu tu* which sounds like a sarcastic laugh.

The *Poliscena* of Leonardo Aretino is written, like the *Philogenia,* in prose, without division into acts, and with little respect for the classical unity of time. It is a story of love and seduction. Gracco, son of the old Macario, wishing to possess the young Poliscena, is aided by his servant Gurgulione and the old serving-woman Yaratantara. When this wretched female is unable to persuade the mother, Calfurnia, to sell the girl for ten *mine,* she finds Poliscena, tells her how Gracco is dying for love of her, entreats her to be merciful. Poliscena, already in love, arranges to receive him secretly. When Calfurnia discovers Gracco's seduction of Poliscena, she tells his father, and threatens the son's condemnation to death unless he marries Poliscena. Old Marcario consents to the nuptials; and thus the story ends.[2]

The *Poliscena* comedy is classic in form. The character of Gurgulione (from the *Curculio* of Plautus) differs little from the servants of the Plautinian and Terencian theatre. Marcario and Gracco are the figures of father and son as they were represented by the Roman theatre.

But the influence of classicism is even more evident in the *Chrysis* of Enea Silvio Piccolomini, written in 1444. It is written in Latin iambic verses imitating those of Terence and Plautus. The personages in the *Chrysis* are those of the ancient theatre; the crude representation of the customs and sentiments of the prostitutes is lifelike. Cassina says to Criside, "No lover pleases me for more than a month. Always do the new calends bring me new loves." And Criside replies: "Thou lovest with too much constancy, since it is fitting to celebrate with new unions both the nones and the ides: in fact, with every new sun I procure new lovers." Although originality is not lacking in the *Chrysis,* Piccolomini's imitation of the Plautinian Comedies extends even to particular expressions, as may be seen by comparing the *Chrysis* with the *Asinaria* and the *Curculio.*

The *Cauteriaria* of Antonio Buzario (1469) is a gay little tale, although suddenly the action takes a tragic turn. Bracco, the husband, exhausted by the excesses of sensual love, and having through ill treatment killed both his first and his second wife, is now able to fulfil his marital duties only "vix semel in anno." Sintilla, his third wife, desires compensation from the priest Auleardo, handsome, vigorous, fresh-coloured, "of just stature, of worthy form." Salamina, her maid, suggests the means, while suspicious Bracco charges his servant Graculo to spy upon his wife. Graculo sees his mistress in church exchanging gestures of love with the priest. After the sermon, Sintilla, on returning to the house, feigns illness, and begs for a priest for the last rites; and Salamina introduces Auleardo into the chamber where the dying woman lies. While the woman is "confessing" in her own way, and the faithful Salamina guards the door, Bracco rushes into Sintilla's bedroom; but Auleardo has fled. He returns; and Bracco finds the two in flagrant adultery. The man escapes; the terrified woman implores mercy. Here comedy changes into savage drama. The old man says to Graculo, "Hide thyself under the table in the room so that thou mayest aid me when I bind Sintilla upon it to cauterize with a red hot iron that part of her body which erred." Auleardo, with his friends, breaks into Bracco's house, learns from Sintilla of the horrible torment inflicted on her, and furiously determines to inflict the same punishment on Bracco. Bracco trembles with horror. He implores Auleardo: "I will offer you a splendid supper . . . I will give you five hundred pieces of gold . . . I will make you master of my house . . . I will be always your servant . . . I will cede to

thee, my Sintilla." Auleardo is not moved; but the woman intercedes for her husband. Freed from the prospect of torture, joyous
and grateful Bracco orders a banquet which offenders and offended
enjoy together. The three principal personages of the comedy, the
husband, the wife, and the priest, form a triad which was dear to
all story-tellers of that age. Even Bracco's method of punishing
Sintilla is not original with Buzario. He has borrowed everything
from the mediæval *Novelle*.

In 1483, Tommaso de Mezzo (or, in Latinized form, Medio), a
Venetian patrician, published his comedy *Epirota*. The young Clitifone loves, and is loved by, the maiden Antifile, who had sailed
from Epirus with her father, who dies during the journey. On her
arrival in Sicily, she is welcomed by Clitifone's uncle who, having
fallen in love with her, gives her a little house and supports her.
He does not dare to make the girl his wife, she being poor and an
orphan. Hence, he delays things; and at the same time flatters old
Pamfila, who is determined to marry him. But at this point, Epirota, the uncle of Antifile, comes from the Epirus to Syracuse. He
gives his niece a rich dowry and marries her to Clitifone; and he
himself marries Pamfila. There is originality in the first scene in
the *Epirota,* where Pamfila's serving-maid rouges the old woman's
cheeks, and fills with ointments the wrinkles in her foolish face.
The woman is not a prostitute as in the *Mostellaria* of Plautus. The
figure of the charlatan, unknown to the ancient theatre, also appears here on the scenes for the first time, and is well depicted.[3]

Antiquity and the Middle Ages both influenced the fifteenth century humanistic theatre. The technique and the subjects of these
comedies were suggested by the surrounding social activity, and
reproduced scenes of Italian university life. Toward the close of this
century, however, classic antiquity stimulated Italian Humanists
to attempt the drama. In the *Epirota* of Medio, the *Stephanium* of
Armonio, the *Dolotechne* of Zamberti, classicism is supreme. Sub-

ject-matter, situations, characters, language, style, structure, are all in direct imitation of the Roman theatre.

Closely imitating this Roman theatre also, but entirely different in dramatic composition, are the *Orfeo* by Poliziano[4] and the *Timone* by Boiardo. Poliziano's *La Favola di Orfeo* is a dramatic poem, similar in form to the *sacre rappresentazioni*, but with a classical instead of a religious subject. The *Orfeo* combined tragedy, the pastoral, and the opera in a mixed work of melodramatic art in which the songs of the shepherds and wood-nymphs anticipated the style of Tasso's *Aminta* and Guarini's *Pastor fido*. If, in form and movement, it adhered to the traditions of the *sacre rappresentazioni*, its originality consisted in the substitution of a Pagan for a Christian fable. Poliziano says that he "wrote this play at the request of the Most Reverend the Cardinal of Mantua, in the space of two days." Poliziano wrote the *Orfeo* at the age of eighteen. It could not have been played later than 1483, for in that year the Cardinal died. The merit of the piece is in its charm of musical language, its subtlety of musical movement, a limpidity of thought and feeling, in which the very words evaporate and lose themselves in floods of sound. Orpheus himself is a purely lyrical personage.

Boiardo by his *Timone* and Poliziano by his *Orfeo* gave the earliest specimens at Ferrara and Mantua of secular plays written in the vulgar tongue. The *Timone* must have been composed before 1494, the date of Boiardo's death; and the *Orfeo* was in all probability represented in 1472. It is significant that the two poets who were mainly instrumental in effecting a revival of Italian poetry, should have written for the stage. In the *Orfeo* we find a direct outgrowth from the *sacre rappresentazioni*. The form of the Florentine religious show is adapted with very little alteration to a pagan story. In substance the *Orfeo* is a pastoral melodrama with a tragic climax. Boiardo in the *Timone* followed a different direc-

tion. The subject is borrowed from Lucian, who speaks the prologue, as Gower prologizes in the *Pericles* of Shakespeare. The
comedy aims at regularity of structure, and is written in *terza
rima;* yet the chief character leaves the stage before the end of the
fifth act, and the conclusion is narrated by an allegorical personage,
Lo Ausilio.

·NOTES

CHAPTER IV

1. Neither the greedy Nicolosa nor the wary Ursula have much in common with the women of the Latin theatre; they are figures from real life, and they belong to that tribe of women of whom it is not difficult for a youth like Vergerio, a student at the university of Padua, or of Florence, or of Bologna, to acquire direct experience.

2. Love and seduction are here, as in the *Philogenia* of Ugolino Pisani; but the catastrophe is utterly different. There are, however, two monologues which remarkably resemble each other. In these monologues of Poliscena and of Filogenia, both lament the sad servitude in which social conventions and family education hold unmarried women. These girls both long for the pleasures of love.

3. The hero of *Epirota* (1483) has just arrived in Syracuse and, accompanied by a "Civis Syracusanus," sees, upon the public square, a charlatan who speaks to a crowd of people: "As I told you, O young men, this herb from the garden of the Hesperides possesses infinite virtues. A thief will be able more easily to hold fire in his hand than this root; and for that reason, in Mauritania, where this herb grows, there are no thieves. It possesses another memorable virtue. If anyone shall carry it with him sewn into his clothes, he will never perish by an evil death. . . . I turn to you, O navigators, to you who sail over the salt waves of the sea. Those who carry with them this root cannot drown. This herb has very great virtue against the bites of scorpions, and calms disturbances of the belly, and loosens the bowels, and heals the diseases of the chest and cardiacal defects, and is the sole remedy against the bite of a mad dog, and prevents the falling out of hair, and can heal many other ills."

4. Poliziano (b. 1454), whose real name was Angelo Ambrozini, was the son of a lawyer named Benedetto. At the Studium of Florence,

he studied under Argiropulo and Landino, and soon became distinguished for the elegance of his Greek and Latin epigrams. About 1470, Lorenzo de' Medici first took notice of him, and soon came to esteem and love him, and extended to him his powerful protection. In 1480, he was appointed professor of Latin and Greek Eloquence in the Florentine Studium, and held the position until his death in 1491. Like most of the Humanists, Poliziano believed that his *epistolae,* which he collected in twelve books, and his other philological and poetical works written in Latin, would be the foundation for his lasting fame; and certainly some are worthy of preservation. The classic revival has nothing superior in faultless form, warm affection, and sweet serenity, to the elegy on the death of Albiera degli Albizzi; and many of his other odes and elegies, modeled after those of Catullus, Ovid, and Horace, are of unusual merit. His *sylvae,* compositions improvised in moments of poetic inspiration, in imitation of Statius, are full of life and vigor. Yet it is certain that Poliziano's works written in the Italian vulgate, in moments of relaxation, are the chief foundations of his fame.

CHAPTER V

(AN INTERCHAPTER)

ITALIAN UNIVERSITIES AND THE MIDDLE AGES

The rise of the universities: Ecclesiastical Schools: Lay instruction: The *Schola*: University at Bologna: Emigration to other schools: Character and customs of the scholars: Relations of students and professors: Rivalry between the universities and reasons for their decline.

THREE great forms of association controlled the social and political life of Italy during the Middle Ages, and, taken together, had a large influence upon the evolution of liberty in Europe. As the association of workmen in the corporations of the Arts or Guilds consecrated the freedom and dignity of work, and exerted a large political influence, especially in Florence, and as the Communes gave to the world a new conception of political liberty through their aggregation of all the elements of the ancient civilization and the participation in the government of the popular classes in a common democracy, so, too, that third great form of association, the Italian universities, so highly developed during the Middle Ages, by their own will-power acquired very great authority in the social order in Italy and no small influence to the farthest confines of Europe. Without extraneous aid, and sometimes in opposition to those two universal powers, the Church and the Empire, these first centers of modern culture were being developed. Filled with the enthusiasm of youth and enamoured with ideals of democracy, untrammeled by ecclesiastical or political imposition of a formula of theories and limitations, they contended for freedom of thought, liberty of instruction, and right methods of science.

Since these universities form so large a part of Italian life, it is evident that they must be considered in any history of the Italian Theatre which pretends to keep the reader in contact with the environment in which these plays were written and performed. Especially is this true when we consider how much of the literature of the Middle Ages is occupied with these universities, and how often the life and love-adventures of their scholars are mentioned in the tales of Boccaccio and the other novelists, and how many of the plays were either written by university students or describe university life.

We shall not attempt to inquire into the relative importance of the Germanic and Roman influence in the gradual revival of learning and culture which preceded and culminated in the formation of the Italian universities, or to determine the comparative value of ecclesiastical and lay schools. It is certain that, in the first period, Roman society was submerged through its own corruption, that its disruption was completed by the barbarian invasions, and that the early Christian church opposed Roman culture and viewed classical learning with suspicion.

Then came the second period, when the church was obliged to adapt itself to the changed conditions and to avail itself of the profane studies and historic culture in order to propagate its faith and in order to combat the schisms and heresies that were rending it. The universal use of the Latin tongue in the rites of the church was also an element in the preservation of the ancient learning, which also found asylum and cultivation in the monasteries. There the remnants of ancient learning were collected, and in process of time the profane authors were transcribed; and, to many of these institutions, schools were attached for the instruction of the youth. The most famous of these schools was that attached to the monastery of Monte Cassino. This monastery was also richest in the ancient codices, especially in those of medicine and philosophy; and here arose the first asylum of medicine in the West, where many monks both studied and wrote books on this science. There were schools also at Arezzo and Lucca; and throughout Italy the chapters of the cathedrals maintained schools and it was customary for such of the parish priests as possessed sufficient learning to give private lessons.

In regard to lay instruction we have little information. Undoubtedly there were always some lay teachers of letters and grammar; and it seems probable that the study of Roman Law was never entirely interrupted. It was, however, the hated Lombard king who, in his capitol city of Pavia, founded the first juridic school of the Middle Ages, one hundred and fifty years before that of Bologna. And it was the Frankish king Lothair who first sanctioned lay instruction, by his decree ordering a Scotsman, Dungallo, to found schools in many Italian cities, in order to free the intellectual development of the people from ecclesiastical influence.

First in origin and importance of Italian lay centers of culture was the medical school of Salerno. Its doctors were already famous in 984; and its world-wide renown brought students from every part of Europe. Here, for the first time, was assured the intellectual emancipation of the laity from centuries of ecclesiastical dominion in the study and practice of medicine; and, in its earliest period, it was also free from government control. As the most ancient centre of lay culture, and because here for the first time academic degrees were conferred, the Salernian school occupies a notable place in the history of general scholarship as well as in the history of medicine. So great was its fame that the city of Salerno was called *Civitas Hippocratica*.

Although there is mention of a Pisan school of law before 1000, the historic importance of the Ravenna school overshadows all others of that date, because, under the Greeks, Ravenna was the seat of the *Exarchate* and of Greek culture in Italy, and later was the capital of the *Pentapoli*, in which are found the earliest germs of Italian liberty.

Although it was soon to overshadow all other Italian schools, and ultimately to develop into a great university which should rival that of Paris as the largest and most renowned in Europe, little is known of the school at Bologna previous to the coming of Irnerio. Through his original methods of teaching—by the use of glossaries and by separating it from the other branches of knowledge then taught—Irnerio gave to the study of law the character and importance of an independent science; and thus, in the law school of Bologna, recalled this study to its original Roman sources.

These first forms of scholastic association previous to the universities were called *Schola,* and represent a free association between masters and students bound together by a love of learning, and not subject to political or ecclesiastical control, the methods of teaching, the customs of life, the amount of compensation for the instruction given, all being matters of informal agreement—a spontaneous development of culture through the fertile exchange of ideas and information between master and disciple. Such were the schools in the dawn of the new Italian life. Rapidly these schools spread through the principal centres of population; the ardour for learning became common in all classes; new schools were founded everywhere, which prospered or were discontinued according to the fame of their teachers.[1]

In this very brief consideration of the rise and progress of education and culture in Italy in the centuries previous to the universities, we see how, from the first timid beginnings of lay and ecclesiastical instruction up to the widespread and sometimes famous *Schola,* it was—as in those other great and contemporary social institutions the Guilds and the Communes—a gradual evolution which, taken together with the simultaneous development of those Italian Guilds and Communes, explains the Middle Ages.

The second phase in the evolution of the school at Bologna, through which it ceased to be a mere concourse of private activities, a free association between masters and students, was due to the

German emperor Frederick I. Believing that the approval and support of this renowned school of ancient Roman law, and of the traditions of the ancient empire, would consolidate to the monarchial principle and legitimatize his claims of universal dominion, the Emperor by legal sanction raised it into a privileged and independent corporation. Through this imperial decree (*autentica*) giving to the Bolognese school a special jurisdiction and recognition of the privileges of the scholars which might not be interfered with by the citizens of Bologna, it took the name of University (*universitas*).

The city of Bologna not only sanctioned the privileges conveyed to the University by the *autentica* of the emperor, but sought to prevent the rise of other universities in Italy, by threatening with serious punishment any professor who proposed to go elsewhere. Another cause of disturbance, however, was the creation of the University of Liberal Arts (*Universitas Artium*). This caused such grave conflicts between the *giuristi* and the *artisti,* that many of the professors and students braved the threatened penalties for so doing, and emigrated to other schools where they could tranquilly pursue their studies without danger to life or limb. In 1222, many scholars with their professors went to Padua, which from that time had its university. In 1321, many went to the *Studio* of Sienna. As a final result of these migrations, almost every city became a centre of study; and there was keen competition between the different universities to attract students.

This scholastic life, made up of such varied and multiform elements and inspired by enthusiasms and passions so different from those of our own times, represents one of the most picturesque sides of mediæval Italian society. Between those free and nomadic colonies of students and the modern assemblies of scholars, there is nothing in common; and it is this fact that renders interesting the study of those students and of their uses and customs.

Let us transport ourselves in imagination to the period in which there hastened by tens of thousands, to the Italian cities from all parts of Europe, individuals of every age and every social grade; often accompanied by their families; of different nationality, languages, and customs; united among themselves by a common tie, the worship of learning (science); subjected to a special jurisdiction; favoured by innumerable immunities and privileges; wandering here or there without either restraint or law; proud in a profound and limitless sense of independence; often turbulent and quarrelsome: and we shall have a vague and distant idea of what was the scholastic life in the ancient universities.

These scholars with their families formed separate colonies called *nazioni,* named according to the foreign countries (*ultramontani,* from beyond the Alps) or the various provinces of Italy (*citramontani,* of this side the Alps) which they represented. Tumults between scholars of different nations sometimes arose from the most trifling causes. In Bologna, moreover, some scholars introduced themselves masked into the schools while the doctors were giving their lessons, arousing disorders and tumults.[2]

The licentious life which some students led, arose in part out of the customs of the time and the general corruption. Among the students of the Middle Ages were certain individuals called *Goliardi,* who wandered from one university to another leading a licentious life.

That which rendered the scholastic life of the Middle Ages very varied and characteristic, was the frequency of the festivals which were celebrated by the students at certain periods of the year, the professors and other persons connected with the university contributing to the expenses. Every university had also its own special civil and religious festivals. The election of a new Rector was celebrated with great solemnity. Cavalcades, jousts, tourneys, banquets, balls, brightened not only the university but the whole city, which took part in this ceremony as in a public fête. So also the conferring of degrees on the richer scholars was fêted with great banquets and balls; and the arrival of some famous professor usually set the whole city in movement.

The life and love-adventures of university scholars is frequently pictured in the literature of the Middle Ages. Boccaccio and other novelists mention the scholars in their tales.[3] History records frequent rapes of maidens and many other amorous adventures of students, in which the authors had frequently to pay with grave penalties and even with their lives.

In the great multitude of scholars in many cities, private liberality founded numerous colleges.

The scholastic authorities from the earliest times of the foundation of the universities ordered the professors and students to wear a dress different from that of the other citizens, so as to be recognized by the citizens and to profit by the rights and privileges appertaining to their position. Each scholar was obliged by statute to dress in the prescribed way, no matter to what social class he belonged by birth and degree.

Those scholars, however, who wished to lead a life apart from the citizens, could do so without difficulty; for the universities were at that time so constituted that—whether on account of the number of those who flocked to them, or whether through their privileged condition—the students could dwell for long in a place without extending their relations beyond the school. This exceptional state of things gave the scholars who came to study in Italy the conviction that there was no power superior to themselves.

We come now to the relations between the scholars and their teachers. The scholar of the Middle Ages was left to choose his own teachers; and following their lessons and scientific precepts and the traditions of the school, the student showed the real esteem which he had for his teachers and the lofty concept he held of them.

Scholars and professors represented, as it were, a great family. The scholars shared all the immunities and privileges of the professors; coöperated in their election; contributed to the perpetuation of their fame. The scholars were accustomed to call their professors *domini,* and these latter named their disciples *socii*—a title that perfectly corresponded to the place they held as companions and familiars of their masters, and to the coöperation which usually existed between them in the building up of learning. He who was called *dominus meus* was the favorite preceptor of the scholar, who accepted without hesitation his scientific opinions and traditions, perpetuating his name with loving solicitude.

The scholars had the custom of collecting the oral lessons of their professors into volumes and spreading them among other schools. These lessons which formed the numerous commentaries that are still preserved and that witness to the industry of the doctors of the Middle Ages, were clear and simple "conferences" wherein learning was imparted to the hearers without pedagogical bombast or ponderousness, but with a free and familiar exchange of ideas.

These intimate relations between professors and scholars manifested themselves in various ways in the university life of the Middle Ages. The school was then a spontaneously formed company: a clientele which each teacher aimed to create by his personal merits, and which brought him emoluments and fame in proportion to the number of hearers whom he succeeded in acquiring.

The arrival of a professor in a city was highly honoured. Thus, when Filelfo passed in 1429 from Bologna to Florence, all the people went out to meet him; and Cosimo de' Medici went in person to visit him several times. "All the city," wrote Filelfo, "has its eyes upon me, all love me, all honour and praise me in the highest degree. My name is on the lips of all. Not only the most notable citizens, but even the very matrons when they meet me in the city give place to me, and respect me in such wise that it makes me blush. My scholars number about four hundred every day, and perhaps more, and these are for the most part of high standing and senatorial."

We have seen heretofore what was the origin of the ancient universities, and what were the causes of their rapid increase in the Middle Ages. Now, with the same brevity, we shall examine the principal causes of their decline.

Among these causes of decline must be enumerated the incessant and disloyal war which the greater universities made upon the less, so as to increase the fame and splendour of their own schools. The universities, says Savigny, carried in themselves the germ of their ruin, in that the splendour with which they shone depended in great part upon accidental, personal, and transitory causes. Frequent pestilences, intestine wars, discords, famines, very often put a city in the hard position of having to close its university, when the exchequer was exhausted.

The excessive number of Italian universities during the Middle Ages was another cause of their decline. There were not enough doctors and scholars to fill all the universities. Hence, the minor universities were unable to sustain the competition of the richer and more powerful.

Another cause of decline common to all Italian universities was that spirit of discord which reigned in the schools and continually excited hatred among the teachers and tumults among the scholars. In the Middle Ages, society was disturbed by profound rancours and party passions which communicated themselves also to those who cultivated learning, so that the schools changed to veritable centres of riots and battlefields.

Moreover, in the place where the prince had his seat there were founded—almost as ornaments of the palace—academies, libraries, and other centres of scientific activity. The rise of these academies contributed to lessen the scientific importance of the Italian uni-

versities. These new centres of culture rendered learning, like nobility, a caste privilege and a title of honour reserved to few. Many
of those learned men who taught in the universities were guests of
the princes, and divided the cares of their Chair with the offices and
affairs of the courtier, and had necessarily to sacrifice the independence of their reason and scientific convictions to the wishes of
their patron. It naturally followed that, in these associations of
men of letters and artists, all the vices and corrupt manners of the
courts were introduced.

Amid so much emulation for the resuscitation of the ancient remains of the classic culture (even though copyists had multiplied
and found in the exercise of their art large gains), it was not possible with the patient work of the hand to cope with the extraordinary demand for books and the numerous requests made for them
by the studious. Printing, propagating knowledge with marvellous celerity, extended the benefits of learning, and rendered possible for all—without the aid of masters and at small expense—the
acquirement of knowledge. But the invention of printing lessened
the importance of the universities. In the preceding centuries
learning was within the dominion of the universities, and they
made a monopoly of it. Oral teaching was the only means of com-
municating ideas; and one could not become learned except by
hearing the living voice of a professor. Printing, together with the
courts and the academies, drew away a great number of those who
were previously frequenting the universities, and led them to give
up seeking the investiture of academic degrees.

To hasten the decline of civilization and the corruption of manners, there contributed also not a little the predominance which—
in the sixteenth century and yet more in the succeeding ones—the
ecclesiastics took in the institutions of public instruction. The monastic orders having in a short time spread throughout all Italy, to
them was entrusted, almost exclusively, the education of the young

people, who had to accomplish the probationary period of studies under their direction.

The universities also experienced the serious injuries of the ecclesiastical influence, because the censorship and the Inquisition limited the field of learning; and many branches of teaching were abolished by them under the pretext that they were contrary to the dogmas and precepts of the catholic religion. Moreover, to the bishops was entrusted supreme power over the universities.

NOTES

CHAPTER V

1. The chronicler Landolfo attests that such schools were flourishing in Florence, Rome, Milan and other cities, in which were to be found "excellent preceptors of philosophy and other arts" and "famous scholars."

2. This singular custom is recorded in the University of Ferrara; and there survives a very curious edict of 1478 which prohibited anyone from entering the public schools masked. The Edict runs thus:

   "On the part of our most illustrious Lord Duke Hercules, etc., etc., command is given to all and every person, either native or foreigner of whatsoever condition, that, from henceforth, they neither dare nor presume to go in *Mascara* (mask) to the Schools of the Studio (University) of this City of Ferrara, to annoy the Legists and the Doctors or the lessons of the Scholars under penalty of ten gold Ducats to be applied to the Ducal *Massaria* (funds) and to stay eight days in prison; notifying every person that any such Masqueraders will have the masks taken from their faces, and they will be led to prison, and will not come forth if they do not pay the penalty."

3. In the seventh *novella* of the eighth day, Boccaccio narrates a bad joke played on a Florentine scholar named Rinieri by a cunning widow whose love he had sought, and of the vengeance which he took upon her. As the moral of the tale, the writer teaches what it is to scorn the scholars. "Such then," says Boccaccio, "were the consequences of her flouts to this foolish young woman, who deemed that she might trifle with a scholar with the like impunity as with others, not duly understanding that they . . . I say not all but the more part . . . know where the Devil keeps his tail. Wherefore, my ladies, have a care how you flout men, and more especially scholars."

CHAPTER VI

THE SIXTEENTH CENTURY: THE COMEDY

Popularity of the comedies of Plautus and Terence: their influence on the *cinque-cento* Italian comedy: The adjustment of the innovators of the Latin comic types to Italian types, and the reflection of Italian life in the new comedies: Ariosto's *Cassaria,* an example of the new comedy: his *Suppositi: Negromante: Lena: Scolastica:* Machiavelli's *Mandragola,* the most important Italian comedy of the sixteenth century: his *Commèdia in Prosa:* his *Cliza:* Bibbiena's *Calandria:* Aretino's comedies: his *Cortigiana,* a great picture of contemporary society: Lorenzino de' Medici's *Aridosia:* Lodovico Dolce: The *Gelosia* and *Strega* of Grazzini: Cecchi's *Assiulo:* Gelli's *Sporta:* Giambattista della Porta: Secchi's *Interesse:* Bruno's *Candelaio.*

GREAT was the excitement among cultured Italians when, in 1429, after centuries of oblivion, Niccolo di Treviri, that is, Cusano, discovered in Germany a codex containing twelve new comedies by Plautus.[1] Soon these and other comedies of Plautus and those of Terence lived upon the Italian stage as they had formerly lived in Rome, being recited in the original Latin at the courts of princes. Because of the recent invention of printing, their comedies were widely read. Terence's comedies were first printed in 1473; and, in 1476, Giovanni Rufoni (called Planco) published six of Terence's comedies in Venice, with a commentary by Donato. Printed translations of these plays soon followed, were read by many, and were performed upon the stage before numerous and cultured audiences.[2]

You may be sure that those slaves of classic tradition, the humanistic writers, strove to make their own compositions close copies of the form and content of the Roman theatre. Thus, through familiarity with the Roman comic poets and the Greek Aristophanes, the humanistic comedies assumed a purely classic form; and the historic and legendary personages and the Olympic gods of Greece and Rome occupied the Italian stage. According to the rhetoricians of the *cinquecento,* Plautus and Terence were gods, and all good

105

comedy must exactly imitate the Roman, and woe be to the presumptuous writer who failed to follow their infallible rules.[3]

A prologue or argument must be succeeded by exactly five acts; then, after all the knots had been untied and all difficulties solved, the happy ending. And, with slight exceptions, the material which was poured into this mould—the types, characters, plot: fathers and sons as rivals in love, braggart soldiers, finding of lost children, strange recognitions, foolish youths enticed by greedy prostitutes, and all the rest of the Latin theatre—is repeated in the sixteenth century Italian Comedy.

Even the language was fixed by those popes of practice, the rhetoricians. Since comedy characters must be servants, courtesans, parasites, and merchants, the particular language used by these stereotyped characters must also be stereotyped to fit the character. It was a theatre of anachronisms and improbabilities, lacking in psychological analysis; for true literary criticism—born of contemplation and unprejudiced judgment of works of art, and conscious of its own limitation—did not exist in the sixteenth century.

Even when original as to subject, the *cinquecento* comedies remain faithful to the Latin in unity of time and place. The action develops in a few hours—at the most in a day—and the unchanged scene always remains an Italian street or piazza between the houses of the actors.

Comedies composed under such limitations inevitably exhibit a desolating uniformity. Fortunately, there were innovators: some timid, cautiously feeling their way; others more bold, who rebelled against tyrannic tradition, and insisted that the new age demanded a new type of comedy that should more truly reflect the new social conditions. Close or slightly varied translation gradually merges into free rehandling of Latin originals. The fusion of subjects from Latin comic writers with those of modern novelists, and with classic themes especially from Plautus and Terence, was worked into the dramatization of real events of recent times. There are frequent examples of an old father as his son's rival in love, and of marriages forcibly prevented or imposed. Intricacies are produced by the guile of servants, and solved by one or more recognitions (*agnizioni*) of persons believed dead, lost, or stolen in childhood. The same artifices are continually repeated, with a multiplication of disguises, substitution of persons, pretended illnesses, and dangers. Many comic types also have their origin in the Latin theatre: the old blockhead, the miser, the grumbler, the lover, the crafty and rascally servant, the parasite, and the bragging soldier. But, in Italian comedies, these Roman stock characters are modified and adjusted to the modern conditions in which the scene is always placed.

Real life has also suggested the creation of new types: the necromancer who deceives clowns with his charlatan arts; the noisy, awkward, and roguish boy, either as servant or as page; the hypocritical friar, as the imposter ready for any vile service; and the ignorant pedant tutor, who, with great ostentation, speaks a hybrid language larded with Latin. These innovators saw real contemporary life, of which they themselves were a part. Was the writer a citizen of Venice or Naples or Rome, walking through the streets, stopping to converse in the piazza, listening to some good story— some choice bit of scandal about Messer So-and-so or Madonna Such-a-one, told in the local vernacular—this local contemporary life was inevitably reflected in the comedy he produced.

The plots will be improbable, the characters exaggerated; the social life of the city not quite as immoral as the story makes it; the sins of the personages depicted will be made at least as black as reality, for there was little reticence in that age. But those *cinquecento* audiences found truth at the theatre, else they would not have favored these plays. And, if the writer of this history did not believe that you, gentle reader, would find in these plays a true picture of an important moment in the Italian social evolution, he would not have undertaken the huge labor of attempting to present it. Here you will find a whole world of folk: types and characters which have passed directly from Italian every-day life into the scenes of the Erudite Comedy, where they confusedly move in a jovial medley, which now, for the first time, entered the modern drama. Even when the traditional personages of the Latin theatre are brought upon the scene, they have a new air and a special significance which is *cinquecento* Italian and not antique Roman.

It is the old masque and dress, but a new manner of interpretation. The exterior form of the plot is classical, and the classical tradition still remains; but, though many of the episodes are still derived from antiquity, they are strongly mingled with, or modified by, mediæval tales. Here young lovers deceive parents or guardians, and resort to every cunning device to attain their ends. They wander in distant lands, pretend to be servants, dress in clothes of the opposite sex, resort to a thousand stratagems in order to be near the dear one and fulfil their dreams of love. Here are ardent young wives unhappily married to old and cold and jealous husbands. Conjugal infidelity is a favorite theme.

The time was ripe for the birth of the regular Italian Comedy of classic type; and, notwithstanding its improbabilities and exaggerations, the Italian Comedy of the *cinquecento* is a truly national theatre, reflecting social conditions, moral tendencies, sentiments, customs, in a clear and faithful picture of the society of the Renaissance. The lack of originality of this comedy has been exaggerated. Its importance in the history of the Italian Comedy is evident when we consider that it produced comedians like Ariosto, Aretino, and Della Porta; comedies such as the *Frate* by Grazzini, the *Assiuolo* by Cecchi, the *Vedova* by Cini, the *Straccioni* by Caro, and the *Ingannati* of the Siennese academician. It is a century which opened with one of the world's greatest masterpieces, the *Mandragola* of

Machiavelli, and closed with another masterpiece, the *Candelaio* of Giordano Bruno.

Lodovico Ariosto, because of the great influence which his work produced, was the father of the Erudite Comedy. The *Cassaria,* his first original play, was performed at Ferrara in 1508. Of both the *Cassaria* and the *Suppositi* (which was first represented in Ferrara in 1509) two versions exist: the first is in prose; the second in verse.

In the prologue (in *terza rima*) of the prose *Cassaria,* the poet declares to the spectators that he presents to them a "new comedy,"

> full
> of various plays, which never either Latin
> or Greek tongues did recite upon the stage.

The plot of the comedy is complex and involved. Erofilo and Caridoro love Eularia and Corsica, who are in the power of the pimp, Lucrano. During the absence of his father, Crisobolo, Erofilo gives to his servant Trappola a casket full of gold which Trappola leaves with Lucrano as a pledge and gets Eularia in exchange. Erofilo goes to Bassa, father of Caridoro, and denounces the theft of a coffer, and suggests that Lucrano has stolen it. Bassa sends the police officer to the house of Lucrano, the pimp; and, having found the coffer there, arrests him; thus Caridoro possesses Corisca. Indeed the pimp will offer her to him when Caridoro, in order to save Lucrano's life, promises to intercede with his father, Bassa. That is Erofilo's plan. But, alas, the other servants, ignorant of the plot, met Trappola and beat him, and seize the maiden and hand her over to Erofilo. Old Crisobolo unexpectedly returns; and the terror-stricken servant Volpino tells the old man that he has been robbed of that coffer which, probably, is to be now found with Lucrano. Crisobolo penetrates into the pimp's house, and carries away the coffer. The treasure is safe; but not equally safe is Volpino. Fortunately, another servant, Fulvio, placates Crisobolo's anger and obtains from him the money to purchase Eularia, and to bring Corisca to the arms of Caridoro. Thus the play ends with the full satisfaction of the two young friends.

Cassaria is not derived from Plautus or from Terence, but is invented by Ariosto. Nevertheless, it reproduces the spirit and form of the Roman theatre; and the intrigues, although original, are modeled upon those of the Latin comedies. In the poetic adaption of the *Cassaria,* Ariosto changed the scenes, modified some of the names, suppressed some parts, introduced the waiting maid, Stamma, and developed the dialogue. Though the intrigues of Ariosto's comedies may be complex, they are easily followed. Often he seems to talk directly to the audience, instead of through his characters.

In 1513, Pope Leo X opened a theatre upon the Capitol, and here in 1519, surrounded with two thousand spectators, he witnessed an exhibition of Ariosto's *Suppositi*. The *Suppositi,* originally written in prose and afterwards versified by its author, first appeared in 1509 at Ferrara.

The prose *Suppositi* is of the author's time. Young Erostrato, son of Filogono of Catania, comes to study in Ferrara and loves Polimnesta, daughter of the Ferrarese Damone. Erostrato changes name and dress with his servant Dulipo. The false Dulipo (Erostrato) lives as servant in the house of Damone, and secretly enjoys his beautiful daughter; Erostrato (Dulipo) surrounds himself with servants and frequents the University. Filogono unexpectedly arrives and goes to the house of Erostrato; but the servants refuse to admit him. Filogono appeals to the magistrates; and his lawyer, Cleandro, discovers that the false Erostrato is his own son and false Dulipo is Erostrato. Damone's anger is appeased and the two young people are married. As sources of the play, Ariosto indicated the *Eunuchus* of Terence and the *Captivi* of Plautus. Our only interest in this play is as a picture of contemporary Italian Society. In the *Suppositi* in verse, Ariosto followed the text of his prose work.

Ariosto's *Negromante* was first performed at Ferrara in 1530. The scene is at Cremona, where, before the action of the play begins, young Cintio, adopted son of rich Massimo, has already married Lavinia, supposed daughter of Fazio, a modest and honest burgher. Massimo, suspecting nothing, proposes to marry Cintio to Emilia the daughter of his old friend Abbondio; and he acts with so much authority and haste that Cintio becomes the husband of Emilia—a strange husband, for he, recognizing Lavinia as his wife, feigns an organic incapacity which he hopes will annul his involuntary marriage. But Massimo resorts to the necromancer to achieve the healing of Cintio. When Massimo discovers the secret marriage of his adopted son and Lavinia, and recognizes that she is his long lost daughter, he welcomes the young married couple. Cintio's second marriage is annulled; and Emilia, who is still a virgin, finds in Camillo a husband who consoles her for her past misfortune. Though Ariosto has borrowed from the plays of Terence, there is originality in the character of the Negromante, who is a vulgar imposter rather than a sincere astrologer.

Less allied to the classical models, and richer in satire than the other plays of Ariosto, the *Lena* is an original comedy notwithstanding the imitations from Terence and Plautus. The play is noteworthy for the author's study of the characters. Those of Fazio, Lena, and Pacifico are especially successful. Fazio is an old man who for long years has been supporting Lena and her husband. He is in love, but he is also avaricious; he needs this woman in his life, but he hates her insatiable cupidity. She not only receives other lovers, but, now that she is growing old and losing her beauty, she will provide for her old age by trafficking in the beauty and youth of others. Pacifico is the vulgar and despicable type of a knowing and tolerant husband, enjoying the easy life procured by his wife's infamy, but yet not wholly brutalized. That Lena should traffic in

her own body to her own and to his advantage is agreeable; but that she should go so far as the infamy of making the daughter of that very Fazio her victim is disgusting to him. Flavio loves Licinia and pays Lena, procuress, twenty-five florins to introduce him secretly into her house. Here Licinia comes every day to learn sewing. When a surveyor comes to visit and measure the house, Flavio hides himself inside a hogshead, which old Fazio, father of Licinia, has carried into his own house. Thus Flavio lives in the home of the maiden and satisfies his desire. When the matter is discovered, the fathers of the two lovers consent to the marriage. In the *Lena* comedy there is much satire of contemporary Ferrarese society. Its action is simple and natural, and avoids the final recognition and accounts of abandoned children found again by their parents, as in the Roman theatre. In the light it throws upon the sixteenth century customs and vices, it is an even truer picture than the plays of Machiavelli or Aretino.

The *Scolastica,* a comedy not completed at Ariosto's death, was finished by his brother Gabrielle, but bears the unmistakable stamp of his ripest genius. Bonifazio, that excellent keeper of lodgings for Ferrarese students, is a truly original character. He identifies himself with their interests, sympathizes in their love-affairs, takes sides with them against their fathers, and puts his conscience in his pocket when required to pull them out of scrapes. Each of the characters has been copied from the life. The taint of Latin comedy has been purged out of them. They move, speak, act like living beings, true to themselves in every circumstance, and justifying the minutest details of the argument by the operation of their several qualities of head and heart. The *Scolastica* is not only the most genial of Ariosto's comedies, but is also the least fettered by his Latinizing prepossessions, and is the strongest in psychological analysis.

The artist Ariosto was greater than the man. Ariosto appeared at the end of the Renaissance; and he remains the best interpreter of his age. Free from passion and serious thought, lacking enthusiasm, with rare analytic powers and an acute insight into human nature, accepting the world as he found it, without hate, scorn, indignation, or revolt, he represented the weakness of the sixteenth century of Italy. But he also embodied its strength, especially that sustained pursuit of beauty in form, that width of intellectual sympathy, that urbanity of tone and delicacy of perception, which rendered Italy the mistress of the arts, the propagator of culture for the rest of Europe.

Without doubt, the most important comedy written in Italy in the sixteenth century is the *Mandragola* of Niccolo Machiavelli; and, equally without doubt, no Italian previous to Machiavelli produced so effectual a picture of the false and evil clergy, or penetrated so deeply into a human soul as did he in the character of Fra Timoteo. His soul is a livid and stagnant pool.

The *Mandragola* of Niccolo Machiavelli drew its title and story from two popular legends: the first, regarding the virtues of a medicinal herb that was called *Mandragola* or mandragora; and the second, regarding a poisoned or poisoning maiden. This latter legend related that a certain maiden had been nourished from her first years on the poisons of venomous serpents, and that, having grown up, she could poison and kill men in various ways, especially in the act of sexual union. As for the mandragola, for centuries there had been current the most fantastic stories. One of its supposed powers was that of rendering women pregnant. Savonarola, who belongs to the fifteenth century, in his *Practicade aegritudinibus a capite usque ad pedes,* published at Venice in 1486, numbered the mandragola among the means most apt to produce fecundity.

From these two popular superstitions, Machiavelli constructed his play, which centres round a presumptuous fool, Nicia, con-

vinced of his own astuteness, but so credulous as to believe the most
absurd tales, provided they are told with big words. He wants to
have children; and the doctors have advised him to take madonna
Lucrezia to the baths. From the first entry upon the scene, messer
Nicia appears as one of the most comical characters known to the
theatre. When Callimaco, having heard his vain desire, says that,
before deciding which is the most convenient bathing station, he
would have to know the true reason of the woman's sterility—"because there can be various reasons. Nam causae sterilitatis sunt aut
in semine, aut in matrice, aut in instrumentis seminariis, aut in
verga, aut in causa extrinsecus"—in his enthusiasm for the learned
doctor, Nicia cries: "This is the most worthy man that can be
found." Callimaco promises that he will give Lucrezia a potion of
mandragola to drink; he will introduce into her bed a youth invited in from the street, so that he may absorb the poison of that
potion and render it possible for Nicia subsequently to approach
the woman without dying of it; he will even assist in the capture
of the unknown youth who is destined to a brief pleasure and a
certain death. When to Nicia's objection "I do not want to make
my wife a whore," Callimaco answers, "What say you, doctor? I
do not hold you for as wise as I believed. What! You are doubtful
of doing that which the king of France has done, and so many
signori," he is immediately persuaded.

If messer Nicia is a caricature, Callimaco, madonna Lucrezia,
and Fra Timoteo are reality itself. Callimaco is a true lover, who
desires ardently, acts resolutely. He has heard of the marvellous
beauty of Lucrezia Calfucci; he has come to Florence; he has found
the woman more beautiful than reported; he loves her violently; at
any cost, he will have her. The violence of his passion is expressed
when he declares to Ligurio: "I know that thou tell'st the truth. But
what am I to do? What part am I to play? Where am I to turn? I
must attempt something, be it great, be it perilous, be it harmful,

be it infamous: better to die than live thus." Sostrata, a woman of
few scruples, tells Lucrezia that it is impossible that she, her
mother, should counsel her "to a thing that was not right," while
Fra Timoteo himself assures her that there is no "burden of conscience" in what it is proposed for her to do. Fra Timoteo weaves
around her his subtle arguments. He says that he has "been over
his books more than two hours studying this matter." He declares
"that where there is a certain good and an uncertain evil, one
should never let go that good for fear of that evil," and demon-
strates that there is here the certain good of winning "a soul for
messer Domenidio" (for the Lord God), and an uncertain evil,
which is the possible but not inevitable death of the young man
put to lie with her. He assures her that there is no sin where the
will does not concur "because the will is that which sins, not the
body"; and he maintains that "the end has to be looked to in all
things," and that when that is good, the means employed to attain
it are good. The pure and virtuous Lucrezia debates and resists;
and, in the end, conquered by the persuasions of the friar and the
exhortations of her mother Sostrata, she resigns herself to her destiny with a gloomy repugnance. "I am content; but I believe I shall
never be alive tomorrow morning. . . . God help me, and Our
Lady, that ill befall me not."

It is a chaste and noble figure of a woman that Machiavelli has
vigorously shaped with a few touches. Afterwards, when it is an
accomplished fact, the power of love effects a transformation in
her conscience. She says to Callimaco: "Since thy cunning and
the foolishness of my husband, the simplicity of my mother, and
the roguery of my confessor have led me to do that which of myself I would never have done, I am not able now to refuse that
which Heaven wishes that I accept. Hence I take thee for lord,
master, and guide. Thou my father, thou my defender, and I will
that thou be my every good; and that which my husband has

willed for one evening, I will that he shall have always." All those whom she held dearest conspired to make her fall into sin: she now knows the stupidity and iniquity of men and has experienced undreamed felicity. Should she renounce love, beauty, youth, joy, should she keep faith with her husband, bear respect to her mother, show herself reverent to the friar?

Fra Timoteo is the chief corrupter of madonna Lucrezia. As we have said, his soul is a livid and stagnant pool. And when he is offered a rich bribe, he lends himself easily to crime. No Italian writer previous to Machiavelli—neither Dante nor Boccaccio—had produced so effectual a picture of the false and evil clergy, and had cast so acute a glance into the interior of their conscience.

In the *Mandragola* Machiavelli put forth all his strength. Sinister and repulsive it may be, but its power is indubitable. More even than Ariosto's *Lena* and *Negromante,* or any other sixteenth century comedy, it nakedly detaches itself from Latin precedents and reveals Florentine life. This play is worthy of the author of the *Principe*. The *Mandragola* is a microcosm of society as Machiavelli knew it, and as it needs must be to justify his own philosophy. Viewed as a critique upon life, in the *Mandragola* Machiavelli exaggerated the stupidity of dupes, and underestimated the resistance which strongly-rooted moral instincts offer to audacious villainy. He left goodness out of his account. What must the people among whom Machiavelli lived have been, to justify his delineation of such a ruffian as Ligurio, a confessor so vile as Timoteo, a mother willing to prostitute her daughter to the first comer. At the date of its appearance, no one resented it. Florentine audiences delighted in its comic flavor and accepted it as true. Leo X witnessed it with approval. His hatred of the monks found satisfaction in Timoteo. Society thanked the man of genius for exposing its infamy and rendering vice amusing. Machiavelli depicted human nature just as he had learned to know it.

Mandragola was composed in the hours of enforced leisure at San Casciano, between 1513 and 1520. The plot seems to be Machiavelli's own invention. The clear and simple action is developed in perfectly logical sequence, and runs straight to its accomplishment. It was intended to be simply a work of art; but since its action rests on a foundation of real thoughts and sentiments and passions, and since the personages who take part in it act and speak as if they were "flesh and blood," the *Mandragola* was accepted by Machiavelli's contemporaries as a vigorous and satirical representation of the Florentine and Italian society of the *cinquecento*.

The *Commedia in Prosa,* for which we might find a title in the name of the chief personage, Fra Alberigo, displays the spirit and the style of the *Mandragola*. This short play combines the chief points of the *Clizia* and the *Mandragola* in a single action. Fra Alberigo is a vulgar libertine, provided with pious phrases to cloak his vicious purpose, but casting off the mask when he has gained his object, well knowing from past experience that the appetite of the woman he seduces will secure his footing in her husband's home. Margherita, the servant, revels in the corruption she has aided. She delights in sin for its own sake, extracts handfuls of coppers from the friar, and counts on profiting by the secret of her mistress. Yet neither Caterina nor Amerigo yields a point of baseness to these servile agents. They speak of things unmentionable with a crudity that makes one shudder, and abuse each other in the jargon of the streets. This comedy of Fra Alberigo is a literal transcript from a cynical *novella*.

The *Casina* of Plautus suggested the story of *Clizia*. Machiavelli, it is true, improved upon Plautus, and his *Clizia* is more beautiful than the *Casina*. But the plot, the characters, the order of many scenes, sometimes even the words of the speeches belong to Plautus, the action being, however, transferred to the Florence of 1506. The *Clizia* is a finished picture of Florentine home life.

Sofronia triumphs over her ashamed and miserable husband, who now consents to Clizia's marriage with Eustachio. Its strength and beauty are the masterly delineation of a family interior. The *dramatis personae* are vigorously sketched and act throughout consistently.

The small but glorious duchy of Urbino also participated in the activity of the new Italian Theatre of classic form. There, in the carnival of 1513, was performed the *Calandria* of Bernardo Dovizi da Bibbiena. The twins of the *Calandria* instead of being, as in the *Menæchmi* of Plautus, two males, upon whose resemblance the action turns, are a male and a female; and the plot also differs from that of Plautus. The name and figure of the protagonist Calandro, however, is derived directly from Boccaccio. A jocund figure of a simpleton is the old Calandro, whose exaggerated stupidity is delightfully expressed. Pleasing also is the servant Fessenio, indefatigable manipulator of intrigues to favour his master's friends. Ridiculous in his magisterial gravity is the preceptor Polinico, in whom is first truly incarnated the figure of the pedagogue, already suggested in the doctor Cleandro of the *Suppositi*.

In Bibbiena's comedy, the subject is immoral; indecent allusions and speeches abound. These defects unfortunately pollute the greater part of the Italian *cinquecento* comedies; nor did the protest of moralists avail to keep them within bounds. The public wished to laugh; and authors knew no better medium of hilarity than open or artfully veiled indecency. Moreover, immorality inundated life, and was thence reflected with exaggeration in comedy, which is obliged by its very nature to depict real life. Machiavelli himself is distinguished in this respect from his contemporaries only in that his representation in *Mandragola* of the evils afflicting family life and religion is more profound and powerful.

In originality, Pietro Aretino's comedies approach *Mandragola,* although far inferior in art. They are five in number, the *Mares-*

calco, Cortigiana, Ipocrita, Talanta, and *Filosofo,* composed in prose between 1525 and 1542.[4] The works of a lively but untrained intellect scantily provided with literary culture, and carelessly composed, they offer but slight trace of classic imitation. The dialogue is lively; tedious monologues are generally lacking; comic and biting wit flows through them in piquant allusions and cunning phrases; and the writer's caprice gives the rich and incisive language an entirely individual stamp. He peoples the scenes with pleasing, hastily photographed figures of all those about him: dissolute youths, crafty servants, practised swindlers, courtiers, stupid men pretending to wisdom, lost women, and braggart soldiers. In the midst of the principal figures, delightful glimpses of real life often appear, as a story-teller, a fishmonger, or a Jewish second-hand clothes dealer. The originality and merit of the licentious libelist's comedies lie therefore in the powerful portrayal of contemporary society in its basest and most trivial aspects. Aretino occupies a most important place in the history of the Italian *cinquecento* theatre. His five comedies were often represented at Venice, Bologna, Foligno, Ferrara, Arezzo, Pesaro, Feltre, and, probably, also at Vicenza and at Torino. Compared with the vast Aretinian work, the dramatic activity of the other comedists of northern Italy is poor.

The *Cortigiana* was written at Rome (1525) and was printed in Venice in 1534. Especially does the contempt for court life flame in the primitive version, which is now preserved in a Magliabecchian codex. All the characters move around messer Maco da Siena and Signor Parabolano. Maco commits the greatest follies, even having himself put in a cauldron, which he has been told is the manner in which courtiers are made; Parabolano, while he believes himself to be with the beloved madonna Livia, finds that he has possessed Togna, wife of the baker Arcolano. The *Cortigiana* is life itself. The ferocious satire against the *signori,* the recollections of

places, facts, and customs, is a great though unfinished picture of
contemporary Roman society.

The procuress Alvigia is the most successful character in the
Cortigiana. A contriver of crimes and corrupter of consciences, who
feigns great devotion, she is entirely unlike the male and female
panders of the Latin Theatre. Rather is she suggested from that
old woman whom Boccaccio briefly represented in the tenth novel
of the fifth day of the *Decameron*. Read the eighth scene of the
fourth act of the *Cortigiana* in which Alvigia promises Togna that
in her house she will procure great pleasure in spite of her husband
Arcolano:

Alvigia: Tic toc.
Togna: Who's there?
Alvigia: It's I.
Togna: Who are you?
Alvigia: Alvigia, daughter.
Togna: Wait, I'm just coming.
Alvigia: Well found, dear daughter.—Ave Maria—
Togna: What miracle is this that you let me see?
Alvigia: This Advent and this weather have so upset me with
its accursed fasts that I'm no longer myself.—Gratia plena domi-
nus tecum.
Togna: You always say prayers, and I no longer go to church;
nor do any longer anything good.
Alvigia: Bless thee. I am a greater sinner than others,—in muli-
eribus,—knowest thou what I want to say to thee?
Togna: Madonna, no.
Alvigia: Thou wilt come at five o'clock to my house, for I want
to put you with the seigneury—et benedictus ventris tui,—and with
other advantage that I did not the other day,—in hunc et in hora—
listen to me,—mortis nostrae,—don't think any more about it.—
Amen.
Togna: From first to last I'll do what you want, for the great
drunkard deserves all evil.

Alvigia: Thou art wise.—Pater noster—thou wilt come dressed as a man because these grooms,—qui es in cœlis—play mad jokes by night—santificetur nomen tuum,—and I would not that thou shouldst rush away in two-twos,—adveniat regnum tuum,—as did Angela from the moor,—in cœlo et in terra.

Togna: Alas, here's my husband.

Alvigia: Don't lose thy chance,—panem nostrum quotidianum da nobis hodie—there's no other fête that I know of this week, daughter, unless the station to San Lorenzo extra.

The Italian comedies of the sixteenth century are numberless. They come from nearly every region of Italy but mostly from Florence. After Machiavelli, Lorenzino di Pier Francesco de' Medici was one of the first Florentine writers of comedy. His *Aridosia* was performed in 1536 at the marriage of Duke Alessandro. The following year, this ambitious and corrupt youth murdered his cousin. He drew the principal plot of *Aridosia* from Plautus' *Aulularia*; but he freely elaborated his Latin sources, tempering imitation with direct observation. The artistic merits of *Aridosia* are diminished by the excessive use of certain ancient artifices that Italian writers had inherited from the Latin theatre.[5]

Among the North Italian comedians, besides Ariosto and Trissino with his *Simillimi,* there is the Venetian Lodovico Dolce (1508–66), an indefatigable writer, the translator of Greek and Latin works, the author of many mediocre poems, tragedies, annotations, and historical, linguistic, pedagogical, and aesthetic writings.

The two greatest *cinquecento* Florentine comedists are Anton Francesco Grazzini (Lasca) and Giovanni Maria Cecchi. Grazzini is a rebel. In the prologue of the *Gelosia,* he ridicules those writers who assert their comedies are new. And he blames "those who bring together the ancient with the modern," and make a medley that has neither head nor tail; and who, making modern cities the scene, and representing the present times, yet introducing old usages, and ancient customs, then excuse themselves by saying, " 'Thus did Plautus, and Terence, and Menandro'; and not perceiving that in Florence, in Pisa, in Lucca, one does not live as formerly in Rome and Athens." In the prologue of the *Strega,* he maintains that times and manners have changed and that thus "comedies must be made in another way," nor is it becoming to mix the ancient with the new. Nevertheless those defects which Grazzini reproved in other writers are found in his own plays. In one thing, however, he is consistent: he believed that comedy ought to be written in prose and not in verse. There is little originality in his plots; yet, when he avails himself of subjects treated by earlier writers, his genius transmutes them into original works. He was a mocking, jesting, and witty man, a pure Florentine type. Thus his plays possess a natural gaiety and laughter of their own. The old traditional types have been transmuted into something more domestic, more modern. The transformation of the classic *miles gloriosus* into the Taddeo Saliscendi of the *Strega* is delightful. His comedies, nearly all composed between 1540 and 1550 (*La Gelosia, La Spiritata, La Strega, La Pinzochera, La Sibilla, I Parentadi* and *L'Arzigogolo*), are uniformly classical or classicalized.

In pure and witty Florentinity, Lasca is surpassed alone by Giovanni M. Cecchi (1518–87), the most prolific writer for the Italian Theatre of the sixteenth century. He was a Florentine notary, "neither lettered nor without letters, and of simple fibre, of a stock that had never been out of sight of the cathedral dome." He composed hurriedly, but was always improving and freely rehandling and altering his composition. He wrote quantities of comedies, farces, moral and sacred performances, scenes, and intermezzos in prose and verse. In his *sacre rappresentazioni (La morte del re Acab, L'esaltazione del la Croce,* etc.), he modified and adjusted the old forms, often twisting facts of sacred history to the satiric representation of contemporary Italian customs.[6] His twenty-one profane comedies are some in prose, some in verse, others in both styles. Some represent occurrences of the author's lifetime; others are derived from the *Mandragola* or from the *Decameron* or are free elaborations of different Latin works. Cecchi is fond of complex entanglements; he cleverly sketches the characters; his scenes are full of life; and he presents a real picture of the Italian society of his time. This reproduction is furthermore aided by the softness of the Florentine language spoken by an educated person. Cecchi, instead of setting up as a rebel, expresses his firm intention of imitating the two admired comedists of ancient Rome.

The *Assiuolo,* Cecchi's finest comedy, is one of the best comedies of the sixteenth century. Giulio and Rinuccio, students of the University of Pisa, both love madonna Oretta, wife of old Ambrogio; and he, although extremely jealous of his own wife, loves Rinuccio's mother Anfrosina. Indignant Anfrosina reveals everything to Oretta; and the two women arrange that Anfrosina shall introduce Ambrogio by night into Rinuccio's chamber, where Oretta will receive him. But Giorgetto, servant of Giulio, having learned of this intrigue, suggests to Giulio the means of attaining his desires.

Thus it happens that Giulio, disguised as a woman servant, himself receives the old Ambrogio, shuts him up in the courtyard, goes himself to the room where Oretta is awaiting her husband, and, after having had his pleasure, makes himself known to her, easily obtaining forgiveness and the promise of future joys. In the meantime Rinuccio, who knew that old Ambrogio was to pass the night out, penetrates into his house expecting to find madonna Oretta, but finds instead her sister, Violante, who had, at Oretta's desire, occupied her bed; nor has he any reason to complain of this misunderstanding when the beautiful woman confesses that she has long secretly loved him. Thus the two young students pass the happy hours of that adventurous night.

Ambrogio, a prisoner, trembling with cold, finally forces the door of the courtyard, rushes to his own house, finds the great door unlocked, hears the sound of voices in his bedroom. The distracted man goes in search of his brother-in-law Uguggione and brings him back so that he may see the ignominious betrayal practiced by the wife and sister. In the meantime, Oretta has already returned home and, with the aid of Violante, plots the final deception against the old libertine. When Uguggione and Ambrogio burst into the room and see an unknown man in the company of madonna Oretta, this latter freely affirms that that man is indeed her lover and that she has sent for him to come to her to punish her husband for his unfaithfulness; but then, having torn the beard from the face of this supposed lover, she reveals her sister, Violante. And messer Ambrogio, cheated in so many ways, patiently listens to the bitter reproaches of Uguggione, who is furious at the false accusation against the chaste wife, who is his sister.

The plot is simple, the interest is spontaneous, the dialogue is comic, and the situations dramatic; the characters are well drawn.

G. B. Gelli's *Sporta* has been called "after the *Mandragola,* the finest comedy of the ancient comic theatre." Published in 1543, it at once roused discussion. Grazzini charged Gelli with having stolen his comedy from Machiavelli. Machiavelli's nephew, Giuliana de Ricci, declared that Machiavelli composed a comedy called the *Sporta*; and that G. B. Gelli, after making a few additions, gave it out as his own. Gelli undoubtedly owes much to Plautus, from whose *Aulularia,* the *Sporta* directly derives.

Among southern comedians, Giambattista della Porta (1535–1615) stands pre-eminent, a man of keen and versatile intellect who also occupies an honourable position in the history of science. From the close study of philosophy, magic, and alchemy, he sought recreation in the composition of plays. Della Porta is said to have composed twenty-nine comedies, three tragedies, and a tragicomedy. Fourteen of the comedies remain, all in prose: the *Olimpia*, the *Fantesca*, the *Cintia*, the *Astrologo*, the *Turca*, the *Tabernaria*, the *Sorella*, the *Trappolaria*, the *Carbonaria*, the *Chiappinaria*, the *Due Fratelli simili*, the *Due Fratelli rivali*, the *Moro*, the *Furiosa*.

Both the Italian Renaissance and the classic Roman period inspired his work. Indeed *Carbonaria* and *Trappolaria*, and other plays, reproduce entire scenes from Plautus' comedies. Boccaccio, Ariosto, and Aretino suggested much to Della Porta, but he is not a mere plagiarist. This varied material is so skilfully blended with his own as to become harmonious and original. Great is the variety of form, even greater the variety of content, in these pathetic, sentimental, romantic, and realistic comedies.[7]

Niccolo Secchi wrote three comedies: The *Inganni*, the *Interesse*, and the *Camerriera*. The *Inganni* (1549) derives its plot from the *Asinaria* of Plautus: young Gostanzo's love for the courtesan Dorotea, whose perverted mother drives him from the house and urges her own daughter to abandon love and to sell herself to rich clients. It is a nimble, dexterous, and lively comedy.

The plot of the *Interesse* (1581) is based upon the permanent disguise of a maiden, Lelio, in male costume, a disguise imposed upon her by her father. She is a beautiful, ardent, and mischievous girl. She knows what her real sex is, but is not permitted to reveal the mystery. She madly loves young Fabio who loves her sister Virginia. Driven by desire, dressed in Virginia's clothes, she receives Fabio in her own house by night, making him enter by a little secret door. This leads to complications, since Virginia loves Flaminio, who rages at Fabio's assertion that he has secretly wedded Virginia and that his friend Achille and two servants assert that they have seen Fabio entering the house and welcomed by Virginia. Liars and calumniators he brands them; violent words lead to threats of beatings, challenges, duels. Finally Lelio confesses her love for Fabio and her deception; and her advanced state of pregnancy dissipates all misunderstandings. The comedy closes amid general joy; Flaminio marries his beautiful and virtuous Virginia; and Fabio takes as wife that one whom he had truly possessed. The personages who take part and the events which take place have all the appearance and force of truth.

And how well Secchi has shown how to set in relief the different moral qualities of the characters! How well he has succeeded in showing the generous trust of Flaminio and his impetuous energy! How skilful he has been in treating the engaging mischievousness of the supposed Lelio, who never betrays herself even in the gravest moments—this merry girl, who, although knowing herself *enceinte* and foreseeing the consequences of her fault, still jests about her own state.

But what brilliancy of conception, profundity of observation, clearness of presentation there is in the *Candelaio* by Giordano Bruno, of Nola, that noble thinker who was burned at the stake in 1600! This comedy was probably written at Paris in the summer of 1582. Figures palpitating with life! Here is the *candelaio* (chandler) Bonifacio, who loves the prostitute Vittoria and hopes to attain his end by magic arts and strange incantations. Here is the old Bartolomeo, the credulous miser, who, bending over the furnaces, amid retorts, eagerly strives to make gold. Here is that monument of empty learning, the pedant Manfurio, who hurls invectives against anyone disrespectful of his authority. These men, vividly representing various forms of human stupidity, are deceived and robbed by a band of knaves. The philosopher of Nola was not an imitator. From his own imagination and his observation of real life came the action, situations, and figures of his comedy. Here the realism of the Neapolitan underworld is mirrored, as are also places, customs, and institutions. The piece is one of the most obscene of the *cinquecento,* since the vulgar and immoral persons who appear in the play knew only vulgar and immoral expressions. But what vivacity, what movement in the tumultuous dialogues and monologues, in the flying questions and answers!

Compare the twenty-fourth scene of the fifth act of the *Candelaio* with that part of the ninth chapter of the third book of the *Pantagruel* of Rabelais, in which Panurge asks Pantagruel's advice as to whether he should or should not take a wife. Madonna Carubina is interrogating madonna Angela Spigna as to whether she should marry Bonifacio.

To her came madonna Carubina and said: "My Mother, they wish to give me a husband; Bonifacio Trucco presents himself, having the wherewithal and the means."

Replied the old woman: "Take him."

"Yes, but he is too old," said Carubina.

Replied the old woman: "Daughter, don't take him."

"My relations advise me to take him."

She replied: "Take him."

"But I don't much like him," said Carubina.

"Then don't take him," she replied.

Carubina added: "I know him to be of good family."

"Take him," said the old woman.

"But I understand that he takes two bites at a cherry."

She replied: "Don't take him."

"I am informed," said Carubina, "that he has a greyhound of good breed."

"Take him," said madonna Angela.

"But alas, I have heard that he is *candelaio* (a chandler)."

"Don't take him," she replied.

Said Carubina: "All esteem him mad."

"Take him, take him, take him, take him, take him, take him, take him," said the old woman seven times: "It does not matter that he is a chandler; never mind if he takes two bites at a cherry; it's nothing to you if he doesn't much please you; never mind if he's too old: take him, take him because he is mad. But mind he isn't one of that rigid, bitter, sour kind."

"I am certain he is not one of those," said Carubina.

"Take him then," said madonna Angela, "take him."

NOTES

CHAPTER VI

1. Niccolo, who in February, 1429, had received news of the discovery from Poggio Bracciolini, thought that it was a hoax. Even Traversari doubted it when Cardinal Giordano Orsini refused him information regarding the precious codex. This codex, however, was really in the hands of the cardinal, who refused all petitions that he should show his great discovery to the new pontiff, Eugenio IV. When finally the cardinal permitted the pope to carry the codex with him to Florence, after an oblivion of centuries, the twelve comedies were published.

2. The humanistic influences of the fifteenth century were scarcely less unpropitious to national comedy at its outset than they had been to tragedy. Humanism embraced the several districts of Italy in a common culture, effacing the distinctions of dialect, and bringing the separate elements of the nation to a consciousness of intellectual unity. Divided as Venetians, as Florentines, as Neapolitans, as Lombards, and as Romans, the members of the Italian community recognized their identity in the spiritual city they had reconquered from the past. The whole nation possessed the Latin poets as a common heritage; and on the ground of Plautus, Florentines and Neapolitans could understand each other. It was, therefore, natural that the cultivated orders, brought into communion by the ancients, should look to these for models of an art that they were intent on making national. We, therefore, find that, at the close of the fifteenth century, it was common to recite the plays of Plautus and Terence in their original language.

   The parasites of Latin comedy found their counterpart in the clients of rich families and the poorer courtiers of princes. The indispensable *Davus* was represented by the body servants of wealthy householders. The *miles gloriosus* reappeared in professional *bravi* and captains of mercenaries. Thus the personages of the Latin stage could easily be furnished with Italian masks.

3. In the sixth division of his *Poetica,* Trissino declares that the Greek "will generally be fickle, untruthful, flattering, apt at learning the laws"; the Italian will be "sagacious, partial, imperious"; the Turk "will be introduced as arrogant, murderous, ignorant, inimical to virtues, talents, and nobility"; the Frenchman, "vehement, reckless, mutable, and ungrateful."

He also declares that "the fathers and mothers love their children most ardently. . . . The children do not love either their father or their mother, and the males love the mother and the daughters the father; brothers do not love each other much; . . . husbands love their wives more than wives their husbands."

Giraldi maintains that two things are necessary to the dramatic fable: "one of which is called *Peripetia* by Aristotle, the other *Agnitione*"; the first is "change from good fortune to misfortune or from unhappy to the contrary"; and the second "is nothing else than a coming to the knowledge of that which was not known at first, hence men, from being friends become enemies, or from happy unhappy, or from unhappy happy."

The action ought to be distributed over the five acts in the following manner: "In the first, let the argument be contained. In the second, the things contained in the argument begin to tend towards the end. In the third come the impediments and perturbations. In the fourth, means of remedying troubles begin to offer themselves. In the fifth, the desired end is given with due solution of the whole argument." In comedy, "never does a young virgin or maiden speak upon the stage." "The mother of a family of honest standing must never come upon the scene or show herself moved by amorous passion, as we see old fathers of families there."

In regard to the use of *intermezzi* between the acts of comedy, Daniello observes that such *intermezzi* are sometimes used as a substitute for the choruses which "are not used in comedies"; Trissino condemns them because *"intermedij [intermezzi]* . . . are things most different from the action of the comedy." Ingeneri approves, declaring that the *intermezzi* "to the pastoral, and to the comedy, are not only becoming, but are most ornamental; and, whether like or unlike the fable, they always enrich the spectacle and delight the spectators."

Trissino deems the Plautinian type of prologue superfluous because such a declaratory office can be better entrusted to the first characters who are introduced to speak upon the stage; Castelvetro, on the contrary, holds it useful and convenient.

Giraldi approves a "double story" in the comedy, describing as double "that fable which has in its action various kinds of persons of similar quality, such as two lovers of differing talent, two old men of various nature, two servants of contrary manners, and such others as one sees in the *Andria* and in other stories of the same poet, where it is clear that these like persons of unlike customs lend great grace to the plot and to the solution of the story"; but Giason de Nores does not admit that "two actions, which are not contrary, be mixed together, for which things Terence has been greatly reproved."

The most violent dispute of these rhetoricians was as to whether comedy could be written in prose or whether verse was absolutely necessary. The majority of the treatise-writers declared themselves hostile to prose; Giraldi affirming that "without verse neither tragedy nor comedy can be laudably composed," and de Nores giving his judgment that "they do ill" who "compose in prose" their tragedies and comedies, since verse is the "inseparable property" of both the one and the other. Alessandro Piccolomini approved of prose, which also was defended by Agostino Michele, who, in 1592, published a *"Discorso* in which is demonstrated how one can write comedies and tragedies in prose." The Paduan Faustino Summo, in certain "Poetic Discourses," after having set forth the arguments of his adversaries, refuted each of them, and undertook to demonstrate the absolute necessity of verse in comedy.

Such were the doctrines preached through all the *cinquecento,* since the *Poetica* of Daniello saw the light in 1536, the *Discorso* of Giraldi in 1554, and the *Poetica* of Trissino in 1562, the *Annotazieni* of Piccolomini in 1575, the *Discorsi* and the *Poetica* of Giason De Nores in 1587 and 1588, the *Discorso* of Agostino Michele in 1592, that of Ingeneri on the *Poesia Rappresentativa* in 1598, the *Disputatio* of Paolo Beni and the *Discorsi poetici* of Faustino Summo in 1600.

4. Ignoring the principles established by the Plautine mannerists, Aretino liberated the elements of satire and of realism from their bondage to Latin comedy. Why should he attend to the unities, or never send the same person more than five times on the stage in one piece? Why should Romans ape Athenians? Why should he shackle his style with precedents from Petrarch and Boccaccio? Why imitate, when his mother-wit supplies him with material, and the world of men lies open like a book before his eyes? Why follow pedants, who mistake knowledge of grammar for genius, and whose commentaries insult the poets they pretend to illustrate?

The merit of Aretino's comedies is naturalness. Each character is vividly outlined, though the study may lack depth. Aretino's plays are a mine of information upon the social life of the Renaissance. Evil is good for its own sake also. He revels in recalling his sensations. The Court, idealized by Castiglione, censured by Guarini, inveighed against by La Casa, in the *Cortigiana* shows its inner rottenness. At the pleasure of a charlatan writer who thrives on this pollution, we shake hands with ruffians and cut-throats, enter the Italian brothels by their back-door, sit down in their kitchens, and become acquainted with the secrets of their trade.

The necessary consequences of his haste are discernible in all his compositions. Aretino left nothing artistically finished, nothing to which it is now possible to point in justification of his extraordinary celebrity. What then, it may finally be asked, was Aretino's merit as an author? Originality and independence. The contradictions of the epoch were concentrated in his character. He was a professed

Christian of the type formed by Rome before the Counter-Reformation. He helped the needy, tended the sick, dowered orphans, and kept open house for beggars. Yet he corrupted youth by painting vice in piquant colors. He led a life of open debauchery. He was a liar, a bully, a braggart, venomous in the pursuit of private animosities, and the remorseless foe of weaker men who met with his displeasure. From the conditions of society which produced Cesare and Lucrezia Borgia, Pier Luigi Farnese, and Gianpaolo Baglioni, it was no wonder that a writer resolved on turning those conditions to account, should have arisen. The social diseases which emasculated men of weaker fiber, he turned to the account of his rapacious appetites. He was the last, the most perfect, and the most vitiated product of Renaissance manners. A characteristic legend is told of Aretino's death. Two of his sisters kept, it is said, a house of ill fame; and the story runs that he died of immoderate laughter, flinging himself backward in his chair and breaking his neck, on hearing some foul jest reported by them.

Aretino wrote his second comedy, *Il Marescalco,* "at the court of the Gonzagas, between the closing days of 1526 and the spring of 1527," but retouched it before printing, at Venice, in 1533. The duke of Mantua persuades a *marescalco* (an officer) and other gentlemen of his court, that he wishes to give a beautiful and rich maiden of the city as wife to the woman-hater. The boy, Giannicco, is a mischievous and impertinent little nuisance, who sings like a lark. It is his joy to put his master the *marescalco* in a rage.

About the end of 1541, Aretino returned to the theatre, writing the *Talanta* in only "eight days," and the *Ipocrita* in "less time." In the *Talanta,* we return to Roman society. Three lovers desire the courtesan Talanta. Orfinio gives her a precious chain; the captain presents her with a little Moorish slave-girl who slept in the same bed with his own daughter Marmilia; and messer Vergolo, gives her a young male Saracen slave, the bedroom-companion of his own son Marchetto. The dress of the two slaves had deceived the parents and procured the felicity of their children; since the Moorish slave-girl was a boy; and the Saracen youth was a girl. But with the coming to Rome of messer Blando and his daughter Oretta, it is discovered that the false Saracen and the false slave-girl are Blando's children, and the former Mucilla openly marries Marchetto whom she had already married secretly; and Antino confirms his already accomplished nuptials with Marmilia.

The *Ipocrito,* unlike Aretino's other dramatic work, mingles a romantic and sentimental element with the comic. Ipocrito is a hypocrite, a worker of evil actions and disorganizer of families, and Liseo represents Aretino's own character and his own view of life.

Aretino's last comedy, *Il Filosofo,* composed in ten days, about the end of 1544, and printed for the first time in Venice in 1546, is the least happy of the five.

5. The *Aridosia* of Lorenzino de' Medici, represented in 1536 with a magnificent setting by Bastiano da San Gallo, results from the perversion of three Latin comedies, one by Terence and two by Plautus, the *Adelphi,* the *Aulularia,* and the *Mostellaria.* In some particulars it also recalls the *Asinaria.* The miser Aridosio, a type so admirably depicted by Plautus, is here cold and ineffective. Noteworthy in Medici's comedy are the picture of contemporary society and the bitter satire against priests and nuns. In this play of Lorenzino de' Medici, the nuns are as unworthy as the priests. Young Fiammetta is shut up in a monastery. Her love for Erminio has gone so far that it will soon be impossible to conceal the consequences. Erminio knocks at the door, and Suora Marietta, comes to the entrance and tells the enamoured youth that the girl's pregnancy is daily becoming more visible; she must be removed at once from the monastery.

6. In Cecchi's spiritual drama *Tobia,* which corresponds to the *Rappresentazione dell' Angiolo Raffaele e di Tobia* (Representation of the Angel Raphael and Tobias), the scene is in Nineveh; the whole action is reduced to the return of the young son of Tobias with his new bride and recently acquired riches. But since the Biblical narrative did not suffice to fill the five acts of the drama, Cecchi added

some amusing scenes, playing up the interest in contemporary events.

Similar burlesque types are found in almost all the spiritual and moral dramas and farces which Cecchi wrote. Not only the old men, the servants, and other personages of secondary importance are derived from the classical comedies, but also the parasites, the braggarts, in the *S. Agnese*, the *Cruccia*, the *Coronazione del Re Saul*, the *Morte del Re Acab*, the *Conversione della Scozia*, the *Riscatto*. But he borrows the *contadini* and the physicians from the *sacra rappresentazioni*.

Sometimes Cecchi modernizes the Gospel account into a bourgeois comedy, as the *Figliuolo prodigo*, which is supposed to take place in Florence in the author's own time. In yet other cases, he substituted pure abstractions for human personages, causing them to speak or act in the same manner as they had so often been acted in the *quattrocento* allegorical representations.

7. Della Porta's *La Furiosa, Il Moro,* and *I Due fratelli rivali* are serious comedies. *Il Moro* fuses two episodes taken from the *Orlando furioso* of Ariosto, and consists of a series of dramatic adventures. Pannuorfo is a bragging Neapolitan, who gives himself out as a great lord and conqueror of women. "Oh, great affliction is it to be handsome! All the day, letters, notes, messages, undertakings. The night comes and I must sleep with ten gentlewomen." In the *Due fratelli rivali,* inspired by a tale of Bandello's (1, 22), two brothers are rivals in love. There is real knowledge of the human heart in the *Sorella,* where a young lover believes he has discovered his own sister in his sweetheart. Though horrified at the involuntary crime committed, he cannot adapt himself to being brother where he has been lover. In the *Tabernaria* and the *Chiappinaria,* he gives to the young girls a direct part, contravening Giraldi's injunction "never does a young virgin or maiden speak upon the Stage." In his amorous dialogues Della Porta sought truthfully to render the deeper emotions of the heart. In the *Fantesca,* the two Spanish captains face each other. Mighty threats, mighty challenges; but neither of the grotesque heroes strikes in earnest.

CHAPTER VII

THE SIXTEENTH CENTURY: THE TRAGEDY

Mediæval Italian tragedies: Influence of the *sacra rappresentazione*: Carretto's *Sofonisba*: Trissino's *Sofonisba,* the first regular Italian tragedy: Giraldi's *Orbecche,* originating the *tragedia avviluppata*: his *Cleopatra*: *Selene*: *Arnenopia*: *Altile*: *Antivalomani*: his use of *tragedia avviluppata*: Imitations from the Greek: Rucellai's *Rosmunda* and *Oreste*: Martinelli's *Tullia*: Cresci's *Tullia feroce*: Gratarolo's *Altea*: Zinano's *Almerigo*: Speroni's *Canace*: Aretino's *Orazia*: Dolce's *Marianna*: Influence of the conventions originated by *Giraldi*: Increasing importance of the romantic element: Tasso's *Torrismondo*: Tragic spectacles, and their lavish display.

IN the Middle Ages, the word "Tragedia" meant merely a canto or song, given in lofty style. Italy was the first country in Europe to revive the tragic form of drama, and the *Ecerinide* of Albertino Mussato (1261–1329) was probably the first Italian tragedy. The metre, the use of the chorus, and the division into five acts were modeled upon Seneca. But the idea is that of mediæval tragedy. Certain situations are most original, and some of the narration is very dramatic. It is written in Latin, and is an historical drama about Ezzelino III and his brother Alberico.[1]

All the literature of the *cinquecento,* and especially that of the theatre, though it owed much to the perception and taste of the whole people, was composed for the most part by men of middle rank for the amusement of citizens and nobles. It partook of those qualities which characterize the upper and middle classes. It was deficient in the breadth, the magnitude, the purity, which an audience composed of the whole nation can alone communicate. The absence of the tragic element in Italian art and literature is all the more remarkable because the essence of Italian history, whether political or domestic, was eminently dramatic. The Italians lived their tragedies in the dynasties of the Visconti and the Sforzas, in the contests of the Baglioni and Manfredi, in the persons of Pan-

136

dolfo Sigismondo Malatesta and Cesare Borgia, in the murders, poisonings, rapes, and treasons that form the staple of the annals of their noble houses.

The failure of Italian tragedy was inseparable from its artificial origin. It was the conscious product of cultivated persons who aimed at nothing nobler than the imitation of the ancients and the observance of impossible rules. It was suffocated by classical imitation on the one hand, or on the other by the hampering adjuncts of court-pageants and costly entertainments. These tragedies were the literary manufacture of scholars, writing without spiritual or intellectual contact with the world of action or the audience of busy cities. Their personages are shadows, formal marionettes. Their passionate movements are the spasms of machinery.

Mussato's dramatic experiment with *Ecerinis* at the beginning of the Renaissance was renewed by a few Humanists in the fifteenth century, who composed historical and mythological tragedies in Latin in imitation of Seneca's. Leonardo Bruni, L. B. Alberti, Piccolomini, imitated Terence and Plautus.

The tragedy *De Captivitate ducis Jacobi,* by Laudivio, though written a century and a half later than *Ecerinide,* is, like all the succeeding Latin tragedies of the Renaissance, greatly influenced by the *sacre rappresentazioni.* All of them are imitations of Seneca, and the direct influence of the Greek theatre is not perceptible. In them the dramatic element is scanty, and they are better adapted for private reading than for public performance. The name of Tragedy had reappeared in Italy, but not the substance.

But the course of dramatic literature, driving the *sacra rappresentazione* from its place of honour and leaving it to languish on the stage of popular theatres and convents, was not based on the movements of these tragic or comic Latin attempts, but on the restoration of scenery and the direct study of ancient examples. During the *cinquecento,* Seneca's Latin tragedies had several times been performed in the original or in translation in Rome and Ferrara, and had certainly contributed elements to the composition of the lay dramas which, although modeled on the sacred performances, showed an alteration in external arrangement.

The *Orphei tragedia* (1494) is a transformation by Antonio Tebaldeo of Poliziano's *Favola d'Orfeo* composed in 1471. It contains neither study of character, nor development of passions, nor unity of interest.

Among many other tragic histories (*storie tragiche*) of this century, the best known is *Filostrato e Panfile* (1499) of Antonio Caminelli, known as *il Pistoia*. It is borrowed from the first novella of the fourth day of the *Decameron,* and relates the tragic story of Guiscardo and Ghismonda.[2] Though Seneca recites the prologue and the author attempts to give the work classical form, its excessive rhetorical ornamentation deprives this early attempt at Italian tragedy of value.

After Pistoia came the "magnificent cavalier and poet, messer Galeotto Carretto," who claimed that his *Sofonisba* was a true tragedy, notwithstanding that in its construction he used the liberty of form of the "mixed dramas" modeled on the *sacre rappresentazioni.* Four books of Livy (27–30) are his material. Unfortunately, Sofonisba herself is the most uninteresting of all the colourless characters.

When we consider that admiration of the Renaissance for the antique was as conspicuous in the Italian tragic theatre as it was in the comedy, it seems strange that translations of Greek tragedy were not generally known before the early *cinquecento,* and when performed met with slight popular favor. Nevertheless, it was under such influence that Gian Giorgio Trissino (1478–1550) composed the first regular Italian tragedy, *Sofonisba,* finished in 1515, and six times printed before the date of its first representation at Vicenza in 1562.

His material was derived from Livy's narrative, the action being restricted to the unhappy queen's marriage with Massinissa, and her stoic death. Sofonisba is overwhelmed when she learns that the enemy is "already within the walls" and that Siface is a prisoner. As the conquerors burst out on the public square, the messenger points out the leader Massinissa, at whose feet Sofonisba throws herself imploring mercy. Massinissa replies that he is incapable of cruelty to a woman, especially when she is young, noble, and beautiful, and will even spare his enemy Siface. He invites Sofonisba to enter into the palace with him. Scipio's lieutenant Lellio appears and is informed that Massinissa "spends his time with his new wife, joyous and merry amid pleasures and songs." Massinissa comes out of the palace and Lellio informs him that he purposes to take Sofonisba a prisoner to Rome, and orders the soldiers to invade the palace; but Massinissa bars the door, crying out:

> Let none of you who here around doth harken
> Presume to set his foot within this doorway,
> For with his blood it shall be dyed vermilion.

The dispute is referred to Scipio, before whom Massinissa pleads in vain. He resigns himself, exclaiming, "Since now I see it is your will, to have this woman I will contend no longer." Sofonisba takes poison.

Notwithstanding some fine verses pronounced by Sofonisba and by the chorus, the work is a mechanical copy of Greek tragic forms, as Trissino intended it to be. It is moulded according to Aristotle's rules and Hellenic examples. Unity of time and place is scrupulously observed. The chorus is always present and, like the Greek one, joins in the dialogue; and the longer songs mark the divisions of the spectacle, which is not separated into acts. Sophocles' *Antigone* and Euripides' *Alcesta* suggest the lyric motifs and dramatic situations. But the discourses are monotonous and the tragedy feeble and not dramatic. Trissino is not capable of finding accents of real compassion, love, and indignation. The historical importance of the *Sofonisba* lies in the fact that here Trissino gave to Italian tragedy the "free verse" (*sciolto*), plain, unrhymed hendecasyllables in place of *terza* and *ottava rima*; and that he established the rule that regular Italian tragedy must follow the Greek model.

Sofonisba marked out the way for Italian tragedy in the sixteenth century, and it never again departed from the close imitation of the classics. The tragedies of the *cinquecento* were generally wanting in genial intuition as to the struggles of human passion, and in the ability to represent them. In order to extend the action, they substituted the narrative for direct representation, multiplied idle chatter, and to preserve the chorus-part they created scenes that are ridiculous to a modern spectator.

Because Greek naturalness did not meet the taste of the time, Giambattista Giraldi Cinzio of Ferrara (1504–73) endeavoured to give a fresh impulse to tragedy by the imitation of Seneca, who seemed to him superior to the Greeks in majesty and dignity. His imitation extends even to the accessories in a series of nine tragedies commencing with *Orbecche,* which was performed in Ferrara in 1541.[3] This play marks a new period (1541) in the history of Italian tragedy. It is a tissue of monstrosities. The incest of Selina with her son revealed by her daughter Orbecche, and the murder of the incestuous pair by her husband Sulmone, precede the play. But the shade of dead Selina informs the audience that other blood will soon stain the infamous palace of Persia. Orbecche, who secretly loves Oronte and has already had two sons by him, is destined by her father to marry Selino, king of the Parthians. When Sulmone discovers his daughter's transgression, he kills Oronte and the children and presents their bleeding limbs to Orbecche, who slays her father and with the same dagger kills herself. The horror of the tragedy is increased by Nemesis, by the Furies, and by the shade of Selina, who form the funereal phantasmagoria of the first act.

Giraldi's tragedy, *Didone* (Dido), maintains the same form, although with a less terrible spectacle. In the *Cleopatra,* for which he was commissioned by Ercole II immediately after the *Didone,* Giraldi has put into dialogue and monologue the Plutarchian story; but he never forgets his Seneca.

In the *Selene,* Rodobano, king of Persia and husband of Selene, queen of Egypt, believes that his wife is unfaithful and that she had also attempted to kill him. He flees with his son into Persia, leaving his daughter Grifina with her mother. He sets a price on Selene's head, while the Council of Egypt, in reprisal, promised a richer reward to whoever should slay Rodobano and his son. Fifteen years later, the loving Selene, sends a messenger to her husband, to convince him of her innocence and persuade him to return. Preceded by Antioco, who is to spread the false announcement of their death, Rodobano and his son arrive at Alexandria disguised as Armenians. They present the severed heads of the king of Persia and his son (Act V. sc. 2). The horrible spectacle of these two miserable women clasping those severed heads to their breasts, the one believing them the heads of her husband and son, the other the heads of her father and brother, is not lessened when Rodobano reveals himself and is reconciled to his wife.

Giraldi never drew directly upon the *Furioso,* but real chivalric poetry is manifest in the *Arrenopia.* Giraldi derived this fable from his *Ecatommithi,* woven, the author stated, "of deeds of chivalry." Astazio, king of Ibernia, is the husband of Arrenopia, daughter of Orgito, king of Scotland. When he loves a lady of the isle of Mona, hates his wife, and orders Omosio, his captain, to slay her, Orgito, to avenge his daughter, invades Ibernia. Astazio and Orgito have agreed to entrust the decision of the long war to three champions. Agnoristo, an unknown knight and one of Astazio's champions, asks the two kings if they would make peace should it be proved that Arrenopia still lives. Then Agnoristo reveals himself to be Arrenopia, to the joy of the father and husband. There are interminable monologues and dialogues in which messengers and confidants speak in place of the more important personages. Since *Arrenopia* is a tragedy of "deeds of chivalry," many of the discourses are about chivalry.

In the *Discorso,* Giraldi claimed that he was the first to follow Aristotle's rules of the tragic art. To form an idea of this technique, consider the *Altile*. We are in the "illustrious Syria"—so says "My Lady Tragedy" in the prologue—in Damascus, "the royal seat of the realm"; and the king Lamano, angry that his sister Altile had "submitted herself to a man of foreign country"—that is to Norrino of Babylon—discourses upon feminine unchastity. "A single unchaste woman is enough to fix eternal stain upon all lofty blood." Lamane orders Liscone to arrest Norrino, so that "the villain manifest to all his great crime by his death." Astano, the black Iago, who has failed to win Altile's love, secures the confidence of Norrino so as to betray him. Bruno, faithful servant of Norrino, tells Norrino of Astano's wicked plot and urges his flight. Altile pours out her lamentations over the flight of Norrino and her own dishonour; and threatens suicide by Norrino's sword. Then comes Lamano; and, in a stormy scene, his cruel wrath contrasts with Altile's wild despair. To Lamano's reproaches she opposes the rights of nature. As a maiden she took the husband whom father and brother gave her; now as a widow, she rightly chose the godlike man who pleased her best. It is the only living scene of the tragedy. Altile is the typical Italian tragic heroine modeled upon Boccaccio's Gismonda. While Altile weeps and despairs with the chorus, Lamano's soldiers clamorously lead Norrino to execution, and Altile rushes towards her lover, wishing to die with him. In the fifth act, however, Lurcone, king of Tunis, father of Norrino, arrives at Damascus. Norrino is saved and the court passes from despair to joy. Perfidious Astano kills himself. In the fifth act also, Venus appears. Giraldi discourses upon terrestrial love and that morality which forbids lovers to seek the supreme delights of love "against the common use of marriage."

In the *Antivalomeni* (1548), the most intricate of Giraldi's tragedies, from the first discourses of the first act, the spectator is informed of what has taken place and of that which is about to take place. This is characteristic of all his plays. *Antivalomeni* means *interchanged;* but the interchanges arise out of the perfect likeness of four young people, which renders possible the disguise of youths as girls and of girls as males. In the *Antivalomeni*—and it is a characteristic of all the Italian tragedy of the sixteenth century—the monologues and dialogues suffocate the action.

The *Eufimia,* like Giraldi's remaining tragedies, has a happy ending. But the author, who had begun his career with the *Orbecche,* did not renounce that horribleness which characterized his first tragedy.

Giraldi drew the subject of *Orbecche* and of his six other tragedies from his collection of novels called *Ecatommithi,* and was herein an innovator, giving a dramatic form to fiction, that is, to his own invention. In Giraldi's theatre, people of every country act and speak, save Italians, French, and Spaniards. But to whatever country and to whatever period the Giraldian personages belong, their characteristics, ideas, and social conventions are the same. The morality is that of the sixteenth century, for, as Giraldi said in regard to tragedies, "It is not well to have them other than such as the similitude of the times in which the poet writes, demands in regard to costumes, to the decorum, and other circumstances of the personages."[4]

Much has been said of Giraldi as a renovator of tragedy and a true forerunner of the romantic drama. Rather than a precursor of the romantic drama, Giraldi is a formulator of that neo-classic type of involved tragedy (*tragedia avviluppata*) which for many years was regarded as the perfection of drama. *Tragedia avviluppata* meant that the *denouement,* whether happy or sombre, depended upon the final recognition of some person whose real individuality was at first unknown. Parents ignorantly kill their own children, and children are unconsciously parricides; princes disguise as private persons; women disguise as men; those believed to be dead are found yet living: with all the equivocal situations and extraordinary accidents which could arise from these things. All these abound in Giraldi's plays; and, because of his authority and out of respect for classical tradition, they appear in every well-constructed Italian tragedy of the period.

In the quarrels of men and women, Giraldi sided with the women and praised matrimony. It was a vital question in the literature of the time, and he brought it also on to the tragic stage. All his women are devoted, sincere, virtuous; all are victims of men's cruelty. Had his talent equalled his sympathies, his women would all have been sweet and interesting figures.

While Trissino was writing *Sofonisba* (1515), Giovanni Rucellai, the author of the *Api,* composed *Rosmunda* derived from Longobardian history; but both are fashioned after the identical manner. The Florentine, however, modifies Paolo Diacone's account more radically than Trissino does that of Livy, and transfers situations, many verses, and nearly one whole scene from Sophocles' *Antigone.* Rucellai's *Oreste* has all the defects of the *Rosmunda,* aggravated.

Falisco persuades the king to marry Rosmunda instead of torturing this daughter of Cunimondo. "Then thou dost counsel me to take her?" asks the king in amazement; and since Falisco assures him that the match is a good one, Alboino replies, "I am content to carry out thy counsel." Rosmunda's horror of becoming

Alboino's wife is overcome by the exhortations of Falisco and the persuasions of her nurse. Rosmunda must consider her own danger and that of her maidens from the licentious Longobard warriors. "And if so be thou art disposed to avenge thy father, the better canst thou do so being queen, and wife of Alboin, than being servant." Rosmunda speaks of a man who loves her and who, she hopes, will come to rescue her. This Almachilde appears and learns that Rosmunda is Alboino's wife, and, having heard her lamentations, plots vengeance. All succeeds perfectly. Almachilde, disguised as a woman, enters Alboino's chamber and cuts his throat.

Rucellai's other tragedy, *Oreste,* is a free handling of Euripides' *Iphigenia among the Tauri,* with ill-advised amplifications and sentimental exaggerations whereby the dramatic force of the original is lost.

In the course of the sixteenth century other tragedies followed, in which there reappeared either a tale already treated by the great Athenian dramatists, but now transferred to new personages, or a Greek tragedy rehandled with more or less freedom and good taste. The rigorous simplicity of the ancients was neither understood nor appreciated; and it was considered an improvement to fill out the original with bombastic rhetoric in the amorous parts and to distort delicate expressions by coarse paraphrasing.

Greek tragedies abound in atrocities, and Rucellai was the first Italian playwright to follow their example. In spite of the happy ending of both Rucellai's tragedies, in each the evildoer perishes and the atrocious appears in both. The ferocity of Toante is horrible in the *Oreste;* the decapitation of the corpse of Cunimondo in the *Rosmunda* is monstrous, as is the horrible cup which Alboino prepares from the severed head; and the cruel scene of the decapitation of Alboino, as described by the messenger.

The *Antigone* was translated into Italian (1533) by Alamanni and is notable for the simplicity and elegance of the language.

Allessendro de Pazzi translated the *Efigenia in Tauri* (1524), the *Ciclope* (Cyclops) (1525), the *Elettra* and the *Edipo Re*. His sole original tragedy is the *Dido in Cartagina* which precedes these.

Pazzi introduced the mythological supernatural into Italian regular tragedy, and also a new form of verse resembling the Greek in sound.

The *Tullia* of Lodovico Martelli is an extreme example of Greek imitation. To the ferocity of Tullia (daughter of Servius Tullius), Martelli adds the horrors of the Aristides legend; and, from the combination of the two legends, there emerges a monstrous tangle of wickedness. Servius is a usurping tyrant who seeks to maintain himself upon the throne by terror and artifices; hence he proscribed every adversary and gave his two daughters in marriage to the two sons of the murdered king. Tullia, the daughter of Servius, has already murdered her own sister and her first husband.

Highly praised was the verbose *Giulio Cesare* (Julius Caesar) of Orlando Pescetti. Two scenes of the fourth act are almost dramatic: the third, in which the conspirators, meeting with Caesar, persuade him to repair to the Senate; and the fourth, where the conspirators are anxiously spying on the secret colloquy of Lennate with Caesar and fear betrayal. The rest of the play is monotonous dialogue, monologue, narrative, song, or lamentation.

Cresci's *Tullia feroce* is preceded by a prologue recited by Ambition, who, after having discoursed of herself and her own power, sets forth the argument of the tragedy. Finally Tullia comes on the stage (Act III, sc. 1). She is resolute and will reign; no fear that she will change her mind. In some hundreds of verses of seven feet (*settenari*), she persuades Tarquinius that they ought to ascend the throne at once, acquiring it by parricide. The fifth act consists wholly of lamentations and narrations; the chorus—carrying on a dialogue with the *Nunzio* (messenger), the Servant, and the Nurse—mourns the good Servius, and imprecates the ferocity of

Tullia whose chariot has crushed the wretched body of her father.

Aniello Paulilli, a Neapolitan, composed an *Incendio di Troia* (Burning of Troy); Angelo Lottini, a *Niobe*. Bongianni Gratarolo began with a mythological tragedy overflowing with learning, the *Altea* (Althea). Meleagro, Altea's son, kills the boar sacred to Diana, and gives the spoils to Atalanta from whom they are taken by Altea's brothers. Meleagro slays them; Altea, to avenge her brothers, kills her son; then, after her daughter, Deianira, has announced to her the death of her own husband, Ercole (Hercules), consumed by the famous shirt of Nessus, Altea also dies; and thus finally the wrath of Diana is appeased.

At short intervals, the subject of Merope was treated by three different authors; and these works remain among the most celebrated tragedies of the *cinquecento* owing to their frequent comparison with the famous "Meropes" of the *settecento*. Following Aristotle's *Poetics,* which excluded the happy ending from all tragedies, Pomponio Torelli's *Merope* (1589) does not end in a festival like that of Liviera and like the three famous "Meropes" of the *settecento*.

Another mournful love-romance characteristic of the period is the *Almerigo* of Gabriel Zinano. Almerigo, prince of Spain, secretly abandons his father's court, lured by the fame of the beauty of Elvira, daughter of Amurate, emperor of the Turks, and goes to Constantinople. His father dies. The Spanish realms, "not knowing where their lord is, call to their government Rotilda, daughter of the king of France, already destined to be the wife of Almerigo." Formindo, his tutor, reveals his hiding-place to Rotilda, and, disguising herself, she goes to summon him. They meet at Constantinople. Almerigo confesses to unhappy Rotilda his immense love for Elvira. Elvira, who loves Almerigo and knows herself to be promised in marriage to the king of Persia, laments, and consults with Estilla, her "friend and sister-in-law." The two maidens decide to flee (Act V, sc. 5), while Rotilda, who unseen is present at their colloquy, offers herself as their companion. In the meantime Almerigo also has decided to flee to rejoin his dear Elvira. In the darkness of the night, Almerigo perceives three persons who seem to wish to cross his path. With his sword he kills Rotilda, Estilla, and Elvira! While he deals this last fatal blow, a ray of moonlight illumines the face of Elvira and he recognizes her. Almerigo raves, faints and revives many times, until the Nurse arrives and has Elvira, yet living, carried to her apartments. The emperor, Amurate, tears out the eyes of Almerigo, mutilates him with bestial fury. Dying, Elvira desires from Almerigo one last embrace, but Almurate refuses, "and the one is cast to the tigers, the other exposed to the panthers." Thus, with a description of an accursed repast of wild beasts, Zinano's tragedy ends.

Luigi Groto's *Dalida* (1572) is another example of the horrible. Candaule, king of Battriana, although already husband of Berenice, marries Dalida, kills her father, Moleonte, and usurps his kingdom. Ferocious Berenice has Dalida bound and guides her hand to torture the bodies of the two children with daggers; then with their flesh and that of Dalida, she prepares a supper for the king. All of the principal personages are killed, since Candaule and Berenice poison each other.

A year after the performance of *Orbecche,* Sperone Speroni (1542) finished *Canace* which was to be performed at Padua, and which is famous for the long and bitter controversies it called forth. The incestuous love of Canace and Macareo was a repugnant subject, and its treatment is most unhappy. It is the most striking example of the *horrible* type of tragedy. Published without the author's consent in 1543, it was republished in 1546 at Padua, with Speroni's knowledge.

To be avenged on Eolo, king of the winds, who had sought to prevent the fatal journey of Eneas, Venus caused the twin brother and sister, Marcareo and Canace, to burn with incestuous fire; and from this love a child is born, whose *shade* appears upon the stage to relate its own unhappy fate. In order that her little baby may escape from the fury of Eolo, Canace arranges with the nurse that the child shall be carried out of the royal palace, hidden under flowers which she proposes to offer to the goddess Juno. The stratagem fails, for, while the king admires Canace's flowers, the child hidden beneath them "raises a loud cry," and all is thus discovered. Eolo murders his daughter; the son kills himself; and the child is thrown to the dogs to be devoured by them. The unavailing repentance of Eolo follows. Speroni introduced the division into acts and added the prologue, recited by Venus, who descends from "the third Heaven" to magnify her own power to the spectators.

Pietro Aretino's *Orazia* (1546) is far better than *Canace;* it is indeed the least bad of Italian *cinquecento* tragedies. It follows Livy's tale of the Roman Celia's grief for the death of her husband, one of the Curiazi, her sorrow contrasting with the joy of Rome, which drives the surviving Orazio to kill his sister. Aretino's historical fidelity is noteworthy, and, in spite of the canons of criticism to the contrary, he does not disdain to express his beautiful and powerful images in figurative language, as when Orazio is led prisoner before the king, and looks at Spurio:

> And meeting with his own mine eyes,
> He smiled, and smiling seemed a sun,
> Which sudden 'mid the clouds is born and dies.

In the conflict between the law demanding the death of the slayer and clemency for the victorious champion, the latter prevails; and the tragedy ends happily.

It is also to Aretino's credit that most of the action occurs before the eyes of the spectators, and that he banished the chorus and suppressed the anonymous "messengers" with their interminable monologues, and that the narratives are few and brief compared with those in other tragedies of the period. This praise for Aretino must be tempered by the fact that Publio and Spurio speak too often, and that the dialogue is frequently commonplace.

Another butchery is the tragedy *Marianna,* by L. Dolce; but in it the horribleness is partly retrieved. It has been said that, aside from some defects, *Marianna* is the best tragedy of the *cinquecento*. It had a clamorous success in 1565. Almost unique for the Italian tragic theatre of that time, the two principal characters, Marianna and Herod, are complex souls: Herod especially so. His ferocity arises from a morbid jealousy so great that before departing for Rome, he commands Soemo to slay Marianna, should he not return. The woman he so passionately loves must never belong to another. That is a fine scene (Act II, sc. 2) in which Herod seeks to induce the cup-bearer to deny that Marianna had urged him to poison the king. The cup-bearer, to Herod's great relief, confesses that, upon the instigation of Salome, he falsely accused Marianna. *Marianna* is not the best tragedy of the *cinquecento,* but its second act is notable for real psychological content.

In spite of its merits, *Orazia* had no imitations. Giraldi's tragedies on the other hand, especially *Orbecche,* determined the direction and form of the greater number of Italian tragedies in the second half of the century.[5] Hence, division into acts was steadfastly adhered to, personages were more numerous than they had been in purely Greek imitations, and frequent use was made of prologues, delivered by supernatural beings. The most unbridled passions were put upon the stage. The heralds related with horrible details the most repulsive atrocities. Frigid dialogues and long monologues were put into the mouths of superfluous counselors, servants, and nurses. Moralizations on the instability of fortune, human wickedness, and the need of resignation, became longer and more frequent. In short, among the abundant productions of tragedy in the second half of the sixteenth century, there is not one work that excels in art.

Luigi Groto, called Cieco d'Adria (the blind man of Adria) from his misfortune and native town, under the name of *Adriana* staged a novel of Bandello's, that of *Giulietta and Romeo,* thus becoming a precursor of the great English tragedian. There are some happily conceived scenes in Orlando Pescelli's *Cesare* (1594); and Torquato Tasso introduced a conglomeration of the most admired Hellenic tragedies into his *Torrismondo.*

The half romantic tone which begins to appear in some of Giraldi's later tragedies, becomes an erotic current toward the close of the sixteenth century, as is seen in the *Recinda* of Forzati and the *Calestri* of Turco. The personages of the drama and its construction are on the old classic model; and there are moral and political speeches which have the same familiar monotony as before. And yet, notwithstanding these old classic forms and fonts of inspiration and imitation, a new element has entered into Italian tragedy and has so changed it that in some cases the tragedies have become real romances set in tragic form. The drama has become modern. This new element is love. Love is discussed and sighed over. Love is the theme of every plot: pure love and impure love, fortunate and unfortunate love, timid love and audacious love.

The *Torrismondo* of Torquato Tasso is an excellent example of this mingling of past and present in the drama, of the new romantic element still confined in the old classic mould. *Torrismondo* was highly praised for its conformity to the rules of the art, for the "involved story," and for the author's research into the "principles of Aristotle." But it was not praised for the human, impassioned, vivid, dramatic reality that is sometimes revealed in the souls of the characters.

The nymphs had predicted to the Gothic king that his daughter, Rosmonda (Rosamund) would cause the death of her brother

Torrismondo; hence the king secretly sends Rosmonda into Dacia, and substitutes for her the child of Rosmonda's nurse; and this supposed Rosmonda is educated in the royal palace of Gotia as Torrismondo's sister. Seized by pirates, the true Rosmonda was given to Araldo (Harold) king of Norway, who adopted her as his daughter, calling her Alvida.

Germondo, king of Sweden, seeks Alvida in marriage; but, Araldo refusing, Germondo persuades a trusted friend to ask Alvida in marriage for himself, and after having obtained her, to give her to him, *virgo intacta*. This friend was Torrismondo, now become king of Gozia. Torrismondo sails for Norway, obtains Alvida's hand from Araldo, and sets out with her, saying that the marriage must be celebrated and consummated only in Arana, the capital of Gozia. The ship is wrecked on a desert shore; Alvida and Torrismondo seek refuge under the same tent; she believes that she is giving herself to her husband; he forgets his friend; and thus destiny is fulfilled.

This is the situation at the beginning of the drama (Act I, sc. 1 & 2). When a messenger announces to him the imminent arrival of Germondo (Act II, sc. 1), Torrismondo is filled with fear, but he hopes (Act I, sc. 2) that Germondo may consent to yield Alvida to him and take Rosmonda in exchange. Germondo consents. When the false Rosmonda says to Torrismondo, who has always considered her his sister, "O King, I am your servant; and your servant I was born, and lived in swaddling bands" (Act IV, sc. 3), Torrismondo learns of the substitution. But where is his sister? Is she still living? A messenger, coming from Norway, announces the death of Araldo, and reveals the horrible reality; Torrismondo had committed incest, as well as proved traitor. In the fifth act, Alvida and Torrismondo die.

During the eighty years between *Sofonisba* and *Torrismondo*, the subjects, the styles, and the metres of Italian tragedy vary. They

are divided or not divided into acts and scenes; they are of happy
or of unhappy ending; gallant sentimentalities came into favour;
atrocities spread; but, in technique, they varied little. The drama
still consisted of monotonous narratives; the dramatic personages
remained either vague, without depth of human significance,
empty, or false.

Other causes afterwards concurred to obstruct the fortune of the
Italian tragedy. Though the *Accademici Olimpici* (Olympian Aca-
demicians) of Vicenza gave magnificent tragic spectacles in their
famous theatre, and the representation of the *Edipo* of Giustiniani
in 1585 was especially splendid, Ingeneri noted that the tragedies
"as imitations of royal actions and of royal persons" demanded too
sumptuous settings, and the "royal purses" did not willingly open
to such heavy expenditures. In the public theatres, tragedies were
performed only when some munificent lord subsidized them. The
decoration of the scene, which ordinarily showed the perspective
of a royal palace glittering with lights, was magnificent; and the
spectators demanded this magnificence in tragedy. The scenes were
constructed in great part of timber covered with plaster and stucco,
illumined by wax candles; and hence the representation of a tragedy was an expensive luxury. Thus the *Erode re di Giudea* (Herod
King of Judea), which, according to the *Memorie* (Memoirs) of
Pallavicino (Ediz. Daelli, I, 127), was recited at Rome "publicly
. . . with great applause" in 1602, was delayed until, by getting together "money from every side," they succeeded in putting together
the 3000 ducats which were spent on that spectacle.

NOTES

CHAPTER VII

1. Albertino Mussato was born in Padua in 1261, a year after the destruction of Ezzelino da Romano, the imperial vicar, who had threatened Lombardy. Into his tragedy, Mussato put all his hatred of the tyrant, and the joy of Padua at his fall. The *Eccerinus* was probably never represented on the stage; and it is an exaggeration of its excellences to compare it with the greater Greek tragedies.

2. Pistoia changes the names: Tancredi becomes Demetrio, King of Thebes; Gismonda becomes Panfila; Guiscardo is rechristened Filostrato. But the *argomento* repeats all the particulars of Boccaccio's *novella*. Demetrio, "to pass the time," discusses the snares surrounding the powerful, and asks his daughter's opinion upon this subject. She considers that these melancholy conditions are largely imaginary, and suggests that her father, instead of trembling and making others tremble, should think of pleasure and of giving his subjects happiness. The old man agrees, and praises Filostrato, the most faithful, wise, and discreet of his servants; then, seeing the day dawning and the joy of spring returning, laments the restless quest for gold and power, and sends his daughter to breakfast. "I know," says he, "being time, thy appetite." But Panfila's appetite is of another kind. A young ardent widow, she loves Filostrato, and seeks the secret satisfaction of her desire. To Boccaccio's story, Pistoia added the hesitation of Filostrato at the lofty amourous fortune which offers itself to him (Act II), and the veiled love-declaration of Panfila. When Demetrio discovers the amour of Filostrato and Panfila, he swears, "Before the sun hides its bright ray, I will take such vengeance that their punishment will make more than one lover wise." Filostrato's heart is torn out; Panfila poisons herself; thus all takes place and is achieved within that famous *giro di sole,* that round of the sun.

3. Giraldi's *Orbecche* was acted at Ferrara in Giraldi's house before Ercole II, Duke of Ferrara, and a brilliant company of noble persons, in 1541. The music was composed by M. Alfonso della Viuola, the scenery by M. Girolamo Carpi.

4. *Discorso,* p. 39.

5. Antonio Decio da Orte, author of the terrible and famous *Acripanda* (1591), is one of the writers who followed the counsel of Giraldi, that mournful and horrible spectacles should be enacted before the eyes of the spectators.

   Ussimano, king of Egypt, after having murdered his first wife, Orselia, also tries to kill their only son, who escapes and grows up at the court of his grandfather, the king of Arabia, upon whose death he becomes king. He then moves against Ussimano, to avenge his own mother, defeats him in battle, and then proposes to make peace, on condition that Ussimano's two children, by Acripanda, his second wife, be given to him as hostages. When he gets the two children, he cuts them in pieces, wraps the pieces in a bloody sheet and sends them to Acripanda, who, with loud shrieks (Act IV, sc. 2), lays them in a tomb, in which she also shuts herself, and dies. The besiegers break into Memphis: Ussimano is slain; Acripanda's corpse is dragged through the streets; the city is sacked and burnt; and thus the king of Arabia finally revenges his mother's murder. Mortal hatred between father and son, massacre of innocent children, outrage of a dead body, slaughter and ruin, ghosts of the dead Orselia and of the sons of Acripanda—all that is horrible was poured by Decio into his tragedy.

CHAPTER VIII

THE SIXTEENTH CENTURY: THE PASTORAL DRAMA AND OTHER FORMS

Performances of the classical drama in Rome: in Venice and Urbino: in Bologna: in Mantua: Latin comedies at Ferrara: Boiardo's *Timone*: Theatre at Parma: The vogue for bucolic poetry: Dramatization of the eclogue: Beccari's *Il Sacrificio*: Tasso's *Aminta*: Guarini's *Il Pastor fido*: The history of the actor-companies: Popularity of Allegorical Representations: the *contrasti*: Rise of the farce: the *Il Frate* of Grazzini: the *frottole*: the *farsa rusticale*: Carracciolo's *farse caviole*, simple pictures of contemporary society: the *La Ricevuta dell' Imperatore alla Cava*: Alione's farces: The Siennese pastoral comedies of the *Rozzi*: Calmo's use of the different dialects in his eclogues: Detailed descriptions of the farces:

IN Rome, the classic drama was probably first popularized by Pomponio Leto. He gave plays by Plautus and Terence, and modern imitations of them, in the palaces of several cardinals. Giovanni Sulpizio da Veroli instructed the Roman youth in the recitation of tragedies for which he says Raffaello provided the scenery. The *Asinaria* and the *Hippolytus* were also performed at this time. During a splendid banquet at the palace of Cardinal Pietro Riario, a magnificent representation was given. On January 1, 1476, in the house of Cardinal Francesco Gonzaga, were represented the "Vices and Virtues," which disputed before a "king," who was a *cameriere* (man servant) of the cardinal. In 1502, for the marriage of Lucrezia Borgia with Alfonso d'Este, on the same evening in which the *Menæchmi* was recited in the papal palace, before the Plautinian comedy, was performed a complicated allegory of Virtue and Fortune disputing. Cesare Borgia was one of the actors. In 1504, the princess of Bisignano wishing to repair from Rome to Milan, a representation was performed before her in the house of Cardinal Sanseverino. France and Lombardy appeared, "who prayed the princess that she should go into their said

156

Proscenium at Parma

Dom.co M.auro del.

Stage of a S

Gio. Ant. Lorenzini intaglio

provinces, promising her great things," and Rome lamented at "being deprived of her presence." Vanquished Rome was "sorrowful, and the competing provinces rejoiced at their victory." In the carnival of 1508, for the celebration of the marriage of a nephew of Julius II with a Colonna "tre pasti e due comedie" (three banquets and two plays) were prepared. In 1509, two eclogues by Pietro Corsi were recited, Pope Julius and four cardinals being present. With Pope Leo X, plays and spectacles were common in Rome, the new pope saying to his brother, "Let us enjoy the Papacy, since God has given it to us." The Siennese company of the *Rozzi* probably performed some of their plays every year in Rome before this pope; before whom also, in 1513, the *Pœnulus* of Plautus was performed in honour of the citizenship conferred on Giuliano de' Medici. For these Medicean fêtes a magnificent theatre was built seating more than three thousand people. In 1514, to celebrate the visit of Isabella Gonzaga, the *Calandria* of Bibbiena was given in Rome; and Baldassarre Peruzzi arranged for it "marvellous" perspectives. In 1519, the *Suppositi* of Ariosto was given with scenery by Raffaello; and, only a few days before his death, Pope Leo X was present at the performance of a comedy in the villa of Majana.

At Venice, at the end of the fifteenth century, certainly before 1502, there was represented in the courtyard of the convent of the Eremitani, a Latin comedy entitled *Stephanium*. Its author, Giovanni Armonio Marso, a young Abruzzese, was a friar of the order of the *Crociferi* and, from 1516 to 1552, organist of the chapel of St. Mark. The representation of his comedy aroused great enthusiasm. Sabellico wrote to him that, while the *Stephanium* was being acted, it seemed to him that he "was present at a comedy of Plautus or of Cicero, in the theatre of Marcellus or in that of Pompey." On December 29, 1499, however, there was a decree of the Signoria, prohibiting such plays in Venice.

At Urbino, on February 13, 1488, when Elisabetta Gonzaga went there as bride to Guidobaldo di Montefeltro, a representation was given. All the gods of Olympus, "dressed according to allegory, with their emblems in their hands," gathered together to fête the princely nuptials; and Juno and Diana, with most elegant rhymes, disputed before Jove, which was the better life, matrimony or virginity. Jove sustained that conjugal life was best, observing "that if all served virginity, human generation would be lacking and it would be against the divine institution." In 1494, many festivities were given, in Urbino to honour the returning duke and duchess, and also worthily to receive Isabella d'Este Gonzaga, returning from a pilgrimage to Loreto. On February 6, 1513, the *Calandria* of Bibbiena was represented at the court of Guidobaldo, duke of Urbino, and from there the play continued its triumphal course through the princely theatres of Italy.

At Bologna, January 29, 1487, in the great sala of the Palazzo Bentivoglio, on the occasion of the marriage of Annibale Bentivoglio with Lucrezia d'Este, a performance was given by the Riminese, Domenico Fosco. Four grandiose edifices, a tower, a palace, a wooded mountain, and a cliff, were made to advance upon the stage; and there took part in the action Juno, Venus, Cupid, Diana, Infamy, Jealousy, two youths, eight nymphs.

At Mantua, the first in order of time as in artistic value is the *Orfeo* of Angelo Poliziano, represented in 1471, when Galeazzo Maria Sforza and his wife Bona di Savoia visited Lodovico Gonzaga and Barbara of Brandenbourg. Poliziano was then only seventeen years old! And he composed his dramatic fable in the brief space of two days. The marvellous fruit of a great student of Greek and Roman art, the *Orfeo* is profoundly classical. It is composed with sobriety and harmony of rhyme and verse. It exists in two forms, of which the first has the construction of a *sacra rappresentazione*. In the greater part of the *Orfeo,* Poliziano retains the

Oly

tc.

metre of the *ottava* (octave). He retains also the Annunciation; but, since this cannot be delivered by an angel of God, it is spoken by Mercury the messenger of the gods. The scene is immovable and duplex, that is, Earth and Hell. As Paradise opened in the sacred dramas, so now Olympus opens, that is, the upper part of the theatre, and Mercury is let down by mechanical means.

The *Orfeo* was not followed by other representations, and the actual foundation of the Mantuan theatre, the splendour of whose dramatic tradition endured much longer than that of Ferrara or of any other Italian city, is due to Francesco and Isabella Gonzaga. Fame celebrated the young prince Francesco Gonzaga as a perfect knight and cultured lord. Isabella d'Este became his bride and *Marchesana* of Mantua in 1490. She was beautiful, graceful, and reputed the most cultured girl of her times. Her husband and the Mantuan court favored her desire to introduce the classic theatre which, under the encouragement of her father, Duke Ercole I, was already so flourishing in Ferrara.

The Court which accomplished most for the resuscitation of Latin Comedy was that of the Estensi at Ferrara. Latin comedies were recited at Ferrara, as at Rome, in the original; and, at the same time, both Plautus and Terence were presented in translation for an audience that was imperfectly acquainted with the Latin language. After the presentation of the original plays, came translation; and after translation, imitation.

We first hear of the Ferrarese theatre in 1486: "on the 25th day, the duke Ercole da Este had a fête made in his courtyard, and there was a *facezia* (a merry piece, or comedy) of Plautus, called the *Menechino* . . . and the cost of the said fête came to more than 1000 ducats." Next year, for the wedding of Lucrezia d'Este with Annibale Bentivoglio, "a di XXI di Zenaro" (on January 21st) there was given the *Cefalo* of Niccolo, relative and courtier of Ercole. It was "beautiful and of great cost." *Cefalo* is a mythological fable suggested by the seventh book of Ovid's *Metamorphoses*.

About five years later than the *Cefalo* is the *Timone* "Commedia by the Magnificent Count Matteo Maria Boiardo, count of Scandiano, translated from a Dialogue by Lucian, for the pleasure of the most illustrious prince Lord Ercole d'Este, Duke of Ferrara." There are stage directions similar to those of the sacred dramas; it takes place upon a fixed stage divided into two *piani* (levels). A multitude of personages, human, divine, and allegorical, pass from place to place and between Heaven and Earth as required by the play. The *Timone* being a work of Boiardo, author of *Orlando innamorato,* we should expect a work of art of rich imagining, echoing with arms and trumpets and glowing with a thousand lights. In fact, however, Boiardo almost translated the dialogue of Lucian's *Timon,* and strung *terzine* together with desolating uniformity.

In 1499, "the Duke Ercole, in the great sala of his Court, had wooden tribunals set up so as to give some of his Fetes." The *Sosia* of Terence was given, and the next evening, "a Comedy of Plautus," and the following Sunday, "one of the Comedies composed *etiam* this Carnival."

The year 1502, when Lucrezia Borgia came as Alfonso d'Este's bride to Ferrara, marks the climax of these Latin spectacles. His troupe, recruited from Ferrara, Rome, Sienna, and Mantua, numbered one hundred and ten actors of both sexes. Accomplished singers, dancers, and scene-painters were summoned to add richness to the spectacle. The occasion was memorable. In those five evenings, the Court of Ferrara presented to the fashionable world of Italy a carefully studied picture of Latin comedy framed in a setting of luxuriant modern arabesques. The simplicity of Plautus was thrown into relief by extravagances borrowed from mediæval and oriental associations and enhanced by music. The plays began February 3rd. The first was the *Epidico*—in the vulgar tongue;

Fran. M.ᵃ Francia fecé

then the *Bacchides;* third the *Miles Gloriosus,* fourth the *Asinaria,* and finally the *Casina.*

The practice of the Ferrarese stage, culminating in these marriage shows of 1502, determined the future of Italian comedy. Scenic exhibitions being merely an extravagant court luxury, there could be no development of an independent theatre which would inspire the genius of poets. The lack of permanent buildings devoted to acting, in Italian cities, also checked the expansion of the drama. To act a play, a stage must be specially erected for the occasion. After 1550, however, theatres were attached to many princely residences. Such was the Theatro Farnese at Parma, erected in 1618 by Ranuzio I, after the design of Galeotti Aleotti of Ferrara. It could accommodate seven thousand spectators, and is magnificent even in its ruins. What Italy lacked, however, was a theatre open to all classes and at all seasons of the year.

In the second half of the sixteenth century, the pastoral drama, a new kind of dramatic poetry, arose to share with tragedy and comedy the honours of the stage.

The love that men of the Renaissance affected to feel for simple and placid country life produced a harvest of eclogues by Ariosto, Trissino, Alamanni, and many others in imitation of Florentine quattrocentist idyllic poetry and Sannazzaro's *Arcadia;* the Latin idyllic epigram valiantly treated by Navagero and Flaminio gave rise to the idyllic sonnets of Claudio Tolomei, the noted restorer of classic metres; and Virgil, the father of bucolic poetry, was also imitated both in Latin and in Italian.

During the great vogue for pastoral poetry, eclogues, generally arranged as dialogues, also came to take a place among dramatic compositions; and many were composed after the beginning of the fifteenth century to enliven or vary court festivals, as intermezzos recited by actors in pastoral costume with or without scenery. Baldesar Castiglione's elegant *Tirsi* recited at Urbino in 1506 thus imitated *Orfeo;*[1] and others follow Sannazzaro's example in metre and sentimentality.

Gradually the subjects became less simple; the number of the personages was augmented; and various satiric, jocular, and tragic elements were sometimes worked into the scheme of the pastoral tale; the *terzine* and *ottave* were interchanged with and superseded by *stanze di canzone* freely rhymed; and they were performed with pomp of costume and of scenery.

The modest eclogue gradually developed into a multiplication of personages and complexity of scenes which suggested that it be raised to the dignity and amplitude of drama. This happened in Ferrara where tragedy was invigorated with a new spirit by Giraldi, and where comedies and tragedies were continually being performed on stages erected by the prince's munificence.

Here *Il Sacrificio* by Agostino Beccari was performed in Don Francesco d'Este's house in 1554 in the presence of Ercole II and his son Luigi. The value of Beccari's pastorale is chiefly historical. A few elegant imitations of Virgil and Ovid and some happily conceived scenes are not sufficient to give it importance.

The new kind of literature did not bear the solemn name of art till Torquato Tasso's *Aminta* was performed on July 31, 1573, on the island of Belvedere in the Po, a pleasure resort of the Este family, not far from Ferrara. The subject dramatized by the author of *Gerusalemme* is simple. Aminta, a shepherd of divine lineage, loves Silvia who is devoted to the service of Diana and flies from him and despises him; nor is the beautiful nymph's cruelty overcome when he delivers her from the attack of a coarse satyr. Then, at the false rumour of her death, the despairing shepherd throws himself from a rock and Silvia's compassionate heart is fired to love and she becomes Aminta's bride. The slender thread of the action is worked out naturally by scene and episode so arranged that *Aminta* acquires the aspect of a regular drama without

Pastoral Drama

Pastoral Drama

losing its beautiful simplicity. The idealization of pastoral life already practised by ancient bucolic writers is here suffused by an entirely modern sentiment of gentle voluptuous melancholy which is not the least of the attractions of this most singular jewel of Italian literature. The style is graceful and elegant, yet simple and clear; and a soft charm flows harmoniously through the delightful little work. *Aminta* had a triumphant reception all over Italy even before it was printed (1580). Everywhere there were imitations.

In Ferrara, another courtier of the Este, Battista Guarini (1538–1612), drew inspiration from it for the composition of his tragicomedy *Il pastor fido* (published 1590), which is the only pastoral drama worthy of comparison with *Aminta*. Its construction was the consummation of long and laborious effort. Baretti says there cannot "be any doubt that he began it in 1569."

As in Greek tragedy, the principal action of *Pastor fido* is based on the will of Fate. As in the Latin comedy, the drama ends happily, thanks to a recognition. Mirtillo and Amarilli love each other; but the priest, Montano, desires her for his son Silvio, believing thus to interpret an oracle which declared that the misfortunes of Arcadia should cease only when love should unite two young hearts of divine lineage—Amarilli descended from Pan, and Silvio from Hercules. Through the malicious designs of Corisca, a lascivious and corrupt woman, Amarilli is condemned to death. Mirtillo, the faithful shepherd, takes her place, as is allowed by the law; but when he is about to be sacrificed, Carino arrives from Elide and, by his revelations, Montano recognizes in Mirtillo the son he lost as a child. The marriage predicted by the oracle then is to be that of Mirtillo and Amarilli. Thus the will of Fate concurs with that of Love; Silvio, till now in rebellion against the son of Venus, submits to the love of Dorinda; and Corisca, pardoned and penitent, makes amends for her sins.

The *Pastor fido* has some of the characteristics of the regular sixteenth century drama. It follows classic models as to unity of place and time; but it fuses tragic and comic elements into one harmonious unit. Two other actions run by the side of the principal one, Dorinda's love for Silvio and Corisca's for Mirtillo. Guarini thus attains to a wider and fuller representation of life, anticipating the artistic liberty that has given rise to the modern drama.

The *Pastor fido* lacks innate dramatic life, as, however, for that matter, does all Italian sixteenth century tragedy. As in *Aminta,* a lyric tone prevails over the dramatic. The style is splendid, though sometimes pompous and studied. The verse is fluent. Guarini is as exquisite an artist as Tasso whom he rivaled and sometimes imitated. Thus, although the *Pastor fido* surpasses the *Aminta* in plot and invention, it has not the latter's feeling and gentle melancholy.

The performances took place upon a temporary stage, in palaces, in the halls where the *accademie* met, and also in nuns' convents. Very famous artists like Raffaello, Baldassare Peruzzi, and Vasari, often prepared magnificent scenic appliances. Intermezzos of various kinds took place between the acts. These sometimes consisted of short songs and dances, or of vulgar buffoonery; and then again pompous mythological tales were acted in praise of princely spectators.

It is evident that so long as the performance of the drama was merely an intermittent pastime and the performers merely chance actors, there could be no great and regular growth of the art. The sixteenth century, however, witnessed the foundation of durable theatres and the formation of permanent companies of actors; and the drama now became a part of the city life.

By the order of Cardinal Ercole given in 1549 to the architect Bertani, such a theatre, of magnificent architecture, was erected in Mantua. It was semicircular in form, with the seats for the audience rising in tiers.

TENPIO DELLA PACE INTERMEDIO SESTO

Come rapp. nelle notte del
Ser.mo Principe di Toscana
l'an 1608. Giulio Parigi I.

NAVE DI AMERIGO VESPVCCI INTERMEDIO QVARTO

Come rapp. nelle notte del Ser.mo
Principe di Toscana l'an 1608
Giulio parigi I.

Remigio Conta Galino F.

Spectacles

The first regular company of Italian actors of which we have record was the *Gelosi,* first mentioned in 1569 as united into a company. In 1571, they performed at the *Hotel de Nevers* in Paris, and at *Nogent-le-Roi* for the baptism of Charles Henri de Clermont. Whether they amalgamated shortly afterwards with the *Confidenti,* forming the company of the *Uniti,*[2] and then separated afresh to reassume their old name, is doubtful. The *Gelosi* performed in 1572 at Genoa, and in 1574 at Venice in honour of Don Giovanni d'Austria, the victor of the battle of Lepanto.

Of signora Vittoria, a native of Ferrara, who was known on the stage as *Fioretta,* Garzoni says, "But worthy above all of the highest honours seems to me that divine Vittoria, who metamorphoses herself upon the stage; that beautiful enchantress of love, who gladdens the hearts of a thousand lovers with her words; that sweet syren, who binds with suave enchantments the soul of her devoted spectators, and without doubt deserves to be held up as a compendium of the art, having proportioned gestures, harmonious and becoming movements, majestic and graceful action, words sweet and affable, sighs delicate and subtle, laughter agreeable and charming, comportment lofty and noble, and showing in her whole person a perfect decorum such as belongs to, and is becoming to, a perfect actress."

In 1583, the prince Vincenzo of Ferrara, merged three companies of actors into one, and placed Francesco Andreini and his wife, the celebrated Isabella, at its head. The Pistojese Andreini, born about 1548, who after his escape from the Turks and return to Italy, probably joined the *Gelosi,* first acted the part of the *innamorato,* then created that of a vainglorious and braggart soldier with the name of *Capitan Spavento della val d'Inferno.* He died in Mantua on August 20, 1624. His wife, who was born in Padua in 1552 and married to him in 1587, was even more famous. Under the direction and counsels of her husband and Flaminio Scala, *capocomico* (head) of the *Gelosi,* she became the most celebrated Italian actress of her time. Beautiful, cultured, and gentle, she was equally expert in recitation and in song. She died at Lyons in 1604, while returning from Paris to Italy. Her death in the zenith of her glory made her name yet more famous. Living, she was lauded by Tasso and by Chiabrera, by Maria de' Medici and Henri IV, and dead, by the greatest poets of the times.

In 1584, the performance in Mantua of the *Pastor fido* was considered by Prince Vincenzo; and the same year it was put into rehearsal at Ferrara. Its performance at Mantua in 1598 is most important in the annals of the Italian Theatre.

With the performance of the *Pastor fido* finally carried out, after so many rehearsals, there closes an epoch of the classic Italian Theatre. And the correspondence between the beginning and the end of this first stage of the renovated scenic art is noteworthy: between the *Orfeo* at the beginning (1471) which has the external form of *sacra rappresentazione,* but is at the same time pastoral and heroic, popular and courtly, and embraces the earth and inferno; and the *Pastor fido* (1598) at the conclusion. Mantua, through the munificence of its princes, saw within its walls both these spectacles, and had in this way a great part in the creation, the maintenance, and the vicissitudes of the freshly arisen Italian Theatre.

In the second half of the *quattrocento,* there was a rich blossoming of allegorical representations.[3] Jacopo Sannazzaro, Pietro Antonio Caracciuolo, Giosue Capasso, and Antonio Ricci are the principal Neapolitan writers. Among the very numerous recorded festivities, suppers, triumphs, hunts, masquerades, mimic spectacles, their representations are those which have the closest relations with dramatic literature, and which present a more decisive allegorical character. In all except that given in Milan in 1449, we find either the mingling of angels and saints with divinities and heroes of mythology and ancient history, or else absolute classicism; and

Allegori

resentation

classicism dominates yet more widely over the mythological fables, which are closely akin to the allegorical representations and were profoundly influenced by the sacred theatre, which directly affected their formal construction and technical details.

The *Contrasto* was a form extremely popular in Italy during the Middle Ages; and traces of it still survive in Tuscany. *Contrasti* have varied nature and approach to the burlesque, although they always contain devout moral reflections. It is thus in the *Disputazione nobilissima del Vino e dell' Acqua* (the most noble dispute of Wine and Water). If the former boasts that without him the Mass cannot be celebrated, the other points out that without him baptism, which is the door of the Faith, cannot be given. There are also *Contrasti* between the Lovers and Love, of lovers between themselves, of Man and Woman, of women who dispute over their lover, of Winter and Summer, of the Months, of Appetite and Reason, of Rustics and Clerics. Some approach to farce, and, while keeping the name and action of *Contrasti,* bring upon the scene various human characters, as in the *Contenzione di Monna Costanza e di Biagio contadino* (the Contention of Monna Costanza and Biagio the peasant) by Bernardo Giambullari, in which the mistress accuses her farmer before the *Podesta* for neglecting the *podere*. It is full of obscene allusions.

The *Contrasto* is an embryonic drama, in which the imagination endows abstract ideas and material with life and word. The idea is the intrinsic opposition to one another of different facts and objects. Each fictitious personage expresses sentiments appropriate to his character.

The *Contrasto* was recited, not acted. Indeed, the true dramatic representation of it would be impossible, because such forms as *the body, the living, the devil, etc., "says"* and *the soul, the dead, the angel, etc., "replies"* are incorporated in the verse. Only the *Contenzione di Monna Costanza puossi fare in comedia,* "can be acted as a play." Nevertheless, the dramatic character of these compositions is evident.

While the cultured classes of Italian society delighted in sumptuous performances of tragedies, comedies, and pastoral dramas, the people continued to enjoy monologues, dialogues, disputes, and farces of simple plot, which the actors and jesters often improvised with grimaces and plebeian buffoonery before a chance audience. They drew their essential elements from classic models, from other literary sources, and also from direct observation of life. Even when treated with less crude notions of art, they themselves gave rise to compositions of a humble character.

At a very early date, the farce arose in Florence to compete with the *rappresentazione*. During the entire Middle Ages it was perpetuated by the historians and minstrels of the *piazza*. Simple in plot, trivial in form, without art, improvised or filled in at the moment upon a mere outline, depending upon the vivacity of the *lazzi*, the smartness of the expressions, the appositeness of the themes, and the exact representation of the commonest characters, it was acted at the street-corners and in the booths.[4]

Grazzini (Il Lasca) wrote three farces: the *Giostra*, the *Monica*, and *Il Frate*. *Il Frate*, represented at Florence the evening of January 6, 1540, in the house of the courtesan Maria da Prato, and printed at Venice in 1769, was formerly considered as the work of Niccolo Machiavelli. It is a little masterpiece.

Contrasted with the love of Frate Alberigo for Madonna Caterina is the love of Caterina's old husband, Amerigo, for the wife of his friend Alfonso. When Amerigo arrives, after Frate Alberigo, at Alfonso's house, instead of his lady-love, he finds his own wife. The situation is most comical; but amid the ridicule poured forth on the poor deceived husband there flashes a keen satire to illuminate the evil malice of the friar who has just had his pleasure of the woman. With words which would suggest an honourable and de-

Allegori

vout priest, he exalts her chastity and advises old Amerigo to conquer his guilty caprices. "You must know, Amerigo, that to sin is human, to amend angelical, but to persevere in sin is downright devilish. And since living in this world you will always be in mortal sin, I will that you be content, first for the love of God, and then of me, and then for the good of your own honour, to give up this practice and attend to your wife, who is indeed honest and worthy, who devoutly loves you and holds you dear" (Act III, sc. 6). Thus the friar speaks to the sincerely repentant man, and in the meantime, in his thought, foretastes the fresh and frequent joys which the love of Caterina will continue to procure for him.

From the last decades of the fifteenth century, certain burlesque *frottole,* half narrative, half dramatic, had been in vogue. They were called *mariazi* (matrimony), and gave theatrical development to a dispute between two rival lovers or a quarrel between husband and wife or to other themes of popular poetry. They were recited by mountebanks in open squares; and the characters they impersonated were mostly country people speaking their own dialects, i.e., rustic Paduan or *Pavano.* A great deal of the theatrical work of the Paduan Angelo Beolco Ruzzante (1502–1542) comes from these farces of the people. His comedies, especially *Fiorina,* the most beautiful, give a successful picture of country life, full of freshness, vivacity, and good humour.

In Tuscany, where the *sacre rappresentazioni* were usually preceded by *frottole* of comic or moralizing dialogues and mixed with burlesque scenes of beggars, peasants, and inn-keepers, these prologues and intermezzos, like the popular monologues and farces, acquired independent life and art, characterized by liberty of time and place, and variety in events and personages. Country clowns were put upon the stage also in Tuscany; and Berni, for instance, composed *Catrina,* pleasantly ridiculing the customs and speech of the peasants round Florence.

Though given in Florence and elsewhere in Tuscany, the real seat of the *farsa rusticale* was Sienna, where already, in the second decade of the sixteenth century, a few tradesmen, gathered together in a merry assemblage, wrote these humble compositions and recited them before the people.

The most celebrated of these merry companions was Niccolo Campani, called Strascino from the protagonist of his first farce, entitled *La Strascino* (1511). The subjects of their *farse, egloghe,* or *commedie rusticali,* are simple and vulgar: disputes between peasants and their master about the harvest; their loves, jealousies, quarrels, and festivals; and the language is mostly that of the Siennese populace.[5]

The farces of Pietro Antonio Caracciolo, the so-called *farse cava-iole,* were most popular in Naples. Three of the farces of Caracciolo were but monologues recited by the author himself at the Neapolitan court; now in the garb of a "Merchant who sells two slaves, one male and one female"; now "under the guise of Ciraldo"; now "in the person of a *turcomanno*" (Turk). But his other farces extended their action to more personages, representing scenes and episodes of real daily life or dramatizing some novelistic subjects.

Here is the farce "wherein is introduced *La Cita, lo Cito* (a bride, a bridegroom), an Old Woman, a Notary, the Priest with the Yacono (Deacon) and a Third"; here is another farce in which there take part "A Sick Man, three Physicians, a Lad, and a *Magara affattocchiara* (witch)"; and that of another "Sick Man with his Mother and two servants, where there intervened a Physician and a Practitioner"; and the "Dialogue of two Beggars"; and the colloquy or dispute of "A Peasant, two Cabbage-venders, and a Spaniard"; and the farce of "a Physician, a Peasant, and the Wife of the Peasant"; and finally that one "of four peasants who match their wives with others" (or, "who yield their wives to others").

These titles reveal whence Caracciolo drew his inspiration: simple pictures of contemporary society; no old misers and astute servants and dissipated youths and venal courtesans and insatiable parasites, but peasants of the Campania, citizens of Cava, doctors, notaries, priests, witches, beggars: the populace which was around him, and whose passions, weaknesses, prejudices, and customs he observed and reproduced on the stage. The farce *della Cita e dello Cito* (of the Bride and Bridegroom) first brings before us a dialogue between *la Cita,* the Bride, and the old donna Mattalena, in which the former expresses her desire to marry Vito de Baptista, and the latter promises to use her good offices; then, another dialogue between donna Mattalena and *lo Cito,* who is persuaded to marry the girl; then the nuptial contract drawn up by the notary Fiorillo; and finally the celebration of the marriage performed by the Prevete with the aid of the Yacono. Two clauses of the marriage contract determine the reciprocal duties of husband and wife. In the first clause the bride

> binds herself for life to fail
> never in being caressing with the Bridegroom
> if he himself has appetite to take her
> by night and embrace her, and if instead
> she should do the contrary, that he be allowed
> to break all of her bones and drive her out,
> and then to take unto himself as wife
> whomever it might please him.

And in the second, the bridegroom

> promises and swears from now henceforward
> that if she should some lover wish to take,
> he will not grieve at this, and should it happen
> that he should ever find a lover in her bed,
> he promises no worse affront to offer
> than to go out himself and stay outside

for four or five hours and not to return
unless she send to call him; but by compact
requires that the thing his wife has done
she be obliged to make known unto him.

An adverse destiny seems to lie upon the popular theatre of that age, since, of the numerous and very popular *farse cavaiole* composed in the *cinquecento,* the only one surviving is *La Ricevuta dell' Imperatore alla Cava* (The Reception of the Emperor at Cava). This is based upon a real event, the visit which Charles V, returning from the Tunis expedition, paid to his possessions of Sicily and Naples. The emperor arrives, but, amid the general confusion and stupefaction, passes on without stopping. "Oh, cursed be the day I was born!" cries the Sindaco; to think that "at Salerno he has been four nights" and "to us he has offered this affront!" Certainly the fault is that of the prince Salerno himself, who must have "suborned" the emperor and told him to pass "straight through thus in haste."[6]

The fundamental character of Braca's farces is subjectivity, in which they differ alike from the compositions of Caracciolo and from the *Ricevuta dell' Imperatore alla Cava,* which, as we have mentioned, contains the burlesque representation of an historical fact. Those of Caracciolo sketch *genre* pictures and reflect satirically the reality of life; but Braca's express the state of mind of the author who attacks the race or "sect" of Cava, and imagines fantastic episodes in which he plays a large part.

Giovan Giorgio (Gangiorgio) Alione, a nobleman of Asti, wrote in his native dialect comic jests in imitation of the French farces.[7] These farces of Alione's are not representations of ordinary life. They are derived from those jovial and cunning and salacious and jesting imaginings delighted in by the novelists of every age, who, while satirizing real human types and passions, constructed improbable tales.

TERZO INTERMEDIO DOVE SI VIDE VENIRE AMORE CON TVTTA LA SVA CORTE A DIVIDER LA BATTAGLIA.

SECONDO INTERMEDIO DOVE SI VIDE ARMARSI L'INFERNO PER FAR VENDETTA DI CIRCE CONTRO TIRRENO

Spectacles

In 1531, a few Siennese tradesmen founded the *Rozzi* with the aim of supplying themselves with honest amusement. In the theatrical compositions of the *Rozzi,* called *egloghe* or *commedie pastorali* or *egloghe maggiaiuole,* nymphs, shepherds, and mythological divinities appear, so that sentimental scenes of love, transformations, and miracles take place; and this ideal world is contrasted with jesting caricatures of real life. Although without artistic merit, they had a long life, thanks to the company, which, in spite of being several times disbanded by the government, was always able to rise again, and, when transformed into a true academy, maintained its tradition for rustic drama even in the seventeenth century.

The chief aim of the Siennese theatre of the *cinquecento* is the satire of the clownish country folk. Malicious, fraudulent, covetous, of sluggish sensuality, grotesque jealousy, and rough, often obscene language, bold in words and pusillanimous in act, these peasants, such as the *Rozzi* delighted to represent them, are, for the most part, limited to ridiculous and vulgar love-affairs with married women and young girls, to scenes of jealousy between rivals, to interchange of insults and threats, to quarrels, fights, and drubbings.

While the Astian farces of Alione and his unknown contemporaries seem never to emerge from their place of origin, the popular comedies of the *Rozzi* of Sienna passed beyond their local confines, and were even performed before Pope Leo X at Rome.

The pastoral comedies of the *Rozzi* are imitated in the four eclogues of Andrea Calmo, an eccentric Venetian (1510–71). But while the Siennese use only their own dialect, Calmo uses not only Venetian but the dialects of Padua, Bergamo, Dalmatia, and the hybrid speech of the Stradioti (Greek mercenaries), a mixture of Venetian and Neo-Greek. This use of different dialects and even foreign languages in a single theatrical composition became more frequent; and Calmo in adopting it also increased the variety of

tongues. This he did both in eclogues and comedies, which he too
sometimes composed on the lines of learned models and more often
by amplifying popular farce. He is wanting, however, in that
knowledge of the human heart and skill in creating living personages that belong to Ruzzante. It is probable that Calmo improvised some parts of his comedy and wrote them down only after
the first performance. The improvisation and fixed types that
Calmo probably borrowed from plebeian farce finally became essential characteristics of a special kind of dramatization which was
destined to depose regular written comedy. Angelo Beolco (Il Ruzzante), Andrea Calmo, and Gigio Artemio Giancarli form the connecting link between the learned and the popular theatre, and facilitate the natural passage from the literary comedy of classic type to
the *commedia dell' arte*.

All these little popular dramas, though especially designed to
amuse the uncultured, also delighted princes, prelates, cavaliers,
and ladies. In Veneto and Tuscany, not a few of them were composed by writers who were not of the people. They compare favor-
ably in their free and capricious movements and their broad au-
dacities, with the regular structure of the erudite comedies.

The outstanding characteristic of most of these farces is that each
was a dialogue and altercation, between two or more personages.
One impersonator usually took all the parts; but sometimes these
were distributed among several street-corner actors. Varchi in the
Suocera recalls to the old Simon "those *filastrocche* (idle tales)
which twenty or twenty-five years ago blind Nanni and messer
Battista dell' Ottonajo told; which lasted an hour every time one
met them on the street, without concluding anything, and the
people stood around open-mouthed to listen; and many times some
good person thrust himself in between them to make peace before
the thing should go before the *Otto*, thinking that they were in real
earnest."

Pastoral Drama

Pastoral Drama

Like the *Commedie* of the *Burattini,* the farces generally ended in beatings and scuffles, which took the place of "morality." But after the example of the *rappresentazioni,* the farces also sought to rise to greater dignity; becoming a mixture of which it was said, in the Prologue of the *Ingratitudine:*

> It is not Comedy, Farce or Feast,
> But a certain manner of reciting
> More Natural.

NOTES

CHAPTER VIII

1. To the first act composed of the dialogue between Mopso, Aristeo, and afterwards Tirsi, the writer who rehandled the *favola d'Orfeo* added nothing. The second act begins with the second amorous song of Aristeo, which is also in the *favola* (fable); but, in place of Orpheus, the Dryads are substituted. In the third act, Orpheus learns of the death of Eurydice. The exploits of Hercules are recited by a Dryad instead of by a shepherd, but in the same words as in the fable; and Orpheus announces his purpose "to go to the Tartarean gates, and prove if mercy there may penetrate." Act IV is the same as in the *favola* except for a few fresh touches in the form. In spite of Cerberus and the Furies, Orpheus penetrates into Tartarus, and conjures Pluto to restore Eurydice to him. Pluto consents on the condition that Orpheus, in reascending from Tartarus, shall not turn to look at Eurydice "until she be returned among the living." But while the poet proceeds joyously towards the exit from Tartarus, singing verses of Ovid, he turns round to look on the beloved face of Eurydice; and, as a result, she is taken from him. In Act V, as in the *favola,* Orpheus laments, and swears that he will never love any woman again; and then the *Mænades* slay him. The spectacle ends with the singing of the famous Bacchic dithyrambus. (Condensed from Bertana's *La Tragedia.*)

2. The following is a collective letter from the company of *Uniti* to the Prince dated April 3, 1584, from Ferrara:

"We, *Comici Uniti,* most humble servants of your Serene Highness, having afresh joined the Company of Pedrolino, as it formerly was, and even bettered by personages famous in the comic art, and desiring to come to recite at Mantua with the good favour of your Serene Highness, humbly pray and entreat you to concede us license so that we may come, which we shall be immediately

176

most ready to do. We should have come confiding in the goodness of your Serene Highness, but signor Filippo Angelonni, the musician, does all in his power to prevent our coming. We have first wished to make it known to your Serene Highness, so that you may deign to treat of it with the Most Serene Highness of the Lord Duke, your Father, and arrange so that we may freely come to serve you."

In 1585, the *Uniti* again returned to Mantua, as this patent of the Commissioner Carlo Luzzara dated May 4, 1585, attests:

"In virtue of the present we concede to the *Comici Uniti* permission to recite in this city, beginning from to-day for all that time that they shall stay here: and, as assurance of this, we have conceded the present license, subscribed by the hand of our notary and sealed with our great seal."

In Rome in 1586, the *Amore Costante* by Alessandro Piccolomini was performed "in the presence of the Pope's Sister of Montalto, and of the Cardinals Alessandrino and Dezza and the Spanish Ambassador, besides the great concourse of other leading signori" (gentlemen and ladies). And two years later after a great dispute, license was conceded to the *Desiosi* to act comedies by day, but without women and "without the audience being allowed to carry any kind of arms, and that they should have license that noise be not made beneath the same scenes." *Senza donne* would seem to mean without actresses, their places being taken by boys as was the custom in Rome.

Returning to the Duke of Mantua, we find that in April he summoned a company which was performing in Milan, probably the company of the *Gelosi*, which, after the death of San Carlo Borromeo in 1584, recited in Milan until forbidden by Federigo Borromeo in 1596. The Duke, however, continued to protect the actors of 1591, relative to a visit of the *Uniti* to Verona.

In 1594, the most noteworthy spectacle of northern Italy was that given by the City of Milan, by means of the Company of the *Uniti*, to the conte di Haro, son of the signor Contestabile di Castiglia,

Juan Fernandez de Velasco, governor of Lombardy, a spectacle of which we have a minute account transmitted by the ducal ambassador at Milan, Lodovico Falletti, to the ducal counsellor Tullio Petrozani.

The other Martinelli, Tristano, was with the company of the *Diana,* or of the *Desiosi,* after having abandoned that of Pedrolino. He returned to France in 1613, after long negotiations, in which he addressed himself *alla Regina mia comare,* and Marie replied, *ad Arlecchino mio compare.* In July of 1614, Arlecchino with *Lelio* (G. B. Andreini) and Florinda (Virginia Andreini) and the *Capitano Rinoceronte* (Girolamo Garavini) and the entire company again crossed the Alps; nor did they return to France before 1620. Tristano died in 1630 at about the age of 75.

At this time appears Pier Maria Cecchini, known as *Fritellino,* a native of Ferrara, who acted with applause under this mask the parts of the second *zanni.* He died towards 1645.

Another actor who now first appears is Silvio Fiorillo, a Neapolitan, an ornament of the companies of the *Accesi,* of the *Affezionati,* of the *Risoluti,* inventor of the part of *Capitan Mattamoros,* father of *Scaramuccia,* and author of several comedies, drawn for the most part from Ariosto, and of the *ridicolose disfide e prodezze di Pulcinella.*

3. One of the first allegorical representations recorded is that given at Naples. At Milan in the last two decades of the century, among the many fêtes which enlivened the Sforzescan court, two allegorical representations by Bernardo Bellincioni have historic interest. The first was entitled *Il Paradiso* and was presented in Milan, January 13, 1490, in the presence of Lodovico *"il Moro,"* many princes and nobles, and "all the Orators, Councilors, Magistrates, and Gentlemen."

The second allegorical representation, which was without any special title, was recited at Pavia in 1493 for the *famosissimo dottorato del reverendo Monsignore della Torre* (the most famous doctorate of the reverend Monsignor della Torre), Lodovico and Gian

Galeazzo Sforza being also "with their consorts and the most illustrious Duke of Ferrara." On this occasion there was seen "constructed with great skill and art by maestro Lionardo Vinci, Florentine, the Paradiso with all the seven planets which gyrated, and the planets were represented by men in the form and habit as they were described by the poets."

At *Reggio Emilia,* for the entrance of Borso d'Este, July 4, 1453, there were several performances of representation conceived by Malatesta Ariosti, who also wrote the text; angels and saints and virtues personified and personages of ancient history paid homage to the Estense duke.

4. It should be noted that, at this very moment of the ultimate frustration of the comic stage, there existed this germ of a national drama, the *Farsa.* Cecchi, the most prolific, original, and popular of Florentine playwrights, thus describes it:

"The *Farsa* is a new third species between tragedy and comedy. It enjoys the liberties of both, and shuns their limitations; for it receives into its ample boundaries great lords and princes, which comedy does not, and, like a hospital or inn, welcomes the vilest and most plebeian of the people, to whom Dame Tragedy has never stooped.

"It is not restricted to certain motives; for it accepts all subjects— grave and gay, profane and sacred, urbane and rude, sad and pleasant. It does not care for time or place. The scene may be laid in a church, or a public square, or where you will; and if one day is not long enough, two or three may be employed. What, indeed, does it matter to the *Farsa?* In a word, this modern mistress of the stage is the most amusing, the most convenient, the sweetest, prettiest country-lass that can be found upon our earth." (Prologue to the *Romanesca,* Firenze, Cenniniana, 1874.)

The *Farsa,* in the form it had assumed when Cecchi used it, was, in fact, the survival of an ancient, obscure species of dramatic art which had descended from the period of classical antiquity.

5. Similar characteristics are found in the *Strascino,* the *Magrino,* and the *Coltellino* of Nicolo Campani. Berna, Tafano, Togna, and Lenzo, the four characters of the *Coltellino,* are peasants. The first, vainly enamoured of Togna, thinks to imitate the example of a shepherd who slew himself for love of a nymph. The desire for death contends with the fear of it; and the ridiculous man now sharpens his knife, now blunts it so that it may not penetrate farther than be necessary. Then he decides that he will use force to gain his sweetheart. He seizes Togna by the throat, but alas! He only receives a beating from the girl's brothers who rush up on hearing her cries. Thus knocked about, his only desire is for vengeance against the false friend who gave him such dangerous advice; but pacified by Lenzo and by Togna, the friends sing in full accord "a fine song."

6. In this farce we have not only a noteworthy document of what the *cavaiolo* theatre of the middle of the sixteenth century was, but also a proof of the enmity existing between the two neighbouring cities of Salerno and Cava—an enmity that inspired, at the end of the same century and the beginning of the next, the greater part of the works of the Salernian Vincenzo Braca (1566–1625), who dedicated his talent to furiously deriding the Cavesi.

In the fantastic two *Saltimbanci* (quacks), the figure of the charlatan is satirically represented. Another physician, Vernaudo, tells the great man what has befallen the young Arcella: she is pregnant, and cannot now bring her "creature" into the world; what is to be done? Ramundo expounds a complicated and grotesque prescription; but Patrasso and Gorgillo think "that, as one nail drives another, so another man who gets her with child will be able to bring about the evacuation of the first." In both the *Saltimbanci* there is a life-like picture of glorious impudence of the charlatans who exalt their own learning and magnify the virtue of their specifics.

7. Alione's work is closely related to the popular French theatre, which inspires both its contents and its form. The *Farsa de Zoan Zavaline* and the *Farsa de Nicolao Spranga* are the best. In the former is represented the sinful love of a woman and a priest and the exemplary punishment which the injured husband inflicts upon the unworthy minister of God. Beatrice cunningly succeeds in exchanging words with the priest on the public road, and cleverly gets Zoan away from the house into which the desired *messere* is immediately introduced. In the conversation, the lovers, seated at table, taste in anticipation greater delights; but the husband unexpectedly returns, and soundly beats the unfortunate priest. The situation is comical, and the figure of the pusillanimous priest is portrayed with truth.

CHAPTER IX

THE ITALIAN RENAISSANCE
(AN INTERCHAPTER)

Necessity of understanding the Renaissance in order to know the Italian theatre of the fifteenth and sixteenth centuries: Political and ecclesiastical conditions of the age: The rise of Humanism: Lorenzo il Magnifico and Poliziano, poets: Philosophical doctrines: The skepticism of Pomponazzi: Bruno : Moral corruption during the Renaissance: Summary of the period:

IN religion, science, philosophy, humane letters, and the fine arts, that period in the world's history known as the Italian Renaissance is important. Whether as modernists we would trace the current of present-day problems to their source, seeking the dawn of the modern era, or as classicists, are fascinated with Greek and Roman culture, to every thoughtful man the Italian Renaissance looms large.

How contradictory, individualistic, debatable, and perplexing, that Renaissance! How many writers have essayed the subject and will continue to do so; yet no book will ever be so impartial, informed, and adequate in its treatment of the subject as to be final.

Why then, in a short "Interchapter" in a history of the Italian Theatre, even try to fill a small corner in so vast a canvas? For the very good reason that it is impossible to understand the Italian Theatre of the fifteenth and sixteenth centuries without having at least some slight knowledge of Italy at the time when those plays were being written and performed. Those plays were written by Renaissance men. The play and the age, each in its turn, is father and son of the other: each explains the other.

That Renaissance was more than the frame about the picture, more than the atmosphere and environment of the play. That age could have produced no other type of play and have been true to itself; and no other age could have written those plays. They are of the same blood and heart and soul and mind. Each is of the other significant, essential, interpreting.

In 1494, when the French King Charles VIII invaded Italy, the Republics of Venice and Florence, the Duchy of Milan, the Kingdom of Naples, and the Papacy, were federated and free from foreign dominion. In 1527, the Bourbon's sack of Rome ended the Augustan age of the papal city in a horror of fire and blood. After the signing of the treaty of Cambrai in 1529, soon to be followed by the meeting of Charles at Bologna with Pope Clement VII—from whom he received the imperial crown and the iron crown of Lombardy—of all these federated states, Venice alone, though mutilated, was free. Sforza held nominal rule in Milan; Naples was a Spanish province; and Charles in return for his crowns had promised that Florence should be converted into a Medicean duchy. But the Papacy had profited by these disasters.

Though the succeeding seventy years were almost free from the terrors of war, the physical condition of Italy was deplorable. Plagues and famine depopulated cities; depression of commerce, industry and agriculture, insane methods of taxation, poverty, profligacy, and brigandage resulted from Spanish oppression and papal indifference. The political, spiritual, economic, and social life of Italy was contaminated by those two cosmopolitan but non-national powers, the Papacy and Spain. The Roman Catholic Church selfishly aimed to keep the Italian nation disunited; and the Holy Roman Empire had a German as its Emperor, and was Germanizing in its purpose. Yet, as facts and ideas, they are both monuments of Italian creative genius.

Consider the marvel of it: in spite of the cankers of the Papacy and of foreign domination that were consuming the nation's vitals, in spite of the characteristic diversity of the Italian psyche, in the midst of an age of despots, from the Italian genius there was again born a clear ideal that should free the human spirit from shackles. To this rebirth we give the name of the Italian Renaissance.

Because it was an idea, a mental and spiritual condition and not an act, no exact date can be fixed for the birth or the death of the Renaissance. The seeds of the Renaissance are found in the Middle Ages; and vestiges of it remained for long after the Catholic Reaction.

Goths, Lombards, Franks, successively blended their several characteristics with the already complex Italic population. In spite of the difference in the type and the conditions of the many Communes, notwithstanding the opposition of feudalism and of the Church, after the hurricanes of a thousand years of disorder, discussion, and obscurantism, Italy became self-conscious, and found that common bond of intellectual and spiritual union which we call the Renaissance.

Vast, complex, is this Renaissance movement; operating in different ways, assuming varied forms. It is the Middle Ages in dissolution; the connecting bond between the age of feudalism and modern life. The Renaissance is vital. It emancipated personality. It was the discovery of man and the world in which he lived. It is positive, secular, exploratory, a period of transition, preparation, and endeavor.

The Renaissance was an attempt to return to the irrecoverable past, through the resurrection of classical literature and its imitation by the new Humanists, which is termed the Revival of Learning. But it means more than that. It was a forward movement, which puts it in relation with modern thought. Pomponazzi's doctrine that moral truth is immutable, that the universe is governed by unchanging laws, is the cornerstone of modern physical science. His teaching that virtue is its own reward: that men should do right because it is right, irrespective of reward or punishment in some distant world beyond the grave, was a new note in religion.

Humanism is a narrower term than Renaissance. It was a mode of thinking, an effort to shake off the pall of theological despotism, an intermediate stage between scholasticism and rationalism, partaking of both. The keyword of Humanism was culture, culture through an imperious personality. In practical life, this idea of imperious personality made self-indulgence lawful and logical, since it was but following the precedent of Greece and Rome.

The Humanists thought, wrote, felt, and acted like pagans. Real Christianity slumbered, but there was no new faith. As secretaries of popes and princes, as chancellors of republics, seated some times in the very chair of Peter, the Humanists leavened society with their doctrine, established a literary commonwealth, and set an example of self-indulgent living. To understand Humanism we must understand the Humanists.

Pietro Bembo is a typical Humanist: with frivolous though cultivated mind, he advises Sadoleto not to spoil his style by reading the Bible. His licentious elegies, odes, and idylls reflect the licentiousness of sixteenth-century Italian life. Fracastoro's verses on *Syphilis,* that terrible disease of the Renaissance age, could only have been written by a pagan of pagans. The Latin verses of Giovanni Pontano were the admiration of his contemporaries. With equal fluency, fancy, and sentiment, he describes homely and innocent domestic scenes and the loves of light women. Sannazzaro's elegies and meditations on love and the joys of country life illustrate the luxurious literature of Naples.

Besides the Latin, there was also a Humanistic literature in the Italian vernacular. It was narrative in form in the North, dramatic and lyric in Tuscany, and more descriptive in the South. Sometimes it was closely modeled on the Latin, sometimes imitated French idioms, and at other times followed the pure Tuscan of Dante and Boccaccio. Lorenzo il Magnifico found time to turn from affairs of state and the pomp of power, to the cultivation of poetry. His *Selve* are brilliant descriptions of the golden age and purely pagan; his *Canzoni* imitate Petrarch; and his *Simposio* contains many reminders of Dante's work. Angelo Poliziano shared with Lorenzo the glory of letters. He is the most truly Latin poet of his century; yet his compositions in Italian are the chief monuments of his fame. His *Fabula d'Orfeo*, in the form of the *sacra rappresentazione,* is a procession of lovely lyric scenes united by dialogues; and follows the classic story. His *Canzoni a Ballo* are exquisite imitations of the Tuscan *Ballata,* and his *Stanze per la giostra* is perhaps the first record of the new Italian Renaissance poetry.

Whether written in Latin or Italian, this Humanist literature is pagan. Its religion was beauty; learning and the Arts were sacred. Faith meant folly and superstition: the masks are varied and beautiful, but beneath them is neither moral earnestness nor spiritual passion. Hence no truly great tragedy was produced. Beccadelli's epigrams, Bembo's *Priapus,* might have been written by the frankest poets of the Roman Empire.

Many elements united in the skepticism of the Italian Renaissance, which found so rich a soil in the naturally skeptic Italian mind. The social immorality shows a profound moral skepticism. Purity of faith and impurity of life were contradictions. The reaction against dogmatic credulity, asceticism, and sacerdotalism; the intimate relation, through commerce and the Crusades, between the Arab world with its culture and philosophy, and the Italian Humanists, promoted skepticism.

Tiraboschi remarks on the enormous influence of Averroës on Italian thought. Averroeism found no place for Creation, miracles, or Revelation. It is a subtle pantheism, and represents idealistic negation. The secularization of literature, the introduction of pagan elements in Mystery Plays, Provençal poetry, which, while employing the language of the Church, blended heathen and

Christian tradition and the free-thinking of the Troubadours, all brought their skeptic influence into the receptive Humanistic world.

The Catholic Church, never truly friendly to republican institutions, since it is itself a despotism founded upon authority, would naturally cause a reaction towards free thought in the free Communes. The skepticism of the Italian universities, where science and philosophy had displaced theology, and reason frowned on faiths, and, above all, the enormous spread of Greek and Latin literature through the invention of printing and the revival of Hellenistic studies and the influence of Roman paganism, were the primary causes of Renaissance paganism.

Pomponazzi is the leading philosopher, if not the leading skeptic, of the Italian Renaissance. Born in Mantua in 1462, he died in 1525. He became a professor at the University of Bologna in 1512, after having previously taught at the universities of Padua and Ferrara. His great work, *De immortalitate animi,* raised a storm in the Catholic Church. It was publicly burned in Venice; and Pomponazzi ran a serious risk of following it in the flames. Insisting that the soul is the form of the body, and that, as form apart from matter is unthinkable, it must perish with the body, he nevertheless asserts that as a Christian he accepts the Church's teaching as to immortality, though as a philosopher he denies it. This doctrine of the "two fold truth"—that it is possible for the same thinker as a Christian to accept the intellectual and religious chains of the Church, and yet as a philosopher, absolutely to deny those teachings—is one of the most curious and interesting characteristics of Humanistic thought. The ethical consequences of Pomponazzi's denial of the immortality of the soul are important. If sin is not to be punished or virtue to be rewarded in a future existence, it follows that death must be despised, that the human conscience is the sole guide as to right and wrong, that virtue must be cultivated for its own sake, that the punishment of vice is in being vicious and the reward of virtue is in being virtuous.

It is noteworthy that Giordano Bruno, the freest thinker of the Renaissance, after entering the Dominican Order, became a priest in 1572; and also that, while in Geneva, Paris, and England, he became acquainted with Calvinism, Anglicanism, and Lutheranism. He was taken as prisoner of the Inquisition to Rome in 1593, and, after seven years of confinement and many tortures, was burned in 1600. We have already considered his comedy *Il Candelaio.* Doubt is with Bruno the starting point of all philosophy, and the preliminary to conviction. He doubted in order to know. Since "our opinions do not depend on ourselves," we should be tolerant of another's belief, and free our own intellect from bonds. From doubt and enquiry, Bruno passed on to a mystic religious faith. He adored the Infinite. He was himself, what is the true meaning of his great work *Eroici Furori,* a "God-intoxicated man." One of the foremost philosophers of his own age, Bruno's influence upon modern thought is greater than that of any other man of the Renaissance.

The immorality of the Italian Renaissance is a favorite subject with writers; many seem to consider it as the chief characteristic of that age. The Renaissance was a period of flagrant and open immorality, and Humanism fostered it. But in the immediately preceding Middle Ages, Italy was also corrupt; and the succeeding Catholic Reaction was not only corrupt, but also brutal and hypocritical.

It is, however, true that the immorality of the Renaissance was characterized by certain conditions of its own. The tendency of new-born freedom is always to excess. The corruption of the Roman Church was brazen; the political conditions of the country were heartrending. The admiration and imitation of the teaching and social life of pagan Rome made of licentiousness a special branch of humanistic literature. The boldest sensuality of the worst days of the Roman Empire became the commonplace of Renaissance society; and force, craft, materialism, and public and private murders were so common as scarcely to excite comment.

Venice was the favored resort of the debauchees of Europe. At Milan, at the court of Ludovico, called *"Il Moro,"* fathers sold their daughters and husbands their wives. In Italy, the clergy were the leading men of pleasure; and profligate convents were the favored resorts of soldiers and the dissolute. In the early sixteenth century, the moral and pecuniary corruption of Rome was beyond permissible description. There was no place in the city for a virtuous woman. In 1490, besides the private courtesans and immoral convents, Rome is reported to have held 6800 public prostitutes. "The Pope," writes J. A. Symonds, "is still a holy being. He rises from the bed of harlots, to unlock the gates of Heaven and Purgatory, and returns to his sty, as chief actor in the comedy of Priapus and Aphrodite. He impartially worshipped Mary and Venus." Innocent VIII publicly acknowledged his seven children, carried on with the aid of his son a campaign of theft and murder, and established a bank where every sin had its price. Popes like Alexander Sixtus harmonized pagan scholarship and sensuality with Christian piety. And the Humanists, not to be outrivaled by the Church, made of vice a fine art and of filthy speech a special branch of rhetoric.

Why, it may be asked, was not this corruption swept aside by that same rising tide of Protestantism which was covering Northern Europe? Because the roots of Protestantism did not strike deep in the infertile soil of the Italian character. Because Italy gloried that Rome was the metropolis of the Christian world, and regarded the Papacy as indispensable to her prosperity. And also, because the Humanists were so dazzled by the Renaissance brilliancy, and themselves so steeped in pagan sensuality, that moral distinctions were obliterated and few men were shocked by these anomalies. A few years of active persecution uprooted Protestantism from Italy. Its churches were suppressed; their pastors fled; and the congregations either emigrated or, except in a few of the mountain valleys of the North, conformed to the Roman Church. Within the Church, however, there were many spasmodic though transient emotional revivals. To vast congregations of weeping listeners, many preaching friars and hermits, with frenzied eloquence, denounced the immorality of monks and priests, of Popes and people. So intense and widespread were these waves of emotion, that both temporal and spiritual powers tried to suppress them through the giving of tournaments and public shows.

The reasons for the extinction of the Renaissance and for the seeming transitoriness of the impression that it made on Italy, are not obscure. Florence, divided between *Ottimati* and *Piagnoni;* Venice, defending herself against the leagued attack of Europe; Milan and Naples, trembling under the threat of foreign invasions, lost all heart for Humanism.

We have seen how in Northern Italy, Urbino, Ferrara, and Mantua continued for a time the Renaissance tradition, while Rome, which had thus far escaped the scourge of war, had become the centre of Humanism. But, in 1527, Rome was sacked and abandoned to the rage of 30,000 foreign ruffians; Clement was imprisoned in Castle St. Angelo; and the age of the Renaissance was closed. Its artificial and unsubstantial life had transformed the upper classes of society without permeating the masses. Evolution does not work backward, and there could be no such anachronism as the permanent revival, after the lapse of more than a thousand years, of the mentality and social life of pagan Rome.

With the coming of the Jesuits and of the Spanish Inquisition came that catastrophe and other anachronism, the Counter-Reformation. And the Counter-Reformation was indeed a catastrophe.

The revival of medieval Catholicism stifled the Italian conscience, promoted hypocrisy and ceremonial observance, assassinated humane letters, destroyed books, trampled upon the liberal arts, and extinguished true learning. Immorality remained; and never were crimes of violence, assassinations, private feuds, and treachery more common.

In this rapid survey of a large subject, we have tried to present the life and source and inspiration and the atmosphere of the Italian plays of the fifteenth and sixteenth centuries, the type of men by whom they were written, and the audience to whom they were presented.

The first stage was a passionate desire for the antique, the discovery and transcription of the lost masterpieces of Greek and Latin literature. Then came the period of acquisition and translation, the age of Cosimo de' Medici and his literary galaxy, and the passing of Humanism from Florence to Rome; the age of Poggio, the literary universalist; of Filelfo, the typical Humanist; and with Lorenzo Valla, Humanism triumphed over orthodoxy and tradition. Finally came the age of Lorenzo de' Medici, of Poliziano, of critics and scholarship, of printers, of Academies; which concluded with the purists, the decline of learning, and the flight of erudition beyond the Alps.

When thinking of this great age of the Italian Renaissance, let us also remember that in addition to its achievements in literature and philosophy, of new ideals of government and wider mental and spiritual horizons, freed from scholasticism and priestly domination, it was also the most important period in the whole history of painting, of sculpture, of architecture. For it was the real beginning of the modern era. It was the age of Raffaello, of Leonardo da Vinci, of Michelangelo, of Donatello, of Botticelli, of Ghirlandaio, of Titian, of Del Sarto, of Perugino, of Brunelleschi, of Bramante, of Sansovino, of Verrocchio, of Cellini and Ghiberti, and of all their glorious company. It was the *Secolo d'oro*. It was the age of Savonarola.

If you have been able to understand the life and thought of this great age, to feel the urge of its spirit and breathe its atmosphere, you will have grasped the significance of these fifteenth and sixteenth century Italian plays and felt the very pulse of the machine.

CHAPTER X

THE SEVENTEENTH CENTURY

Political situation of Italy at the beginning of the seventeenth century: The moral conditions: Corruption of the clergy: The intellectual revival in the seventeenth century: The patrons of the universities and academies: The founding of the libraries.

General characteristics of the tragedy in the seventeenth century Italian theatre: The sacred tragedies: Andreini's *Maddalena*: Tragedies of the Jesuit School: Scamacca's *Oreste*: Other followers of the classic tradition:

The *Crispo* of Savaro: His *Emiddo*, the *Celinda* of Miani: The use of Longobard history, Nolfi's *Romilda*: Mamiano's *Lucrezia*: The use of extra-Italian scenes: Cevoli's *Ormondo*: Delfino's *Cleopatra*: Bonarelli's *Solimano*: Graziani's *Cromuele*.

The meaning of the term *tragicomedy*, the shift from verse to prose: The translation of French tragedies: The pastoral drama and fable: The marine fable, the *Filli di Sciro* by Bonarelli: Andreini's *Florinda*.

Influence of the scenarios of the improvised comedy: Influence of Spanish dramatists: Buonarroti's *Fiera*: The use of *scherzi*, dialect, and satire: Immorality of the seventeenth century comic theatre: Defence of it by Cecchini.

SAD indeed was the condition of Italy at the beginning of the seventeenth century, despoiled of goods, deprived of honour, covered with wounds, tormented, oppressed; her farms uncultivated, her gardens deserted, her woods destroyed, plants uprooted, vines cut, land wasted, towns burnt, castles demolished, forests felled, cities sacked, the inhabitants slain, virgins ravished, widows dishonoured, churches violated, holy things contaminated, fire, sword, blood, and cruelty everywhere. Over the Neapolitan region, over Sicily, over Sardinia, over the Milanese province, over the State of the *Presidi,* in Tuscany, were extended, as Tasso said in the *Secchia rapita* (x, 10), the wings of "the eagle of the great king of the Ocean" (the Spaniard), whose rapacious eyes greedily regarded the rest of the peninsula, seeking further prey. The States of the Church were without arms and open to attack by the Kingdom of Naples. Tuscany was hemmed in by the Portercole, Talamone, Elba, Piombino, Orbetello, and threatened by the spear of

Sardinia; Genoa was more Spanish than Italian; the duchies of
Parma, Modena, and Urbino, were in the pay of the Spaniards;
Monferrato was exposed to the talons of Spain menacing from
Milan. Only the Republic of Venice remained free, but with the
Turk on the East and the Spaniards on the West threatening her
vitals. Thus has Tasso described his unhappy country in the first of
his *Filippiche* (Philippics).

Neapolitan "justice" was notoriously unjust to the native Italian.
The confusion of laws and the dishonesty of judges made the punishment of the innocent and the escape of the guilty almost the
common custom. Bad as were conditions in Naples, they were
worse, if possible to be worse, in the Pontifical state. A cardinal
thus writes in 1667: "The affairs of the state were ill regulated and
full of confusion. Bribery and influence were the sole passports by
which to obtain high office. Justice was administered only to those
able to pay. The minor ecclesiastics were pauperized by the greed
of the major."

France and Spain disputed between them as to which should
control the pontifical court. The Count don Pietro d'Aragona, viceroy of Naples, divided all the personages of the various nations
that made up the papal court, into accomplices of France and accomplices of Spain. Nepotism and greed reigned supreme. The
pontificate of Alexander VII was as ignominious as that of Alexander VI; it could not have been worse.

A contemporary writer speaks of the young gallants of that time:
fops, Adonises, Ganymedes, debauchees, cheats, slanderers, vain,
bestial, crazy; whose eyes knew only how to distinguish the means
for lasciviousness, gluttony, or cruelty; whose hands are surrounded by dice and have as function the fashions of the Aretine;
whose feet know not where to turn save to the theatres, to brothels,
or to churches, merely to transport into these latter all the former
abominations.

The fashionable youth has only such learning as suffices to cover dishonest and obscene meanings, so that feminine modesty may be the more readily corrupted. He always has a dozen impure notes in his pockets, for the women whom chance may suddenly offer him. He sleeps until midday; he lets his hair flow loosely over his shoulders; he is decked with slashes and ribbons and monograms and streamers, with rouge on his cheeks, pomatum on his hands, and roses even on his shoes.

To such frivolity and wantonness is added the desperate wickedness of many hundreds of bandits of whom the Spanish, grandducal, and pontifical governments often made secret use in their diplomatic contests. The bandits were received and sheltered in the monasteries; and the monks sometimes participated in their thefts.

The greed of governors and viceroys, the tyranny and corruption of nobles, were equalled by the avarice and immorality of the clergy, especially in Southern Italy. Many took holy orders in order to escape from the civil law and from taxes. In Calabria, the *Diaconi Selvaggi* (wild deacons) were numerous, lay clergy who could marry. The clerics and friars protected the bandits and shared their booty. In northern Italy the priests went armed and shared with robbers.[1]

Does this true picture of the political, economic, moral, and intellectual conditions of Italy in the seventeenth century justify the assertion that is made by most historians that the *seicento* was an age of absolute decadence? It does not. The evil was indeed widespread and deep, but it was not all-pervasive. The vanity of the great, the servility of the masses, is contrasted by not a few highminded philosophers; the defenders of prejudice and superstition were opposed by some men of true science; two currents meet and strive. The old world is falling into ruin, but the new arises radiant. Tradition attempts a final resistance; but the new philosophy rebels, seeks for truth, and strives to dissipate the darkness.

The political, religious, and intellectual order was profoundly changed. Having lost all liberty by the peace of Chateau-Cambresis, Italy was not wholly drawn into the Catholic reaction. In letters and arts also a strong and vital innovating spirit was revealed. The *seicento* gave a new kind of theatrical representation, wholly Italian—the melodrama; and the Italian *commedia dell' arte*, also, which had risen about the end of the *cinquecento,* was now firmly established. The revolt in Turin (1610) and in Naples and Palermo (1647) reveals the national sentiment and hatred of foreigners. The rebellion against political authority of the Church is shown in the writings of Fra Paolo Sarpi. Such were the developments of the Italian thought in the *seicento.*[2]

The abject servitude of the nobility was great; yet some Italian princes protected culture and the fine arts. Carlo Emanuele I, Chiamrera, Marino, Tassoni, Testi, received honors and rewards from grand dukes of Tuscany. Cosimo II and Ferdinando II favoured sciences and letters; Cosimo III was patron of scientists and scholars. So too the Estensi and Farnesi and Urban VIII and Alexander VII protected arts and letters. The grand dukes of Tuscany gave liberal stipends to the universities. In 1603, in the house of the Roman prince Federigo Cesi, was founded the famous academy of the *Lincei,* which applied itself to the natural sciences; and, in Florence in 1657, Leopoldo de' Medici founded the academy of the *Cimento,* for scientific investigation in the direction indicated by Galileo. The Academy of the *Crusca,* founded in 1582 at Florence, undertook the compilation of the vocabulary which was printed for the first time in 1612 and a second time in 1623.[3]

Thanks to the munificence of the grand dukes, the Medicean-Laurenzian library and the gallery of antiquities were enriched with new treasures brought from every part of Europe. During the seventeenth century, the Vatican library of Rome received notable additions. Paul V collected new Greek and Latin codices in two vast halls erected by him, and so founded the famous library of the Borghesi. Cardinal Francesco Barberini, nephew of Urban VIII, founded the famous Barberiana library; and Cardinal Ottoboni, nephew of Alexander VIII, was not less munificent. The Maruceliana library at Rome had its origin in the seventeenth century. As rival of the Vatican, there arose in Milan, in the first half of the *seicento,* the splendid Ambrosiana library. At Naples there were opened to the public in 1690 the Brancacciana, gathered together in Rome by the Cardinal Brancassio, and by his will transported to Naples after his death.

Notwithstanding Riccoboni's assertion that about 1620 the Italian tragic theatre had disappeared from the stage, and in spite of keen competition from musical and pastoral drama and improvised comedy, the tragic production of the seventeenth century was hardly inferior in quality and not less copious than that of the previous century, whose tradition is continued in essential spirit and attitude.

From the *Sofonisba* of Trissino to the *Orbecche* of Giraldi and the *Canace* of Speroni, the structure and methods of the early models were reproduced. The tragedy of this century generally respected the three unities and the division into five acts; it preserved to the chorus its office of confidante; it preferred the catastrophe, terrible with the slaughter of personages, either before the eyes of the audience or minutely narrated by "messengers," who often exhibited the head or limbs of the slain.

Sometimes the action developed with an extremely simple plot; more frequently the plot was intricate. The characters were conventional, without warmth or life or any strong personal traits. Caesar talks like Tancred, Mary Stuart like Lucrezia; the long philosophical speeches are as often declaimed, are inopportune and inadequate, and lack sentiment.

As in the *cinquecento,* incests, usurpations, and slaughters are favorite subjects; and, for the most part, the technique is unchanged. In the prelude, or in the first act, the ghost recites the events preceding the action; and nuncios, messengers, nurses, secretaries, and captains make wearisome discourses. In other tragedies, brothers ignorantly fall in love with their sisters, or fathers with their daughters; or some murder their parents, and men are believed to be women, or women believed men, and the resemblance between persons is so perfect as to facilitate substitution. Chance and error produce the most lamentable combinations. Unforeseen accidents, unexpected recognitions, thus constitute the most common elements of the Italian tragic theatre of the *seicento;* the genuinely simple tragedies are very few.

Whether subjects are ancient or modern, historic or legendary, romance and love usually participate; and when the subject is wholly imaginative, romance and love, derived often from the poems of Tasso and Ariosto, frequently predominate. The characters also are often borrowed from these poets. Chiabrera and Testi both borrowed from Ariosto and Tasso. It is appropriate therefore that the shade of Ariosto should recite the prologue in Testi's *Isle of Alcina,* which is derived from cantos VII, VIII, and X of the *Furioso.* Thus the greater number of these Italian tragedians combined amorous sighs and mortal misfortunes without which a good tragedy could not be constructed. The exclamation of the Nurse of Semiramide in Gessi's tragedy *Nino il figlio* (Nino the son), "Amid the loves and deaths, may heaven aid me!" (Act III, sc. 4) applies to the great ocean of *seicento* tragedy.

The sacred tragedies are distant types of those *sacre rappresentazioni* which flourished in the fifteenth century. Having lost its primitive simplicity, the sacred drama was modeled upon the classical tragedy, and assumed its solemn, artificial manner. Its original, ingenuous, and popular form, which ill accorded with the more refined manners of the cultured city classes, now took refuge among the common people. In the country districts, altered it is true by inopportune additions and unhappy adaptations, it has survived even in this twentieth century. In the sacred drama of the seventeenth century, the legendary themes were treated according to the classical rules, though the characters, the arrangement, the style, all were influenced by the melodrama and the pastoral fable.[4]

Of the many scenic works of the seventeenth century that have the same subject as the *sacre rappresentazioni* of the *quattrocento* and early *cinquecento,* the *Adamo* (Milan, 1613) and the *Maddalena* (Mantua, 1617) of Giambattista Andreini should be mentioned.

The protagonists of the *Maddalena* are Magdalene, Martha, and Lazarus; there also participate the archangel Michael, many angels, Divine Grace, three lovers of Magdalene, Samson, David, Angelo, Baruc his page, Mordecai his butler, Emanuel his cook, Arone and Lione his dwarfs, besides servants, ladies-in-waiting, and finally three old women who walk bent, leaning on sticks. The first three acts of the *Maddalena* relate the shameful life of the sinner, the festivities and merrymakings held in her house. The fourth and fifth acts represent her conversion and her entry into heaven. As in the melodramas, the serious approaches strangely to the comic, the grotesque, and the licentious; scenic show and music play a great part.

The musical element enters also into the *Adamo.* The action is grandiose. With the Biblical story which forms the groundwork of the picture are interwoven many extravagances and that spectacular display which so greatly pleased the public. That some suggestions for his *Paradise Lost* came to John Milton from Andreini's *Adamo* is not impossible.

Sacred dramas had not been lacking even earlier, but in the *seicento* there was a great vogue for those that have as their subject lives or legends of saints or martyrs, and these were even decked out as romances.

Of many tragedies of the Jesuit school of this period, there remain to us only the "arguments" or the general outlines which were printed for the convenience of the spectators; as, for example, *L'argomento della tragedia intitolata Baltasar* (The argument of the tragedy entitled Baltasar) composed by a "Father of the Company, in the college of Brera in Milan" and there represented on July 6, 1604; or such as the *Breve instuttione di tutto quello che si contiene nella tragedicomedia intitolata Faustiniano da rappresentarsi nel Collegio di Brera* (Brief account of all that is contained in the tragicomedy entitled Faustiniano to be performed in the college of Brera), in July, 1610. There are many similar compositions of which only the *canovacci* (outlines) or *scenarii* remain to us, as though they were *commedie dell' arte.*

The subject of the *Faustiniano* is taken from St. Clement, and is simple. It consists in the conversion to Christianity of Faustiniano who, while vainly trusting in Fortune, journeys over half the world to find his wife and children, and by the aid of Providence finally recovers them.

The principal characteristic of the pseudo-classic tragedy of the *seicento* is the increasing prominence of the love-element and suppression of the chorus. This suppression of the chorus is the most important innovation in the seventeenth century pseudo-classic tragedy.

The Jesuits tried to satisfy the public taste by introducing shepherds, lovers, and warrior women into their tragedies, as appears in the *argomento* of the *Odoardo,* performed at Parma in the carnival of 1648.

Was the public bored by lugubrious tragedy and did it prefer laughter to tears? The Jesuits' theatre tried to satisfy this requirement also. Thus the *Oracolo di Navarra, opera tragicomica* (the oracle of Navarra, tragicomic opera) was performed in the Collegio Clementino of Rome during the carnival of 1692. Already tragedy—even the Jesuitical—to be tolerated, must be reduced, if possible, to a love-comedy.

Sacred subjects were naturally more frequently treated. But, sacred or not sacred, the more notable productions of the Italian Jesuitical theatre point rather to a reaction against the artistic licenses to which the century had abandoned itself, continuing, as far as possible, faithful to the rules of the classic or pseudo-classic poetry. Such was the thought of a fertile Jesuit who conserved even in the eighteenth century the reputation of a "great tragic poet," the Sicilian Padre Ortensio Scamacca; and such was the opinion of another Jesuit, Padre Sforza Pallavicino, not so famous for his simple tragedy the *Ermenegildo* as for his other works.

The *Oracolo di Navarra* is full of love. But how could love-affairs be brought into the Jesuit tragedies if the rules of the order prohibited women from appearing on the stage? Padre Stafonio, in his famous *Crispus,* although he had an amorous subject in his hands, caused the shade of Fedra to appear in the prologue, but excluded women from the tragedy. Padre Pallavicino, on the other hand, got himself out of the difficulty by introducing into his tragedy a woman dressed as a man; "because the domestic laws of his religion forbade him to introduce on the stage any woman in female dress." Scamacca was less scrupulous, for in several of his forty tragedies he made use of women as protagonists, for example, in the *Eufrasia,* a sacred tragedy which reproduces the episode of the Ariostian Isabella, and so also in a dozen other sacred or moral tragedies, either original or derived from widely differing subjects. Like other Jesuits, Scamacca frequently resorted to the devil and angels, even in those places where the classical inspiration should have excluded supernatural appearances. He did so in the *Cristiano.*[5]

All Jesuitical tragedy has as its aim and as its characteristic to use the play for the moral and spiritual benefit of the people. Scamacca's *Oreste* is a good example of this art. The scene is laid in Argo before the royal palace where Orestes has already avenged Agamemnon by slaying Clytemnestra his mother and also Egisto. The action begins just when Orestes is enjoying a short respite in sleep from his horrible torment by the Furies. After long wanderings by land and sea, Menelaus has returned to Argo; and thus uncle and nephew meet and embrace each other. Menelaus promises his nephew assistance. Old Tindaro (Tindarus) coming in is amazed: how can Menelaus tolerate that the matricide should remain unpunished in violation of every law? Enter Orestes, who boasts of his deed. Her punishment was necessary, not only to appease the shade of Agamemnon and the wrath of Apollo, but also to set a curb upon the criminal audacity of the feminine sex. Electra and Orestes are condemned to death. The fourth act relates how Pilades and Orestes attack the house of Menelaus, slay Helen, and take possession of Ermione, daughter of Helen and Menelaus, and drag her as a hostage to the house of Orestes. Menelaus, in consternation at the killing of Helen, rushes to liberate Ermione, followed by a band of "ministers" whom he orders to force the door of the palace in which Orestes has fortified himself. Orestes shows himself with Ermione, whom he threatens to slay before her father's eyes if Menelaus does not desist from the siege and promise to persuade the Senate and people to cancel the sentence of death. Menelaus makes the promise. And now, behold, the earth quakes, opens; first Pluto appears, then Helen, foul semblance of a woman; as, says Pluto, the evil female had always been a monster within. Then Pluto summons Electra and Orestes; reproves them for their misdeeds; restores Ermione to Menelaus; and counsels him and also Pilades.

Thus Scamacca's tragedy offers teaching to all. Wives who imitate Clytemnestra and Helen shall end their days badly and roast in the inferno; children must respect their parents; husbands must

Fable

not be fools like Tindarus; youths must be more prudent than Pilades, etc. Let all, then, learn to follow the precepts of "our holy religion." But while he thus sought to Christianize the pagan play, he also tried classically to regularize the Christian theatre. Scamacca applies to sacred subjects those precepts of the Aristotelian poetics of which he was an intense admirer and imitator, as is shown in the prologue to *San Giovanni Decollato*. In this prologue, he alludes to the corrupt taste of the time, which tolerated the hybrid forms of the tragedy, etc.

Fidelity to the pseudo-classic type is met with also in sacred tragedies of the *seicento,* composed by non-Jesuit authors, as in the *Giustina reina di Padova* (Justine, Queen of Padua) of the Paduan Cortese Cortesi; in the *Assalonne* by Giovanni Ramelli of Castel del Piano, which appeared in the same year (1607); and in the *Gerusalemme cattiva* (wicked Jerusalem) by Bernardino Campelli, (1623).[6]

While the spiritual drama was drawing its material from the *sacre rappresentazioni* of the preceding centuries, the profane tragedy was more independent in its choice of subjects. Mythological fables, Greek and Roman history, knightly legends, all supplied arguments almost unknown to *cinquecento* tragedy.

There were two principal types of tragedy: the *implesse,* or *inviluppate,* in which the plot was most complicated,[7] and *piano e sémplicissime* which was without disguise or entanglements.[8]

In *Crispo,* written by Giovanni Francesco Savarro (1662), there is a psychoanalysis quite unusual in contemporary tragedy. Duty and passion contend in the soul of Fausta, wife of Constantino, who passionately loves her stepson Crispo but struggles against the temptation. Crispo enters her apartment at a psychological moment. She tells him that she is profoundly unhappy, and he promises to console her, if she will confide in him. The horrified youth, besides being the good son of Constantino, is also the faithful lover of Berenice. Fausta dies; and Crispo, having been accused by his stepmother of attempted incest, is killed by Constantino.

An even more pathetic tragedy is the *Emiddio* (1666). Savarro, to render the *Emiddio* "grazioso," that is, grateful to the public taste, continued a most complicated love-intrigue. Polisia, daughter of Polinnio, is loved at the same time by two Ascolanian cavaliers, Teodoro and Costante, both equally valiant, ardent, jealous, and unfortunate. Polisia loves a woman disguised as a man, a noble Roman maiden named Flavia who—she too enamoured—goes through the world seeking Emiddio, the saint; and when she finally finds him she too is, by the venerable aspect of her beloved, purified and sanctified.

The Signora Miani is perhaps the first woman of Italy to compose a tragedy. As an exhibit of contemporary taste her *Celinda* (1611) is interesting. The oracle had predicted that Fulco, king of Persia, would find his son Autilio in Lydia, where he is bound by the sweet chains of love to the beautiful princess Celinda. In order to live near her, Autilio calls himself Lucinia and, disguised as a woman, causes himself to be sold as an "Irish slave" to Cubo, father of Celinda. The pretended Irish slave quickly becomes the favorite handmaiden of the princess, who—but let Celinda speak for herself:

Love, which conspired to my hurt, sought that I should also be minister of my shame; where feigned Lucinia on soft cushions lay languishing; having stripped myself of my rich dress, by her I laid me down, and now her white face, now her neck, kissing and caressing, I made a chain round her with my arms; and she, perceiving the near danger drew back within herself. . . . But so much did and said I in the end, that my right hand I put forth underneath her fair bosom and then became aware that it was not like mine, with breasts adorned!

Celinda yields to Autilio, who becomes "of her first fruits the happy reaper." Thus, in the moment in which the action opens, Celinda has already been four months enceinte.

Cubo also loves . . . Lucinia!! Autilio, as Lucinia, begs a favor of the king. He (supposed Lucinia) in order to merit the position of queen, desires to fight against the Persians. If, in fighting, she is able to save the kingdom, she will be worthy of the throne. Thus Lucinia (Autilio) and, with her, Cubo set out for the camp. The Lydians are defeated; a messenger of king Fulco brings "as a gift" to Celinda the hands, heart, and head of Cubo; Lucinia is wounded and dies; Celinda, who by no means could outlive her dear Autilio, dies also. Along with the mournful the signora Miani makes the tragedy pathetic and tender; but the tenderness consists only in the eroticism which begins to appear in the tragedies of the end of the *cinquecento,* and which, in some of the *seicento* tragedies, is excessive.

From the time of Rucellai, Longobard history has been used by Italian tragedians and was drawn upon by many *seicento* writers. Vincenzo Nolfi, author of a melodrama (*Belerofonte*) and of a poem on the *Santa Casa di Loreto* (Holy House of Loreto), also wrote the tragedy, *Romilda* (1643), which has its scene at the court of Gilolfo, duke of Friuli, who has left Romilda a widow. Romilda boldly carries on the war against the Bavarians and their hated king Carcanno, slayer of her dear Gilolfo. One fine day, the faithful widow of the Longobard duke,

> By reason of an all unknown desire,
> Upon the royal tower mounts, and thence,
> With palpitating heart, with dewy eyes,
> While she the squadrons there encamped beholds,

discovers, emerging from "rich superb pavilion," a "proud and noble warrior" who, "by the signs," she knows to be Carcanno.

Instantly from the hater she becomes his lover: "Marvel of love, which in a flash, changes the poison of hate to vital humor!" (Act I, sc. 1.) Enamoured Romilda ignores Agilmondo, a generous Longobard prince who has come to her defence. Romilda opens the gates to Carcanno, with rejoicing receives him, and their nuptials follow. But Carcanno, on leaving the nuptial bed, says to his soldiers, "Go to Romilda, and with her vile limbs do as you will. . . . No wife of mine is she: As with some impure woman, I lay with her. . . . And let her children be pierced through and through." When Romilda and her children are dead, Carcanno discovers that she was his sister! Distraught with horror at his double sin of incest and murder he attempts suicide; but is prevented by the affection of his subjects.

In these tragedies, historic accuracy is changed to complicated romance. And, among them all, the very few which have Roman history as their subject have this same romanticism. Thus in the *Lucrezia* of G. B. Mamiano (1625) who wished to teach modesty to women, and continence to princes, the prologue is recited by Lascivia (Lust) who presents herself with "Curled hair which almost upright stands," with "dewy flashing eyes," with "mirror in hand" to give "oblique reflection" "of her fair breasts to incite with the sweet heaving of that milk-whiteness to the feast of love the eager lovers." Mamiano's Tarquinius loses his time; for Lucrezia is an honest woman. While Collatino is in the field fighting, Tarquinius enters the house of Lucrezia as a guest (Act IV, sc. 2), and then violates her. Lucrezia recalls her husband from the field, and relates to him, with much detail, the indignity she has undergone (Act V, sc. 1). Her last words are these: "Being conscious in myself of chaste affection, I of the guilt absolve me, but not so of penalty. And never shall it be true Lucrezia should invite by her example others to live if once deprived of honour. May this blow, with which I pierce my innocent heart, declare it."

Few of the *seicento* tragedies are laid in Italy. The poor imagination of the seventeenth century authors wanders preferably in distant lands; because, as Gessi said, "the subject" being "more foreign than domestic," and hence "more removed from our knowledge," it "will the more easily admit the episodes and fabulous parts connected with the true."

Mario Cevoli set at Prague in Bohemia the scene of his *Ormondo* (1650), which is a lamentable comedy of errors. Europa, daughter of Orbante, king of Hungary, loves, and is loved by, Ormondo, son of Boemondo, king of Bohemia. Disguised as a man, she flees to Prague, to her lover, in the company of a faithful lady-in-waiting, Alvida. But Alvida is in fact Aronte, son of the king of Sweden, who had disguised his own sex so as to be able to remain near her. The pretended Alvida sows discord between Europa and Ormondo. Ormondo, to avenge himself on Europa, makes love to Armida, Europa's sister. Europa goes unknown to the camp to punish Ormondo and is slain by him. Aronte then lays aside his woman's dress and challenges Ormondo, who kills him, and equips himself in the arms of the dead Aronte. His faithful friend Alarco, believing him to have fallen under the blows of Aronte, assails and kills him.

In the *Cleopatra,* Delfino depicts a real contrast of passions. The secret love of Augustus for Cleopatra, the waverings of the proud queen, her suspicions of Augustus' sincerity, her despair on seeing herself deceived, and finally her suicide, are truly tragical. Augustus encourages the captive queen to live and to hope. If Augustus would marry her, Cleopatra would consent to live; but she will not offer herself to him. Augustus loves Cleopatra, but political reasons require that he conduct her a prisoner to Rome. Agrippa proposes a secret marriage. "Thou canst make her thy wife in secret; then with joyous heart will she come under the name of prisoner to Rome." While Cleopatra is anticipating the joy of being saluted as empress of Rome, Agrippa begs her to keep secret Augustus' promise of marriage until the fleet, which is to conduct the betrothed couple to Rome, has weighed anchor. Araspe intercepts a letter from Augustus to the Roman Senate and brings it to the queen. The queen reads that Augustus was leading her a prisoner to Rome, making use of "hopes for chains." Betrayed, Cleopatra commits suicide and Augustus laments (sc. 9).

One of the most famous tragedies of the *seicento,* the *Solimano* (Venice, 1619), was by Prospero Bonarelli, brother of Guidobaldo, author of the *Filli di Sciro.* Prospero Bonarelli was born in Ancona in 1588, and died there in 1659. A man of arms and of letters, he passed most of his life in the courts of Ferrara, Modena, Tuscany, and Vienna, for the last of which he composed several theatrical works.

In this play the actors are Turks. Bonarelli claimed that *Solimano* is an historical tragedy as Sansovino, in his *Istorie dei Turchi* (*History of the Turks*), had furnished his data as to Turkish customs and manners. The plot of *Solimano* proceeds from one of the usual substitutions of children. There were born almost contemporaneously to Solimano a child by Selino, the wife who had the title of queen, and another child by Mustafa, a Circassian. The latter, being a little the elder, would have been the legitimate heir to the throne, but died shortly after birth; and the mother, in order to give a successor to Solimano, consigned the little body to a woman, to exchange for a living child. The queen, seeing that her own son would be the victim of the suspicions and hatred of the Circassian, pretended that he had died and gave him to the same woman, and received the dead body of Mustafa's child. The woman had carried Selino's child to the Circassian, who concealed the substitution from Solimano. From this point the action develops naturally and tragically.

The *Solimano* has twenty actors, the principal of which are Soli-

Solimano

mano, "king of the Thracians," the Queen his wife, Mustafa his son, and Despina, "daughter of the king of Persia, in male costume, in love with Mustafa." Mustafa is dear to his father, but two cruel enemies plot against the paternal favor: the Queen, his stepmother, and the ambitious Rusteno, son-in-law of Solimano. Solimano, learning of the love between his son and the Persian princess, is certain that he shall be betrayed by them, and entrusts Despina to the custody of a soldier, ordering him to shut her up "in the darkest prison" until the hour strikes for sending her "to the eternal shades of death." While Despina remains alone with her custodian, Mustafa arrives (Act IV, sc. 7). She attacks him with bitter words; he, astounded, protests his love, but in vain. The lamentations of the two lovers, their final amorous tenderness, and then their barbarous murder, afford ample material for the recital of the Nuncio. In Act V, the Queen, who had been also the principal accuser of the prince and the principal instigator of the bloody counsels, "by strange means . . . has recognized Mustafa as her son." Desperately weeping, she carries her son's head on the stage and then swallows a deadly poison. This horrible final scene is borrowed from the *Orbecche* of Giraldi of the preceding century. Adrasto, at the head of the faithful soldiers of Mustafa, rushes on to the stage to avenge the dead prince in the blood of Solimano and Rusteno. The tragedy ends with the fall of Solimano, "rendered a horrible example of every misery," and with the sack and burning of Aleppo.

On its appearance, this play was hailed as a new marvel by many. Signor Andrea Salvadori swore that through the work of Bonarelli Italy had finally produced a perfect tragedy. The material of the tragedy is partly romantic, partly classical. Bonarelli's exclusion of the chorus and the reasons which he gave for this innovation greatly influenced other writers of tragedy. It also is to his credit that the rhetoric is less excessive and the philosophical speeches are less fatiguing than in most contemporary tragedies. The characters are clearly outlined and possess life. The thousand infamous arts by which Rusteno, a new Iago, instills suspicion into Solimano against his son and the gradual development of these suspicions are skilfully represented. Bonarelli's dramatic effects are good, his situations are natural, and he shows a real knowledge of the human heart.

The greater breadth of design and liberty of movements and of methods adopted to produce the effects, which one notes in the Italian tragic theatre of the *seicento* as contrasted with the timid and cold classicism of the sixteenth century, appear not only in the tragedies of the sacred argument, but also in those whose subject is profane. *Cromuele* (dedicated in 1671 to Louis XVI) by Girolamo Graziana, the most remarkable tragic author of his time, is an example of this. The preface announces "a tragedy of novel mode."

We are on the banks of the Thames, at the mouth of which Anne Hyde, daughter of Edward "who was afterward Chancellor of England," has picked up a youth called Henry who is in fact Queen Henrietta, wife of Charles I, who has come thus disguised to save her husband, Cromwell's prisoner. Cromwell's wife Elizabeth is in love with Charles, and with the aid of Orinda, "a widow lady, her confidante," seeks to save him. In Act II, the pretended Henry— that is the queen Henrietta—in order to escape Cromwell's spies proposes suicide. Edward prevents her. To reassure the queen, Edward summons his daughter Anne, who then proposes the means of seeing her imprisoned husband and planning his escape. Anne is a friend of Orinda; Orinda is the mother of Arthur, governor of the Tower of London. Orinda must persuade Arthur to take the pretended Henry into his service! In fact Orinda, besides the pretended Henry, has already introduced into Arthur's service a certain youth Edmund. Orinda puts the keys of the prison at the disposal of Elizabeth. Does Elizabeth wish that Charles should console her? Then let her go to him in prison; Henry and Edmund will open the door. Elizabeth consents, and Orinda explains to "Henry" and Edmund how they can serve her. When the guard of the king's prison is entrusted to them, let them open the door and allow Elizabeth to enter. Imagine the stupefaction, anguish, and jealousy of the pretended Henry; yet she promises not to hinder Orinda's design, since upon it depend the safety of Charles and the triumph of the good cause, and since it may furnish occasion to "set at nought with innocent deception the go-between, the adulteress, and the tyrant." Edmund, believing himself alone, exclaims, "Already I see the king freed, Elizabeth scorned, Cromwell confused, Orinda deluded!" Orinda, who is present, on hearing these incautious words exclaims, "Ah, perfidious one! vengeance!" Thus are events precipitated. Charles is beheaded, Edmund is executed, and Edward Hyde drags Henrietta away. In the meantime we have Elizabeth and Orinda, the former afflicted, the latter exultant, and both avenged; but while Orinda glories in having punished with death the rash youth who had deceived her, to the consolation of the materialistic Orinda Elizabeth replies: "You speak with your heart, but not with mine."

With this scene in which are contrasted two differing feminine natures, one passionate but faithful, the other inconstant, sensation-seeking, the tragedy might well end; but the measure of the complications was not yet full. That mysterious Edmund was the beloved Delmira, daughter of Cromwell and Elizabeth.

The relief which Graziana gave to the complex characters of some of his personages is new; and new likewise is the way in which he interwove the comic with the tragic.

Because tragicomedy was more popular than tragedy, many compositions were entitled *tragicommedie* when "tragedy" would have been more correct. The title of *tragicommedie* was given to a great variety of plays such as the *Invidia carnefice di se stessa*

(Envy is its own executioner) by the Lucchese, Giuseppe Fivizzani (Bologna, 1693); to *Lo sdegno amoroso* (The amorous scorn), a Spanish tragicomedy of cape and sword by Francesco Bracciolini, from which Chiari later derived his *Vendetta amorosa* (Amorous revenge); to *Le due sorelle* (The two Sisters) by Giov. Francesco Lupi (Pisa, 1625); to *La donzella fedele* (The faithful maiden), an "Heroic" tragicomedy by the Paduan romancer Antonio Santa Croce (Venice, 1648); to *La forza delle stelle, ovvero amore e destino* (The power of the stars, or Love is Fate, Naples, 1693); and to many others. In almost all of these, there are, however, two common characteristics: the long and fanciful titles and the almost constant forsaking of verse for prose.

Almost all the critics had decided at the outset in favor of verse; but, at the end of the sixteenth century, prose found some who made use of it in composing tragedies. Later, Agostino Michiele adopted prose in the *Cianippo* (Bergamo, 1506), and maintained that its use was legitimate and advantageous. Paolo Beni declared himself of the same opinion. The same was demonstrated later by Filippo Ghirardelli, in the *Difesa dalle opposizioni fatte alla tragedia del Costantino* (Defence against the oppositions made to the tragedy of "Costantine"). Even if it be conceded for a moment that Aristotle had prescribed verse for Greek tragedians, it did not follow that the Italians were also subject to such a law. After all, Aristotle derived his precept from Greek customs, not from a necessary and universal principle. "In fact," said Ghirardelli, "who can deny that verse does not occasion very great inconvenience to the representation of the tragedies?" Prose is "more lifelike."

The dividing line between the classical Italian tragedy and the dramatic varieties that supplanted it, eludes any precise determination. In the *Zenobia di Radamisto,* by Carlo De' Dottori, an *opera scenica* in prose, with a happy ending, we delude ourselves that we are recognizing a product of art different from the tragedy

properly so-called, on account of a secondary character who is defi-
nitely comic also in name (the boy Pacchetto). These *favole all'
italiana* held the field for many decades and obliged the true and
genuine tragedies also to adjust themselves to their extravagant
forms.

The many French tragedies translated into Italian about the
close of the *seicento* afford proof of this. Possibly the first of these
translations was that of Corneille's *Cid* made by Andre Valfré
(Carmagnola, 1647). It was a little after 1670 that the translations
of French tragedies became increasingly frequent. Reduced from
five to three acts; prose substituted for verse; plot complicated by
strange episodes; comic and burlesque scenes intermingled with
the tragic; common sense violated, a happy ending often being
substituted for the mournful catastrophe—these foreign tragedies
were denaturalized and spoiled. These French translations demonstrate the low state of the tragic theatre in Italy at the close of the
seicento. Towards the end of the *seicento* the classical or regular
tragedy was almost completely abandoned in favor of the French
repertory, which, however bastardized and disfigured by Italian
translators, the France of Louis XIV furnished for the admiration
of all Europe.

Of the pastoral fable of the *seicento,* Tassoni, in Book X of his
Penseiri diversi (Venice, 1635, p. 383), says: "In the pastorals,
where sweetness and languor of style are required, our poets have
written with such excellence that the most beautiful and graceful
compositions of the ancients do not equal them." The pastorals of
the seventeenth century are almost all modeled on the two pastorals
of Tasso and Guarini, though the *seicentisti* also borrowed freely
from the romances and poems. Though numerous, they were
mostly very poor. Yet Giovanni Savio, an apologist of the *Pastor
fido,* affirmed in 1601, ". . . it seems that to-day men resolve not
to read or to write other than pastorals."[9]

Mythology also supplied material for the pastoral drama. Such is the case with that fable by Carlo Emanuele I, which, under the title of *Transformazioni di Millefonti,* was presented on August 24, 1609, at Millefonti near Turin. Carlo Emanuele had a passion for such dramatic representations, and it was the Duke himself who gave to D'Aglio the first inspiration for his *Alvida.* The representation of this drama of the duke's was entrusted to the *comici Accesi* (the Accessi Company of actors), the head of whom at that time was Pier Maria Cecchini, though dramas were also represented by gentlemen and noble ladies.

The *Aci* (Venice, 1600), a marine fable by Scipione De Manzano, and the *Endimione* (Rome, 1692), a woodland fable by Alessandro Guidi, are the pastoral dramas of purely mythological content. Two famous myths furnished material for these fables; that of Acis and Galatea, and that of the love of Diana and Endymion; the two poets, however, treated them freely. De Manzano represents the type of the marine fable. The maritime fables have as their subject not "simply and only mariners" (as Quadrio states), "but the demigods and all the maritime deities, and whatsoever nymph, deity, and person that lives in the seas."[10]

Guidobaldo Bonarelli (1563–1600) was born in Urbino. His *Filli di Sciro,* produced at Ferrara in 1607, is the most beautiful Italian pastoral of the seventeenth century. The style is often elegant, the construction is graceful and harmonious; but the intrinsic merit of the drama does not equal these exterior beauties. Celia, loving Niso and Aminta with equal ardor, resolves to die to escape so singular a situation. There is no tumult in the dual passion with which the soul of the unhappy shepherdess is agitated, and the details of the plot are not original; the Centaur is the usual Satyr of all the Pastorals. The *Filli di Sciro* bears even greater resemblance to the *Amarilli* (Ascoli, 1580) by Cristoforo Castelletti, and to the *Amoroso sdegno* by Francesco Bracciolini. In both these pastorals, the

fundamental motive is the two youthful lovers who find each other again after long separation, and the two friends both enamored of the same nymph.[11]

In Andreini's *Florinda* (1603 or 1604), there is something of the woodland fable: "The scene is laid in the forests of Scotland"; ancient trees, wild beasts, and birds are mentioned; and a "noble shepherd," Alfeo, plays a part in it; the chorus is composed of "Nymphs of the forest." The king of Scotland, Ircano, seeks among those "friendly horrors" oblivion from bitter memories. He, having seduced Flerida, next yielded to the invitation of Florinda, the beautiful fifteen-year-old daughter of the count of Ancusa. At the sight of graceful, courteous, and valiant Ircano, Florinda "was vanquished, and fired and panting"; she gave him the keys of secret doors, and finally had "pregnant her womb with royal seed." Thus a boy was born; and since an ambiguous response of the oracle of Delphi caused Ircano to fear that this son should bring him misfortune, he decided to kill him. But Florinda, warned by Prince Learco, fled with the child, and found an asylum in Alfeo's retreat. After living for six years in the forest, she is found by her brother Filandro, who tells her of repentant Ircano's grief. Joyful Florinda rejoins Ircano. The meeting of Florinda with Ircano (Act II, sc. 2) is most tender; but the shade of Flerida with terrible voice repeats the menace of the Delphian oracle. Ircano's paternal tenderness vanishes. His soldiers kill the child. Florinda, informed of the child's death, poisons herself, and Learco commits suicide; Filandro slays Ircano and Ircano's household. The tragedy runs to more than five thousand lines.[12]

In the seventeenth century, the written or studied comedy had a meagre life owing to its competition with the youthful improvised comedy or *commedia dell' arte*.

In the first half of the *seicento,* the literary comedy continued the tradition of the preceding century, represented especially by the

Neapolitan Giambattista Della Porta (1535–1613). This great cultivator of natural magic, who to love for science united great credulity and who, in 1610 at seventy-five years of age, had the honor of being inscribed in the academy of the Lincei, exerted an important influence upon the comic theatre of the second half of the *cinquecento*. The comedies of Della Porta are modeled on those of Plautus and have all the savour of the Plautian plays, although they surpass them for the naturalness of the intrigue. Full of movement, they present interesting yet natural situations. The characters, although of Latin origin, are fresh and original. The simple, vivacious dialogue of Della Porta even imparts originality to the timeworn intrigue of a youth and a maiden whose marriage is opposed either by the parents or by the jealousy of a rival, until the obstacle is removed through the intrigues of servants or of parasites, and the marriage takes place amid the rejoicings of all. The satire is keen against pedants and boasters; the style is pleasing; the language is at times elegant.

Most of the early *seicentist* Italian playwrights imitated Della Porta. Of the comedies of his time, Giulio Cesare Capaccio wrote: "The actions are very cold. . . . They always rest upon servants, upon shipwrecks. The ineptitude of the scenes, the soliloquies, the effrontery of the maid-servants and the parasites annoy me. . . . All is affectation. And when the comic phrase is languid, does not sting, I am so irritated that I would tear up all the comedies."

Francesco D' Isa copies Della Porta. He published his five comedies—the *Fortunia* (Naples, 1612), the *Alvisa* (Naples, 1616), the *Flaminia* (Naples, 1621), the *Ginevra* (Naples, 1622), the *Malmaritato* (Naples, 1633)—under the name of his brother Ottavio. These also are imitations of Plautus with the usual intrigue and with the usual characters inherited from the *cinquecento* comedies: the enamoured old man; the courtesan; the intriguing and thievish servants; the timid and base captain, terrible in words; the Nea-

politan braggart, resembling the Pannuorfo of Della Porta, or the
Gian Loise of the *Intrichi d'amore;* and the pedant. These types
were now also crystallized in the *commedia dell' arte.*

The written comedy was injuriously influenced by the scenarios
of the improvised comedy. There is no life in the dialogues, which
are either crowded with metaphors, or loaded with maxims, or vul-
garly scurrilous. In the notice prefixed to his *Antiparnaso* (Venice,
1597), Orario Vecchi justly said: "The unbecoming jests which are
introduced into many of our comedies as food rather than as con-
diment, cause that when one says 'commedia' he means to say a
buffoon pastime." And, although Andreini deplored that all contemporary comedies were stuffed with "either contrary or conform-
able loves, intrigues of go-betweens, escapes, abductions, rages,
furies, jealousies, quarrels, disdain, and the like," in his own comedies he gave the saddest example of the corruption which *seicento*
literary comedy attained under the influence of the improvised
comedy. For Giambattista Andreini, this was almost inevitable,
since, besides being a most fertile playwright, he was also one of
the most famous comedians of the seventeenth century.[13] His
many literary works represent two opposite aspects of his personality: his religious writings are of almost ascetic character, and his
comedies are very licentious. The actor who had no scruples in representing most indecent dramas, is also a pious singer of saints; the
playwright who put in the mouths of his characters the most equivocal jests is a religious poet. Andreini's comedies are considered "as
a true and actual attempt to reduce to writing the *commedia a
soggetto.*"

The influence of the Spanish viceroys in Naples peculiarly favored this development of an Italian spaniardized comedy; and,
moreover, Spanish companies frequently performed there. Lope
de Vega and Calderon de la Barca became the favorite models of
the Italian authors; and the repertories of the dramatic companies

opened to translations, to imitations, to adaptations of the Spanish comedies of *"capa y espada."*[14]

The *Covitato di peitra* attributed to Cicognini is perhaps the first Italian drama on the legend of Don Giovanni. From this was probably derived that scenario which was represented with an extraordinary success at Paris by Italian actors in 1657, a scenario which in its time was a favorite spectacle with the Italian public.[15]

Very different from the dramas of classical type is the *Fiera* of Michelangelo Buonarroti the younger, a comedy of manners in which the plot is skilfully developed. It is a vivid representation of the confusion, the altercations, the bustle, and the thousand incidents that can arise out of the concourse of a great multitude of people of every class on the occasion of a fair. Buonarroti's comedy which is made up of five comedies or days, each divided into five acts, was not intended to be performed in a theatre. His aim was literary and linguistic rather than dramatic; and under this aspect his work is important.

To the same style as the *Fiera* belongs also the *Mascherate,* another dramatic work of Buonarroti's, where with much sparkle and elegance the poet represents the incidents of a *veglia* (a masked ball), with which a gay company of ladies and cavaliers passes the evening.

To the style of the rustic comedies belong also some of the scenic jests (*scherzi*) of Filippo Baldinucci, a kind of farce in the Florentine vernacular for the youths of the oratory of San Firenze, who recited them. These *scherzi* of Baldinucci's have no dramatic interest, but they are noteworthy for their graceful language and have the freshness of the spoken vernacular.

Authors of *seicento* literary comedy used dialect chiefly for rousing laughter; and the *commedia dell' arte* had a very great influence in this respect also. The Neapolitan speaks his dialect nonsensically. In the *Schiavetto* of Andreini, the hostess Succiola

PRIMO INTERMEDIO DELLA VEGLIA DELLA LIBERATIONE DI TIRRENO FATTA NELLA SALA DELLE COM: DIE DEL SER.^{mo} GRAN DVCA DI TOSCANA IL CARNOVALE DEL 1616. DOVE SI RAP.^{va} IL MONTE D'ISCHIA CON IL GIGANTE TIFEO SOTTO.

A Veglia (masked ball)

speaks in a ridiculous Florentine; and in the *Servo finto* (Viterbo, 1634), by Giulio Cesare Monti, Pulcinella speaks *toscanissimamente* (most Tuscanly). In the *Farinda* (Paris, 1622), by the same Andreini, French and German, Venetian, Farrarese, Genovese, Neapolitan, various Lombard dialects, macaronic Latin, and the absurd language of a stutterer are all used.

Satiric and moral meanings are generally absent from the comic theatre of the seventeenth century. Yet the comedies recited in Rome during the pontificate of Urban VIII often assumed the character of political satires against Spain, and are an echo of the anti-Spanish attitude of the Pope and of his nephew the cardinal Antonio Barberini.[16]

The indecency of the seventeenth-century comic theatre has been referred to. Tommaso Garzoni, the bizarre author of the *Piazza universale di tutte le professioni del mondo,* while he praises those famous actresses of his time, Isabella Andreini and Lidia and Vittoria, fulminates against the licence, the immodesty, the licentious nonsense, of many other actors who disgraced the art.

During the sixteenth century, the Venetian Republic frequently prohibited the recitation of comedies, or imposed a rigorous revision of the text. Nevertheless (about 1565) "there resorted" to the theatre "almost all the nobility, and there were nobles who begged the comedians that they should say the filthiest things, and they took their wives and daughters there." And a century later (1666), at Rome in the palace of Cristina of Sweden, there were represented "most filthy" comedies to which the cardinals gathered eagerly, in spite of the anathemas of preachers and moralists.

Against the indecency of the theatre, a Spanish Jesuit, Giovanni Mariana, opened war in 1609, almost continuing the work of San Carlo Borromeo, who, from 1565 to 1584, the year of his death, had been the champion of the Church in the struggle against the comedies.[17]

In defence of the comedies there rose up Pier Maria Cecchini and Giambattista Andreini. The latter, in the preface to his plays, shows what advantages may be derived from these; and Cecchini, with his *Brevi discorsi interno alle comedie, commedianti e spettatori,* and in two discourses—the *Specchio della commedia,* dedicated to the duke of Nemours, and the *Sferza contro le accuse date alla commedia ed a' professori di lei,* dedicated to Marcantonio Morosini, ambassador of the republic of Venice to Louis XIII—as well as in the *Teatro celeste,* already referred to, loyally champions his art.[18] The struggle was carried on also in France and continued in Italy even in the following century; until in France, with Molière, Corneille, and Racine and in Italy with Goldoni and Alfieri, the reform of the comic and tragic theatre was initiated and achieved.

NOTES

CHAPTER X

1. Vain were San Carlo Borromeo's attempted reforms within the church, as were the laws enacted by the government; for the priests threatened with excommunication whoever should dare molest them, and Rome, jealous of her rights, sided with the clergy. Tens of thousands of friars and monks crowded the monasteries. At Padua, a city which in 1600 numbered only thirty thousand inhabitants, there were twenty-three convents of friars and twenty-six of monks. And what kind of morality could reign in so great a multitude of the religious, of whom the larger number devoted themselves to the monastic life either to idle in sloth, or because within convent walls was a safe asylum from punishment for their crimes?

Agriculture was neglected; the peasants were idle; the countryside was overrun with bandits and by mercenary troops who caused ruin and disorder. The Italian coasts were robbed by Turkish pirates; and added to all this were terrible pestilences.

Manzoni's *Promessi Sposi* has described for all time the condition of the Milanese province under Spanish misrule; and Masaniello has revealed to us the miseries of Naples under the Spanish viceroys, who, in order to pay for their drunken and gluttonous revelries, imposed tax upon tax, impost upon impost, which ground the common people and sucked out the life of industry and commerce. How true was the Italian proverb, "The ministers of the Spanish monarchy nibbled in Sicily, ate in Naples, and devoured in Milan."

Even vice paid hugely for the privilege of prosecuting its trade, as, when a Spanish company of actors found business slow in Naples, the viceroy Monterey by proclamation compelled all prostitutes to patronize the theatre every day, or in case of absence to pay the actors three *carlini* a month.

Antonio Abati, in his *Frascherie,* depicts the fashions of the time. Laws against the unbridled luxury in dress were frequent in this century. Thus a decree of the Paduan council (May 11, 1619) prohibited women putting on cloth of gold, of silver, embroideries in gold, silver, and silk, furs of wolves, stags, sables, martens, black foxes; and of being accompanied by more than one servant in the street. It permitted them only one single string of pearls at the neck or a gold chain, forty buttons on the whole person, and a gold girdle but without jewels; gems only in earrings and rings. The men were forbidden gilded swords; only their buttons and the medal in their hat might be of gold; no jewels at all. It forbade gilded coaches, adorned with velvet or other silken stuff, or with embroideries or designs over silk or leather.

Crushed by servitude, brutalized by ignorance, the faith of the people had become superstition, while the more cultured classes held astrology in great honour. The belief in magicians, in spells, in divinations, in witches, was common; alchemy, magic, necromancy, had many followers; legends were spun of journeys taken on the backs of devils changed into rams; the malignant spirits, assuming a thousand different forms, often entered into the body of some poor wretch to corrupt both soul and mind. Thus there were frequent trials before the Holy Office against persons accused of keeping demons in rings, mirrors, medals, and other objects, or who had adopted Satan as their Lord.

The only remedy for such ignorance would have been the schools, but most of these were in the hands of Jesuits whose pedantic methods left much to be desired. Hence the education of the soul was false; that of the body not cared for at all. The heavy weight of grammatical rules and of other like pedantries obsessed the schools where youth was to be formed and prepared for life.

The Academies were a sad inheritance from the preceding century, an evil plant. Their vogue is one of the phenomena that characterize the seventeenth century. But in contrast with the grave and solemn and foolish academies there were others of a character wholly agreeable, joyous gatherings of good friends: in Florence, the *Rifritti,* which had as emblem a frying pan with some little fish; the *Mammagnuccoli,* among whom no one was admitted who had not given proof of his *dabbenaggine* (probity, simplicity) as they called it in their own slang; and the academy of the *Borra.* Even grave *Cruscanti,* at the merrymaking which they held twice a year at the changing of the officers, delighted in certain *cicalate* on the most futile subjects as, for example, "in praise of the pan and the fry," and in broadly burlesque verses.

2. Love of country and desire for liberty still flamed in some Italian hearts. A few voices, fervid and audacious, still pealed forth clarion notes to rouse Italians from their torpor. Amid the flames of the popes, the philosopher Giordano Bruno, strong and serene, ascended the pyre in Campo dei Fiori; and Tommaso Campanella, another follower of freethought, was shut up in horrible prison where he languished for twenty-seven years. In 1607, Fra Paolo Sarpi, bold defender of the rights of the state against the despotism of the popes, was wounded by unknown assassins, "stilo Romanae Curiae." In 1619, Giulio Cesare Vanini was burnt; in 1633, Galileo Galilei was forced by the Holy Office to abjure his doctrines.

3. Ferdinando II endowed the Tolomei and the Cicognini, renowned schools of Sienna and Prato. The University of Rome enjoyed the protection of Alexander VII. The University of Padua, thanks to the provident and enlightened liberality of Venice, maintained its ancient renown and was attended by many foreigners. Bologna University continued its splendid traditions, although many of its most turbulent students went to Naples where they could take degrees without frequenting the courses. In Padua as well as at Naples, however, there are frequent references to violence committed by the students.

4. The sincere naturalness of the *sacra rappresentazione* vanished in the artifice and the pomp of the Spanish drama, which was closely imitated in Italy during the second half of the seventeenth century.

The material was the same; and the spiritual or sacred tragedies on the Nativity, the Passion, and the Resurrection were numerous; but they lacked the ingenuous sentiment which characterized the *sacre rappresentazioni* of the *quatrocento*.

The action was divided into acts and scenes, sometimes called *applausi* and *motti,* or *parti* and *avvenimenti.* Modelled upon the famous Spanish *comedias de santos,* its bizarre dramatic action is divided into three days, and represents the life of some saint with the intervention of angels, demons, and allegorical figures. Real personages are also introduced, such as the parents of the saint, the lovers of holy women, the servants. The favorite subjects of these representations were the snares prepared by the devil, and the victories, the miracles, and the final triumph of the saint. They have their prologue, *intermezzi,* and choruses; also the "Echo," a common element in the pastorals, sometimes has a part; the characters declaim, and speak metaphorically, exactly as in the profane tragedies.

An example of those tragedies which have the Passion as their subject is the *Mortorio di Cristo* by Fra Bonaventura Morone of Taranto, a spiritual tragedy in five acts, with prologue and choruses, interludes that clearly show the union of the traditional legendary and the formal classical elements. Another good example is the *Cristo Morto* by Ortensio Scamacca da Lentini. In his long life of eighty-six years (1562–1648), Scamacca wrote forty-five tragedies, all written with the purpose that his theatre should inspire a lofty sense of morality and faith.

5. Cristiano is the son of Levigildo, king of the Goths of Sicilia, and of Teodosia, a Greek princess. Teodosia having died, Levigildo had entered into a second marriage with Godelinda, daughter of Teodorico (Theodoric), king of Italy. Now it happened that Levigildo set out with his father-in-law to fight against the "French" and that in this interval Godelinda fell in love with her stepson Cristiano. Cristiano refuses the proffered love. Godelinda, offended by his re-

proaches, determines both to kill herself and at the same time to be avenged; and, having written a letter to her husband accusing Cristano, hangs herself. Levigildo, on returning from the war, finds the accusatory letter, believes Cristiano guilty, and orders him killed. But "God who desired the salvation of both" causes Godelinda to rise from the dead, so that she may confess her sin, after which she dies again. Alas, Cristiano's torture had done its work and he dies, pardoned and pardoning.

6. Cortesi prefaced his *Giustina* with an apologetic discourse, in which he defends his own work from the censure of those who condemned *i sacri poemi* (sacred poems). In the *Assalonne* (Absalom) of Ramelli, the Bible story of the impious son of David is fundamentally altered. Ramelli has intermingled the usual romance of the profane tragedy; Amassa and Sirilla are the usual perfect lovers. The customary prologue of the pseudo-classical tragedy is also added. The *Gerusalemme cattiva* of Campelli has the usual wrathful shade, nurse, chorus, and nuncio. But the other religious dramas of the *seicento* have another technique—are of non-classical stamp. The famous *Adamo* (1613) by G. B. Andreini, the author entitled *sacra rappresentazione;* the *Adamo ed Eva* (1644) of Troilo Lancetta, *scena tragica;* the *Cristo passo* (1629), by Francesco Pona, is entitled *tragedia,* although it resembles the *sacra rappresentazione.* The *Cristo passo* has the unities of the regular tragedy and the multiplicity of personages and of episodes of the *sacra rappresentazione.* The only reason for remembering Pona's tragedy is that the author tried to render it impassioned.

7. To the class of the *Implesse* tragedies belongs the *Creso* of Cardinal Delfino. The complicated action of this tragedy is based on the disguises of the two characters. In the *Creso,* the characters all talk too much; and, however tragic the situation may be, each arrives tranquilly at the end of his own discourses, after which the others intervene in order to set forth their ideas.

To the class of the *appassionate* belong also the three tragedies of Ansaldo Cebà, the *Principessa Silandra* (Genoa, 1621), the *Alcippo* (Genoa, 1623), and the *Gemelle capovane*. The second is short. Gelandro, who had vainly sought to seduce Damocrito, wife of Alcippi, condemns her husband to exile. To avenge herself, Damocrito pretends to consent to Gelandro's desires, invites him to supper, and poisons him. Then she sets fire to the temple wherein are gathered the women of the Efori who had condemned Alcippo, and kills herself with her daughters. In the third tragedy, the two Capuan sisters, Trasilla and Pirindra, under promise of marriage, give themselves to Hannibal, their father's guest, and are slain by their brother.

Better than the tragedies of Cebà is the *Aristodemo* (Padua, 1657) of Carlo Dottori. The oracle of Delphi, to placate the ire of the gods, has, with one of its usual enigmatic replies, indicated as the victim to be immolated a virgin daughter of an Epitide. Only two virgins in Itome are found in the condition desired by the oracle: Merope, daughter of Aristodemo and his wife Anfia, and Arena, daughter of Liciso. The choice is made by lot, and the name of Arena comes forth from the fatal urn. Liciso declares her to be only his adopted daughter given him by the priestess Erasitea but, not being believed, he conceals her and relates that she has been killed by one of the archers sent by Aristodemo to pursue her. There thus remains as sole victim the daughter of Aristodemo. But her mother Anfia, her bridegroom Policare, and her nurse spread the false report that Merope, instead of being a virgin, is near to becoming a mother; Policare for this reason claims from Aristodemo all right over the maiden whom he affirms is his. Aristodemo, blinded by rage, penetrates into the inviolable chamber where Merope is shut up, to prepare by purification for the sacrifice; kills her; and then discovers that Policare's assertion is false. Aristodemo perceives that he has killed his two daughters; for the priestess Erasitea reminds him that Arena is the fruit of his youthful relations with her. The Inferi demand another victim; and Aristo-

demo, mad with grief, flings himself upon the sword still stained
with Merope's blood. Thus we have one surprise after another in a
plot deliberately complicated by the author who, in 1654, wrote, "It
seems to me that the *implessa* is the most highly praised form of
tragedy and for this reason I have aimed to make it involved and
dolorous."

Among several similar tragedies are the *Ulisse* (Naples, 1614) of
G. B. Della Porta, who is author of *Georgio* (Naples, 1611), which
is modeled on *Efigenia in Aulide*. It has as its subject the victory
won by St. George over a monster which troubled the city. The
Teodolinda is an imitation of Sophocles' *Electra;* the *Chrisanto* is
drawn from the *Hippolitus* of Euripides, and the *Hernando* is
taken from Sophocles' *Œdipus Rex*.

The *inviluppo* (entanglement) is almost never lacking in the
tragedies of the *seicento;* and where it is lacking, there is a dupli-
cating of actions and persons, as, for example, in the *Gemelle Capo-
ane* (Capuan Twins) of Ansaldo Cebà. It is amazing that Maffei
should welcome, in his *Teatro Italiano,* the *Gemelle* in which there
are two protagonists, Trasilla and Pirindra, daughters of Calavio
and Antandra, both in equal degree enamoured of Annibale, and
both seduced by him. After four acts of pure narrative and discourse, the action begins. Annibale has agreed to leave Capua and
to meet Trasilla and Pirindra, each of whom Annibale has promised to take with him. They wait in vain; for Annibale, to save himself from any encumbrance, has fled. The despairing girls drink a
powerful poison and then withdraw to die decently behind the
scenes.

8. The *Reina di Scozia* (Naples, 1604) by Carlo Ruggeri, is an example of this second manner. It is a tragedy of the first years of the
   seventeenth century, and is derived from contemporary history. The
   recent tragic death of Mary Stuart supplied Tommaso Campanella
   and other writers with the subject for a drama. Ruggeri's tragedy
   is simple in action, only the last hours of the unfortunate queen

being represented. The first act comprises the long lamentations of the chambermaid and the secretary of Mary; in the second, the Queen relates a dream in which the dead Darnley counselled her to escape to France, while an angel held her back by showing her a crown; in the third act the two ambassadors announce to Mary the capital sentence; in the fourth, a Calvinist minister vainly tries to convert her; in the fifth, a councillor of King James arrives to save her, but she has already been executed, and a messenger relates the particulars.

Similar to the tragedy of Ruggeri in its simplicity as well as in its subject and title, is the *Reina di Scozia* (Milan, 1628) by Felice della Valle; but other later dramas entitled *Mary Stuart* by Savarro and Celli are not *simplicissime*.

The *Rosmilla* (1622) of Francesco Partini of Lucca is one of the simplest. But simplicity is not in the taste of the period. The *seicento* saw no dramas in which a passion is worked out without any other entanglement; its tragedies are all *implesse,* all complicated and involved.

In the *seicento,* classical or mythological subjects are never treated unless there are to be found in them the chances and the signs of love. The subject of the *Ippolito* found favor because in it love was indigenous; and it was treated, previous to Tesauro, by Vincenzo Giacobilli (1601), and Andrea Santamaria (1619). The subject of the *Edipo,* although in itself *inviluppato* (involved or complicated), pleased less; but Tesauro complicated the knot and increased the number of personages. Antigone secretly loves her uncle Creonte and is jealous of the "damigella" Neera, who reproves her. To think of love-affairs in a time of such great public calamities seems to Neera a thing unworthy of a princess.

9. The pastoral fables of the seventeenth century, like the tragedies and comedies, hailed the carrying off of children, the exchange of names, disguises, the false interpretation of the reply of an oracle. To these are then added the other conventional details derived

partly from the *Aminta* and partly from the *Pastor fido;* such as one or more of the characters rebellious against love and devoted to hunting; the satyr or other monster who is either scorned or slain by the nymph; the false report of the death of one of the characters; and the "Echo" which replies to the lamentations of the unhappy lover.

10. The *Aci* of De Manzano marks the transition from the "piscatory" to the maritime type, and served as model to other fables, such as the *Consiglio degli dei par la fondazione e grandezza dell' inclita citta di Venezia e dell' excellentissima repubblica* (the council of the gods for the foundation and greatness of the noble city of Venice and of the most excellent republic), Vicenza, 1614, by Antonio Maria Consalvi, and the *Nascimento di Venezia* (Bergamo and Venice, 1617) by Cesare Cremonio. In the *Nascimento di Venezia,* Cremonio, holding scrupulously to all the poetic canons of his Aristotle, wove upon them some famous classical myths, such as that of the loves of Neptune and Amimone, the other of Danae and Perseus, the Syracusan legend of Damon and Pythias, the episode of Bacchus and Penteo which we read in the Book III of the *Metamorphoses,* and so on. And in these myths Cremonio had as sole aim the exaltation of Venice, which—that the nobility of its origin might not yield to that of the origins of Athens and Rome—he imagined founded, by the will of Neptune, by Naulo, the son who was born to the sea-god of Amimone.

11. Bonarelli also had immediate imitators; one was Giovanni Villi-franchi, who already, in the *Astrea,* published in Venice in 1594, had closely followed Tasso's *Aminta,* and who in the *Amaranta* (Venice, 1610) reproduced in great part the plot of the *Filli di Sciro,* tracing the adventures of two young people, Amaranta and Lican-dro, who, born in Cyprus and both carried off by pirates, are taken to Egypt, where they live happily loving one another. There is evident in the *Amaranta* the imitation of the *Pastor fido* as well as of

the *Filli di Sciro;* and it is not surprising, since the tragicomedy of Guarini was always kept in view by the writers of pastorals. Orazio Serono, publishing his *Fida Armilla,* in the same year (1610) at Venice, declared that he had wished to walk "in the footsteps of the *Pastor fido* and to have taken pleasure in planning and weaving his web with the thread of Guarini," transporting "both ideas and words of weight" into his fable.

12. Florinda betrayed by Ircano has no connection with the *Flerida gelosa* (the jealous Flerida, 1635) which was later put into tragic form by the Bolognese count, G. B. Manzini (1599–1664). Flerida is the wife and passionate lover of Labeone, king of Sweden, who is enamoured of Rosalia, maid-of-honor to the queen, who loves Costante, "gentleman to the king," who returns her love. But a good subject will not oppose the desires of his own prince; so Costante carries the amorous messages of Labeone to Rosalia. Flerida orders Terpandro, a "Danish gentleman" who lives at the court of Sweden, to kill Costante. But beneath Rosalia's windows, instead of Costante, there arrives the impatient Labeone; and Terpandro, in the dark, cuts off his head, and brings it still warm and bleeding to Flerida. She, having recognized the features of her adored husband, in despair and fury, orders the soldiers to follow and kill Terpandro. Alas, the so-called Terpandro was Corindo, her brother, long mourned as lost. Flerida has murdered both her husband and her brother.

13. Giambattista Andreini was born in 1578. His father was the great actor Francesco Andreini, who, under the name of "Capitan Spavento di Vall' Inferno," was the most renowned impersonator of the type of the captain; and his mother, even more famous, was the actress Isabella Andreini (d. 1604) who, in the latter *cinquecento* and first years of the *seicento,* aroused such enthusiasm in Italy and France that kings, princes, and poets honored and praised her, and, to perpetuate whose memory, there was even coined a

medal having on the one side her effigy and on the other the figure of Fame with the motto *Aeterna fama*. The son of such parents, the two bright stars of the very famous 'Gelosi' (company), Giambattista Andreini, born in Florence in 1578, was also a member of the 'Gelosi,' assuming the name of Lelio. In 1601, at Milan, he married Virginia Ramponi, who became an actress and singer of great fame under the name of Florinda. Giambattista, together with his wife, entered the service of Vincenzo, duke of Mantua, who, after the death of Isabella Andreini, formed another company, the *'comici Fedeli.'* Andreini went with the *Fedeli* to Germany also. Florinda having died, he married the actress Lidia. Between 1637 and 1640, he left the service of the dukes of Mantua, continuing, however, his wandering life until his old age, when he retired to his own property near Mantua.

14. In the *cinquecento,* the Spanish comic theatre had developed under the influence of the Italian comedy, so that, besides translating and rearranging Plautus and Terence, the Spanish playwrights had drawn largely from Italian sources; but in the *seicento* the parts were reversed. But since the public taste demanded the clumsy *lazzi,* the obscenities and other objectionable features of the improvised comedy, this strange union of two vitally different ideals omitted all that was fine and genial in the Spanish comedies, and, far from imitating their sparkle and realism, contented itself with taking their general lines and most unworthy characteristics.

15. Giacinto Andrea Cicognini is the best known of these imitators and is mentioned by Goldoni in his *Memorie*. Mattias Maria Bartolomei, in the preface of his play *Amore opera a caso* (Florence, 1668), affirms that only eighteen of the many plays attributed to Cicognini are authentic.

16. Literary satire constitutes the principal element of such allegorical comedies as are those of Scipione Errico and Giovanni Giacomo

Riccio, poor imitations of the *Clouds* and the *Frogs* of Aristophanes, comedies in which literary criticism has also a considerable part. All of the many comedies copied from Aristophanes were destined chiefly for reading. Something very different was required for the public. One did not go to the theatre to meditate on the philosophy and morality of erudite comedy. Spectators crowded theatres to laugh over the improvised *lazzi* of the zanies.

17. Mariana was imitated in 1620 by Adamo Contzen di Magonza; in 1621 by Francesco Maria del Monaco; in 1637 by Girolamo Fiorentini; and between 1648 and 1652 by Giovanni Domenico Ottonelli with his *Christiana moderazione nel teatro*. In 1646, Alessandro Adimari translated from the Spanish a sermon by the Jesuit Jacopo Alberto against the abuse of the comedies, and Jacopo Pignatelli repeated much the same things as those said by Contzen.

18. Also the *capocomico* (leading actor) Aurelio wrote a treatise in favor of the *commedia;* and Niccolo Barbieri another on the comic art, drawn from the works of St. Thomas and other saints, in 1627; and in 1629, a discourse dedicated to Louis XIII relative to the modern comedy. Subsequently he wrote the *Supplica,* which is a rearrangement of the previous work.

INDEX